ADVANCED LEARNER'S DICTIONARY *Of* JOURNALISM

ADVANCED LEARNER'S DICTIONARY *Of* JOURNALISM

Compiled & Edited by

A Team of Experts

ANMOL PUBLICATIONS PVT. LTD.

NEW DELHI - 110 002 (INDIA)

ANMOL PUBLICATIONS PVT. LTD.
4374/4B, Ansari Road, Daryaganj
New Delhi - 110 002

Advanced Learner's Dictionary of Journalism

First Edition, 2000

ISBN 81-261-0469-4

PRINTED IN INDIA

Published by J.L. Kumar for Anmol Publications Pvt. Ltd., New Delhi and Printed at Mehra Offset Press, Delhi.

Preface

'Journalism' plays an important role in every democratic state. Often it is considered as 'fourth column' of a democracry. If journalism is taken in true spirit, it guides the society, often instrumental in safeguarding the interest of common mass and builds public opinion and raise the voice of depressed and down trodden. Thus, Journalism is not merely a profession but a mission also.

The *Advanced Learner's Dictionary of Journalism* is meant for the students and teachers of Journalism besides the whole community of journalists. Planned and compiled by a team of experts in the field, this dictionary contains the judiciously selected entries, covering all aspects of journalism.

We are grateful to all the scholars whose definitions and explanations are substantially made use of in this work. We are also thankful to Mr. J.L. Kumar, Managing Director, Anmol Publications Pvt. Ltd., New Delhi who undertook the publication of this dictionary.

To make this book more comprehensive and informative constructive criticism from our learned readers are welcome.

—Editors

A

Academic drama: A dramatic tradition which arose from the Renaissance, in which the works of Plautus, Terence, and other ancient dramatists were performed in schools and colleges, at first in Latin but later also in vernacular adaptations composed by schoolmasters under the influence of humanism. This tradition produced the earliest English comedies, notably *Ralph Roister Doister* by the schoolmaster Nicholas Udall.

Academy aperture: Aperture of a 35 mm motion picture camera or projector with the dimensions specified by the Academy.

Academy leader: *Leader* on a motion picture theatrical release print containing information and synchronising marks as designed by the Academy.

Accent: The emphasis placed upon a syllable in pronunciation. The term is often used as a synonym for stress, although some theorists Prefer to use 'stress' only for metrical accent. Three kinds of accent may be distinguished, according to the factor that accounts for each: etymological accent is the emphasis normally given to a syllable according to the word's derivation or morphology rhetorical accent is allocated according to the relative importance of the word in the context of a sentence or question, metrical accent follows a recurrent pattern of stresses in a verse line. Where metrical accent overrides etymological or rhetorical accent, as it often does in ballads and songs, the effect is known as a wrenched accent..

Accentual verse: Verse in which the metre is based on counting only the number of stressed syllables in a line, and in which the number of unstressed syllables in the line may therefore vary. Most verse in Germanic languages is accentual, and much English poetry of later periods has been written in accentual verse, especially in the popular tradition of songs, ballads, nursery rhymes, and hymns. The predominant English metrical system in the 'high' literary tradition since Chaucer, however, has been that of accentual-syllabic verse, in which both stressed and unstressed syllables are counted: thus an iambic pentameter should normally have five stresses distributed among its ten syllables.

Access: To reach into and secure all or part of a body of data; most often used in relation to the securing of information carried in a computer memory or computerized database, but also far more widely applicable to all stores of human thought, information, and artifacts.

Accession: A book, periodical, or other kind of material acquired by a library for its collections; also to record such acquisitions.

Acknowledgment: An author's recognition of the contributions made by others to a work, printed in that work; usually in front or back matter but occasionally carried in the body of the work. Although cast as appreciations, many acknowledgments are actually listings of quotation and illustration sources; some works, especially heavily illustrated books, list illustration sources separately from other acknowledgments.

Acquiring editor: An editor whose primary responsibility is to find authors, contract books, and see the resulting works through to publication; subsidiary responsibilities often include work with authors in the course of manuscript preparation, and involvement with marketing, financial, and production functions. An acquiring editor's functions vis-a-vis authors, manuscripts, and subsidiary responsibilities depend very much on individual publishing house practices and the editor's personal inclinations.

Acquisition: 1. The Purchase of a publication for a collocation by a library or individual. 2. The process of finding and contracting works for publication; the primary responsibility of acquiring editors, but a process in which many publishing people may participate.

Across the board: Referring to a group of numbers that have all risen or fallen together; for example, the prices paid by publishers for paper or of booksellers for books. Sometimes used to indicate uniform fluctuations, as when all wages in a given group rise by the same percentage, but more often indicates that fluctuations have all occurred in one direction, as when prices all rise, although by different amounts.

Active titles: 1. Those publications in a publisher's body of inprint works which are selling well in their markets, as distinguished from those works thought by their publisher to be selling sluggishly; in this sense rather a spongy term, as publications selling at a rate unacceptable to one publisher—who would therefore describe them as inactive—may be selling at a rate which would be thought quite acceptable by another publisher, who would describe them as active. 2. Any publication in print.

Addenda: Short additions to a published work, usually in the form of no more than a few sheets, either bound into a book after the body of the book has been printed but before casing in, or placed loosely or somehow affixed into the finished book after binding and before shipping. In standard publishing practice this term is used to describe supplemental material, but some publishers use it rather loosely to describe also error corrections, which in standard practice are called errata.

Address: In computer systems, the characters that specify the location or destination of any kind of data.

Address of record: An address stated for legal purposes, such as an address stated for purposes of legal notification under the terms of a contract.

Additive colour: Colour mixture by the combination of light of the three primaries, red, green and blue.

Additive mixing: The addition of two signals on different frequencies at the input of an active device operating under nonlinear conditions. The output will contain the two input frequencies, and a range of sum and difference products.

Administrative editor: An editor whose main responsibilities are in editorial organization management, rather than in the editing of published works, but who does not have the general management responsibilities of a chief editor. A rarely used editorial classification; the more widely used term for roughly the same set of responsibilities is *executive editor.*

Adoption: 1. The choice of a work for classroom use by those responsible for making that choice, as when a state commission chooses an elementary or high school text, or a college teacher chooses a text for use by those enrolled in his or her course. 2. The choice of a work for distribution by a book club.

Advance: (1) In a motion picture print, the separation between the picture image and the corresponding point on the sound track required for correct synchronisation in projection. (2) The command for an automatic slide projector to advance to the next slide. 3. A prepaymen in anticipation of future payments, commonly encountered in publishing as an advance by publisher to author against future royalties due according to the terms of a publishing contract, but also encountered in many other business forms, including commission prepayments to outside salespeople. Most publishing advances against royalties are nonreturnable, whether or not future royalties ultimately equal advance payments. When an advance against royalties is paid in increments over a period of time, it is called a *staged advance,* and is usually dependent upon the author's fulfillment of contractually stated conditions prior to each successive advance payment.

Advance copies: Copies of a publication sent after finished works have been produced, but before normal shipment, as when copies of a book are sent to reviewers immediately after printing and weeks before bookstores receive their shipments.

Advance orders: Orders secured before the official publication date of a forthcoming work.

Advance sheets: Copies of printed sheets sent after printing but before bindery operations, usually for promotional purposes, such as to reviewers for prepublication reviews and to book clubs for selection consideration. Once a common practice, but now little used, advance sheets have in the main been replaced by bound galleys, which are galleys cut and bound together for prepublication promotion use.

Advertising: 1. An attempt to sell anything through paid public distribution of selling material. 2. Selling material publicly distributed through any channels of communication, such as newspapers, broadcasts, mail, and films, and in a wide range of possible forms, such as print, radio, and television commercials, direct mail promotions, and records. A single piece of advertising is called an *advertisement* or an *Ad.*

Advertising agency: A business that specializes in the creation, preparation, and placement of advertisements for its clients.

Advertising allowance: An amount granted by a company, such as a publishing company to independent sellers, such as booksellers, for advertising the company's products. The amount is usually expressed as a percentage of the direct costs incurred by the seller in such advertising, up to a fixed dollar limit.

Advertising manager: The employee responsible for overseeing a company's advertising activities.

Depending on the company, this manager may run the company's advertising department as if it were an in-house advertising agency, or may mainly work as liaison with outside advertising agencies.

Advertising medium: Any channel of communication which is used for communicating the sales messages of advertisers, including all available print and broadcast vehicles.

Advertising rates: Amounts charged by advertising media for carrying advertisements placed by advertisers and their agencies; rates vary, depending upon such factors as the sizes and types of markets reached, the placement of advertisements within the medium, and the frequency of placement.

Affiliate: A company that is closely associated with another company, through partial stock ownership, largely shared boards of directors, shared marketing facilities, or other such relationships, but that stops short of subsidiary status, which requires majority stock control.

Affirmative action: Action undertaken, by employers, unions, and others concerned with employment and equal economic opportunity, to reduce discrimination against minority groups and women. The basic statute mandating such actions in the United States is the Equal Opportunity Act of 1972, since followed by other administrative and legal actions.

Agate: 1. A rarely used old type size, measuring about 51/2 points in the modern point system. The vertical measurement of a line of agate type is 1/14 of an inch, so 14 agate type lines fit into one inch of space. In advertising, agate type lines, shortened to *agate lines,* are still used as a basic unit of measure. The term *agate line measure li* most commonly used in relation to classified advertising, which is usually carried in rather narrow columns, but may be applied to a body of type of any width, as it measures only vertical size. 2. A kind of stone, used in hand binding for burnishing the edges of books, usually in gold, but sometimes in silver or other colored materials. 3. A burnishing tool used in hand binding; the stone head of the tool is usually made of agate, but is sometimes made of other stones.

Agency: 1. A relationship in which one party acts for or represents another, under authority granted by the other. The agency may be express or implied, exclusive or shared, general or limited. 2. A business organization engaged in the representation of others; for example, a literary agency, representing authors in negotiations with publishers, or a subscription agency, representing publishers and making sales on behalf of the publishers they represent.

Agency agreement: A formal and written contract between principal and agent, setting forth all terms and conditions of the agency arrangements, as in an agreement between a publisher and a subscription agent. Authors and agents sometimes have such formal contractual agreements, but often do not, the agency becoming formally expressed in each publishing contract, with the publisher often sending all monies due author and agent directly to the agent, who then subtracts an agency fee, and sometimes other amounts previously agreed upon with the author, and sends the balance to the author.

Agency discount: A reduced price granted to an agent selling goods on behalf of another, as when a subscription agent sells on behalf of a publisher at full stated prices and pays the publisher an established discounted price.

Agency shop: A collective bargaining agreement that requires all employees in the bargaining unit to pay union dues or fees equal to dues to the bargaining agent, whether or not they choose to join the union.

Agent: 1. One who acts for or represents another, under authority granted by the other, as does a literary agent for authors. 2. One who sells goods and services for another, such as subscription, insurance, and real estate sales agents.

Allowance: An amount taken off a debt to offset merchandise returns or claims for such matters as defects in delivery or goods delivered; for example, a credit allowed by a publisher for a booksellers return of unsold books.

All published: Describing a set of books as containing all the volumes of a projected set that were published, when the set was not completed.

Allegory: A story or visual image with a second distinct meaning partially hidden behind its literal or visible meaning. The principal technique of allegory is personification, whereby abstract qualities are given human shape—as in public statues of Liberty or justice. An allegory may be conceived as a metaphor that is extended into a structured system. In written narrative, allegory involves a continuous parallel between two levels of meaning in a story, so that its persons and events correspond to their equivalents in a system of ideas or a chain of events external to the tale: each character and episode in John Bunyan's *The Pilgrim's Progress,* for example, embodies an idea within a preexisting Puritan doctrine of salvation. Allegorical thinking permeated the Christian literature of the middle Ages, flourishing in the morality plays and in the dream visions of Dante and Langland. Some later allegorists like Dryden and Orwell used allegory as a method of satire; their hidden meanings are political rather than religious. In the medieval discipline of biblical exegesis, allegory became an important method of interpretation, a habit of seeking correspondences between different realms of meaning or between the Old Testament and the New. It can be argued that modem critical interpretation continues this allegorizing tradition.

Alphabet length: For each typeface and typeface size, the length of the 26 letters of the alphabet, a-z, set in lower case; usually stated in points, rather than inches.

Alphanumeric: Referring to a` set of characters containing letters, numerals, and often other special characters; also called *alphameric.* An electronically-generated visual display of letters, number's and symbols.

All rights reserved: A phrase attempting to protect against copyright infringement in those portions of the world in which the Universal Copyright Convention may not provide full protection. It is normally printed in a copyrighted publication on the same page as is the notice of copyright.

Alterations: Changes made in copy that has been composed; such changes are made by all those concerned with the process of publication, including authors, editors, publishers, and compositors.

Alternative newspaper: A newspaper that is strikingly different from the main body of the press, as signified by its choice of coverage, audience, style, and sometimes format.

Alternative publisher: A publisher appealing to special audiences; usually, but not always, a small publisher originating books designed to appeal to the interests of those seeking the kinds of alternative life styles that became popular in the 1960's. In the 1970's and 1980's, the distinctions between alternative publishers and all other publishers blurred considerably, with many publishers doing the kinds of books earlier thought to be "alternative" books.

American Standard Code for Information Interchange (ASCII): A proposed set of standards for characters to be used in the transmission of data in computer code over telephone lines and in the transfer of such data between the equipment of different manufacturers.

Amoebean verses: a poetic form in which two characters chant alternate lines, couplets, or stanzas, in competition or debate with one another. This form is found in the pastoral poetry of Theocritus and Virgil, and was imitated by Spenser in his *Shepheardes Calender*; it is similar to the *debat,* and sometimes resembles stichomythia.

Anti-novel: a form of experimental fiction that dispenses with certain traditional elements of novel-writing like the analysis of characters' states of mind or the unfolding of a sequential plot. The term is usually associated with the French *nouveau roman* of Alain Robbe-Grillet, Nathalic, Sarraute, and Michel Butor in the 1950s, but has since been extended to include other kinds of fictional experiment that disrupt conventional narrative expectations, as in some works in English by Flann O'Brien, Vladimir Nabokov, B. S. Johnson, and Christine Brooke—Rose. Antecedents of the anti-novel can be found in the blank pages and comically self-defeating digressions of Sterne's *Tristrarn Shandy* and in some of the innovations of modernism, like the absence of narration in Virginia Woolf's *The Waves*.

Antiphrasis: a figure of speech in which a single word is used in a sense directly opposite to its usual meaning, as in the naming of a giant as 'Tiny' or of an enemy as 'friend'; the briefest form of irony.

Anthology: A collection of portions of the work of one or more authors; published as a single work, usually in one or two volumes and often on a single stated theme. Anthologies can be as divers as their compilers choose, mixing several prose and poetic forms, and stating overall themes so wide as to allow several only slightly related subthemes.

Antiquarian bookseller: One engaged in the business of dealing in collectible books, periodicals, graphics other artworks, and related materials; the works dealt in include a wide range of old and rare, not-very-old but rare, and secondhand publications.

Antique: An old collectible, usually an item more than 100 years old, the worth of which stems in large part from its age and condition as well as from current collecting tastes and value estimates. Some of those dealing in collectibles, including books, periodicals, graphics, other book-associated artworks, and related materials, often misleadingly call quite recent items antiques, in an attempt to enhance the desirability of the goods they are selling.

Antique paper: A variety of Printing papers sharing the characteristic of rough, textured finish and low bulk.

Apology: In the literary sense, a justification or defence of the writer's opinions or conduct, not usually implying any admission of blame. The major classical precedent is the *Apologia* of Socrates as recorded by Plato, in which the philosopher defends himself unsuccessfully against the capital charge of impiety before the Athenian court, justifying his role as 'gadfly' to the state. Later writers adopted the title for various kinds of work from literary theory, as in Sidney's *An Apologie* for *Poetry,* to autobiography, as in *An Apology* for *the life* of Mr *Colley Cibber, Comedian* by the much-mocked poet laureate. John Henry Newman's *Apologia Pro Vita Sua* has a greater element of polemic, justifying his adoption of Roman Catholicism against aspersions cast by Charles Kingsley. An apology is sometimes called an apologetic.

Apostrophe: A rhetorical figure in which the speaker addresses a dead or absent person, or an abstraction or inanimate object. In classical rhetoric, the term could also denote a speaker's turning to address a particular member or section of the audience.

Appendix: A section of a book, appearing immediately after the text, containing material thought to be better published in a separate section than as part of the main text, although it is an integral part of the book, rather than supplementary material; for example, a body of tabular materials, which if published as part of the main text would impede the flow of the narrative, but which is an essential portion of the book as a whole. Whether to include material as appendix or main text is very much a matter of writing and editing choice.

Array: A series of memory locations with a single name, for example a set of related *variables* representing the days of the year could be named day *(1)—day* (365) (a one-dimension array) or named as parts of months *day* (3,9) (a two-dimension array).

Art: In wide publishing usage, all the non-text elements of composition, including such physical elements as drawings, illustration, and hand lettering, and such design elements as layout and pasteup. More narrowly, the physical elements alone.

Art book: A book containing material primarily concerned with the visual arts; while often a heavily illustrated book, the category includes books composed largely or wholly of text.

Artwork: Illustrative copy whether prepared by an artist, camera or other mechanical means. The term is also used in printed circuit layout work.

Article: A nonfiction work on a single subject, usually written for a periodical, such as a newspaper or magazine; can be as short as a few thousand words, but may sometimes be of book size, especially when run serially in the periodical.

Association copy: A book that has acquired value because of its association with a notable person or event; for example, a book that has belonged to a historic figure.

Asterisk (*): A reference mark used mainly to indicate the presence of footnotes, but, occasionally used to indicate imprinted expletives or obscenities.

As-told-to book: A book produced by a writer from conversations with another, with the other being credited as co-author—often the primary author—of the book; such a work often results from the collaboration between a non-writing celebrity and a professional writer.

Audiovisual (AV) materials: Nonbook materials, such as slides and records, used to supplement educational texts; in practice, the term has expanded to include some motion picture material, but does not include computer-assisted instructional materials or video materials.

Audit Bureau of Circulation: A private organization which audits and verifies the claimed paid circulation of newspapers, magazines, and other periodicals; significant because advertising rates are largely based on audited paid circulations.

Automatic writing: A method of composition that tries to dispense with conscious control or mental censorship, transcribing immediately the promptings of the unconscious mind. Some writers in the early days of Surrealism attempted it, notably Andre Breton and Philippe Soupault in their work *Les Champs Magnetiques. W. B.* Yeats had earlier conducted similar experiments with Georgie Hyde-Lees after their marriage in 1917; these seances influenced the mystical system of his prose work A *Vision*.

Author (au): The original writer of a work of any size and in any form, published or unpublished, although the term is most commonly used to refer to published writers.

Authorized: Describing a work that has official sanction or approval from interested parties, such as an authorized biography approved by the subject's heirs or executors, or a version of a religious work endorsed by a major church group.

Authorized edition: An edition produced under copyright protection, rather than one that has been pirated or reprinted when the work was no longer in copyright; may be any printing or edition of the originally copyrighted edition.

Author's alterations (AA's): Alterations made by an author in composed copy, aside from correction of printer's errors (PE's); usually made in galleys but sometimes in page proofs, including alterations in text, heads, illustrations, and design. In newspaper, periodical, and looseleaf publishing, author's alterations are often necessary in order to provide timely publications; their cost is viewed as part of the cost of publishing and is borne entirely by the publisher. In book publishing, who bears the cost of author's alterations is a matter of contractual provision, most publishing contracts providing for a 10-15% author's alteration allowance, and some going as high as 20%; the author bears the cost of all alterations beyond the stated percentage, generally of the original cost of the composition. In contrast, cost of correcting printer's errors is borne by the composition house.

Author's copies: Free copies of a work provided to its author by the publisher of that work on publication; the number of copies, often 510, is specified in the contract between author and publisher.

Author's discount: The discounted price charged an author by a publisher for copies of the author's own work, beyond the number of author's copies provided in the author-publisher contract; also a matter of contractual provision, and usually in the 25-40% range. The author's discount is sometimes allowed on other works from the same publisher.

Author's guild: A major national author's organization, representing its author members, and in some senses all authors, on matters of common interest, such as pending legislative, regulatory, and tax matters; author-publisher relations; professional development; free speech; copyright protection; and public lending right. The Author's Guild and The Dramatist's Guild together comprise The Author's League of America.

Author's interview: An interview of an author by a media representative, for the purpose of generating printed or broadcast materials on the author, and usually on the author's work; generally arranged as part of the promotional activities on behalf of a recently published or forthcoming work.

Author's proofs: Proofs of typeset works, sent to the author for correction and return to the publisher. The first proofs are usually put together in long sheets called *galleys*, which may be paginated, but not in the final pagination of the work itself. After the author returns corrected galley proofs to the publisher, the publisher corrects the composed material, moves to page makeup, and usually produces a second set of author's proofs, called *page proofs*, which are copies of the completed pages of the work, including page numbers. The author makes any final corrections on the page proofs and sends them back to the publisher, who then completes publication. Some publishers move directly to page proofs on certain works, bypassing the galley proof stage, with the author reading the composed manuscript only once, and making all corrections on the page proofs.

Author's questionnaire A form used by many publishers to secure from the authors of forthcoming works information which may be of use in marketing those works, and through which publishers seek to learn more about such matters as special markets, media, book content, competition, and the authors themselves; used very widely in professional and reference publishing, and occasionally in trade publishing.

Author's read: The reading of galleys or page proofs by an author primarily for meaning, rather than for the purpose of correcting typographical errors.

Author's tour: A trip undertaken by an author to promote his or her book, during the course of which the author engages in such promotional activities as television and radio appearances, bookstore autographing appearances, speeches before local organizations, and discussions with distribution personnel. Usually arranged by the publisher of the book, with the publisher paying for travel and associated costs, and the author contributing unpaid time; sometimes arranged and paid for solely by the author.

Autobiography: A nonfiction work dealing with the life of its author; sometimes called memoirs. Many books currently passing as autobiography are actually biographies, written by uncredited ghost writers and published under the subject's name.

Autocode: To use computers themselves to develop programs in machine language from human-developed symbolically coded programs.

autōgraph copy: A copy of a work signed by its author; such works are a staple of the antiquarian book trade, some acquiring great value as they age.

B

Background art: The artwork used to provide a background for Primary illustrations, for example, a line or shadow pattern on which an illustration is placed.

Backlog: All unfilled orders from customers. A distinction is often made between total backlog, which includes all unfilled orders, and active or current backlog, which includes only orders in process or for which material is on hand.

Backlist: All titles a publisher currently carries in print, other than those published recently, usually within the last six months; but some publishers treat books as new, or frontlist, books for considerably longer than six months, with backlist classification reached only after sales or topical interest have subsided.

Back matter: Everything following the main text of a publication, including such materials as glossaries, appendixes, footnotes, bibliographies, and indexes. Where such materials appear in the body of the text, as all of the above but indexes often do, they are not back matter, but part of the text; and indexes may even appear as front matter, as is often true in directory, legal, and topical publishing. Both back matter and front matter are identified entirely by placement within a publication, rather than by form or content. Also called *end matter.*

Back order: An order accepted and held for future delivery, usually because the item ordered is out of stock.

Back to press: Describing a publication in print that is in the process of being reprinted, sometimes with such minor changes as typographical error corrections, but without such substantial changes as would occasion designation of the new printing as a new edition.

Back up: To print material on the other side of a sheet of paper that has printing on one side only; as a practical matter, normally used to instruct a printer to print on both sides of sheet.

Bargain books: Books that are sold far below their list prices; used rather spongily to describe all such books, whether remaindered, reprinted in lower-priced editions but still bound basically in the same way as was the original edition, or discounted down close to the seller's purchase price from the publisher, but does not include paperback reprint editions.

Baskerville: A group of type styles named after their originator, the 18th century English printer and type designer John Baskerville.

Batch processing: 1. Processing of a single load or lot of material or information as a unit, in contrast to continuous processing. Most often used to describe the technique of grouping a number of similar items of input so that they can be processed to completion during a single computer run, as in inventory control and order processing. In *remote batch processing,* jobs or data are entered at remote terminals, batched and processed at a central location, and the results returned to the remote terminals. 2. The serial or sequential processing of computer programs or data.

by the poet Allen Ginsberg and the novelist Jack Kerouac. Writers of the beat generation' dropped out of middle-class society in search of 'beatific' ecstasy through drugs, sex, and Zen Buddhism. Their loose styles favour spontaneous self-expression and recitation to jazz accompaniment. The principal works of the group are Ginsberg's Howl and Kerouac's *On the Road*. Significant contributions in poetry were Gregory Corso's *Gasoline* and Gary Snyder's Riprap; while in prose, the group's mentor William S. Burroughs published *The Naked Lunch in* 1959. The poet Lawrence Ferlinghetti was another leading figure. The Beats had a strong influence on the counter-culture of the 1960s.

Beaver-tail: Beam In antennas, a radiated beam that has a width in the horizontal plane significantly greater than that in the vertical plane.

Belles lettres: Literary writings mainly of aesthetic rather than content value; the term is often used to describe prose thought to be beautiful, whatever its content. The French term for fine writing', originally used to distinguish artistic literature from scientific or philosophical writing. Since the 19th century, though, the term has more often been used dismissively to denote a category of elegant essay-writing and light-weight literary chatter, of which much was published in Britain in the late 19th and early 20th centuries: Max Beerbohm's essays and Andrew

Lanes *Letters to Dead Authors* (1896) are examples. An author of such elegant trifles is a *belletrist*. *Adjective:* belletristic.

Below the line: 1. Unusual items, such as major onetime costs and revenues, which are shown separately on accounting statements. Such items are described as *below the* line, while customary items are *above the line.* 2. In marketing, sales promotion costs other than advertising are *below the line,* while advertising is *above the line.*

Benday: A process through which a wide range of shadings and tones can be applied to line and halftone drawings, either directly to the plate, or, as is more common in modern practice, through the overlay of one or more screens on the original artwork; named after Benjamin Day, the 19th and early 20th century New York printer, who invented the first of the many processes now used to accomplish these ends.

Beneficial interest: The right to benefits flowing from a contract, a will, or an insurance policy; for example, the right to royalties held by an author's heirs, flowing from an author-publisher book contract.

Bestseller: A book selling so many copies in a given period that it ranks among the top sellers nationally for that period, as measured by such standard indexes as the *New York Times* and *Publisher's Weekly* bestseller lists. The main indexes are reported weekly, and the main categories reported on are hardbound fiction and nonfiction, trade paperback fiction and nonfiction, and mass market paperback fiction and nonfiction.

Bestseller bonus: An additional payment from publisher to author in the event that a published work appears on a certain bestseller list, or group of bestseller lists, usually for given periods, as specified in the contract.

Bible paper: An opaque, strong, very thin, fairly light, and rather expensive book paper used extensively in very long books requiring physical compactness, such as Bibles, looseleaf reporters, and dictionaries. Also called *India paper* or *Bible* stock.

Biblio: Pertaining to books, from the Greek *biblion* for book. Used only in combination with other terms other terms.

Bibliographer: One who organizes, describes, and catalogues printed materials; usually describing one who does so professionally, rather than on a onetime or quite occasional basis.

Bibliomania: A compulsion for involvement with books, usually for the acquisition of books; but far more widely used to describe the state of mind of those who love books, and without the social opprobrium accompanying many other kinds of manias.

Bibliophile: A booklover; in somewhat narrower senses, one who has developed considerable knowledge of books, or a knowledgeable book collector.

Bibliopole: One who deals in books; in our time, usually one who deals in rare, old, or valuable books.

bibliotheca: A library or other book collection.

Bid: 1. An offer to buy immediately at a specific price, whether in the course of a unique transaction between buyer and seller, or as one of a group of competing offers, as at an auction. 2. A formal quotation of the price a seller will require to do a job for a potential purchaser, as when a freelance writer or a printer quotes a price on a job to a publisher.

Big book: A commercially successful book. The term is relative; 3 large trade book publisher may consider a book "big" only if it sells tens of thousands of copies in hardcover, reaches one or more national bestseller lists, and enjoys substantial subsidiary rights sales, while a smaller publisher may describe far more modest commercial results as "big." Also called a *blockbuster*.

Big name author: An author who has celebrity status, whether achieved through authorship or in some other way; a term often used loosely by publishers and publicists for commercial purposes.

Bilingual edition: A book in which some or all of the text is written in two languages.

Billboard: An advertising poster or structure, usually placed outdoors and aimed at catching the attention of travelers.

Bimonthly: An every-two-months publishing frequency; sometimes confused with *semimonthly* which is a twice-a-month frequency.

Binder: 1. A cover that is not glued to the contents of a publication but attached in some other way, as by rings, posts, or combs through holes punched in the contents of the book; widely used for looseleaf publications requiring periodic updating. 2. One in the business of binding books.

Binder's board: Heavy paperboard placed under the cloth used in bookbinding to create book covers. Once in book covers, the material is usually called *boards*.

Bindery: A place where books are bound; also a general term describing the performance of a substantial number of publication production operations beyond the printing process and through the production of the printed work, including folding and cutting the printed sheets coming off the press, assembling, casing in or otherwise covering the printed pages, and related functions. Once carried on in a physically separate area in printing plants, bindery operations are more and more being merged into the printing process, for reasons of speed and economy, as when sheets are folded and trimmed as they are printed, or an integrated line of presses and binding machines produces a completed publication in a single pass through the line, bypassing several traditional bindery operations.

Binding: 1. The cover and associated materials in a publication, including cover materials, glue, thread, and any mechanical binding elements, such as metal rings, posts, plastic combs, and staples. 2. The process of manufacturing a finished publication after the printing of contents, including all bindery operations, such as folding, gathering, collating, and trimming the printed pages; sewing or drilling; the casing-in operations; and additional functions, such as covering hardbound books with jackets, or inserting pocket parts or advertising materials.

Binding edge: That edge of a page that is closest to the backbone of the publication, and that will therefore need enough margin in printing to allow for binding, without making the resulting page margin disproportionately small as compared with the other three margins on the page.

Biography: A nonfiction work dealing with the life of another. An *authorized biography* is one commissioned by or actively supported by the subject or appropriate executors; the biographer is often given full access to the subject's papers, but sometimes is required to limit both the enquiry and the portrayal. *An unauthorised biography is* one written against the express wish of, or without the support of, the subject or various heirs and assigns, sometimes resulting in libel or invasion of privacy suits against the biographer and publisher. Publishers sometimes use the label "unauthorized" as a marketing device, hoping to appeal to readers' supposed interest in hostile or sensational portrayals.

Bibliomania: A compulsion for involvement with books, usually for the acquisition of books; but far more widely used to describe the state of mind of those who love books, and without the social opprobrium accompanying many other kinds of manias.

Bibliophile: A booklover; in somewhat narrower senses, one who has developed considerable knowledge of books, or a knowledgeable book collector.

Bibliopole: One who deals in books; in our time, usually one who deals in rare, old, or valuable books.

Block of copy: A body of material that is handled for editing, composing, and other publishing purposes as a connected whole, though not necessarily the whole body of a work; in form may appear to be several parts of a work, as when several chapters are closely connected in content, but should be edited together as a unit.

Block printing: Printing, often in substantial quantity, from carved blocks, in early Chinese and European printing from wooden blocks, and later from linoleum blocks as well. Early Chinese block printing dates from the 8th century A.D., or even earlier; European block printing dates from the 15th century A.D., and resulted in editions known as *block books.* When such printing is done from wooden blocks, it is also called *xylography;* when used for illustrations, called a *woodcut.*

Blueprint: A print of white lines on blue background, produced by contact between an original pen or pencil positive, or a translucent master proof, and sensitized blueprint paper; because it is a contact print, it can be neither enlarged nor reduced, but is the same size as the original. *Book blues* are proofs from film of the mechanicals, and allow for the first and often only checking of placement of halftones and color illustrations, as well as for doublechecking of sequencing and placement of material. The term *blueprint is* often used in publishing and printing to describe prints that are not white on blue, including *brownprints,* which are white prints on brown backgrounds; *brownline prints,* which are brown prints on white backgrounds, sometimes *called silver prints; vandykes,* which are brown and white prints; and other prints that go by brand names.

Blurb: 1. Any piece of advertising copy. 2. The selling copy found on the jacket of a hardcover or the cover of a paperback book.

Bodoni: A group of widely used modem typefaces, originated by 18th and early 19th century Italian printer Giambattista Bodoni.

Body: 1. In metal typesetting, the base of a single piece of type. 2. In any form of composition, the space into which type will be printed, which may be larger than the print itself. For example, a space or body which is large enough to accommodate 12-point type may be used for printing in 10-point type, so that the page will by less crowded with type and have more "air" in it. Such a page would be described as being printed 10 on 12; if printed 12 on 12," then 12 point type would be used to fill a 12-point body. 3. Any piece of copy contained in the text of a publication; often called *body* copy. 4. The main text of a publication, excluding front and back matter.

Boldface (bf): A heavier and darker version of the same typeface used in body copy, often used in headings within a body of copy. It is thereby distinguished from lightface, which is used in body copy. Generally indicated on copy to be composed by a wavy line under the affected words or letters.

Bond paper: Any strong and durable paper normally used for typewriting or for writing with other writing instruments. Although most papers designated "bond" by their manufacturers have some rag content and are watermarked, strong and durable wood paper and unwatermarked papers may also be so designated.

Book: 1. In the widest sense, a body of material capable of being inscribed upon in some fashion, whether or not inscription has occurred; therefore any group of pages or leaves, bound or unbound, and also any scroll or related group of writing tablets of any material. In usual modem conception, a group of pages or leaves bound together in any fashion, whether permanently or in such easily revisable forms as looseleaf, whether blank or carrying printing, and including periodicals, although national postal services define "book" in various ways for mailing status and cost purposes. The term is now expanding to include bodies of text earned in other publishing forms, such as electronic databases delivering text on screens and videodiscs. 2. The script of a play, especially a theatrical work with music; for example, the text of a musical comedy or operetta called the *book,* or the *libretto.*

Bookbinding: That body of operations designed to bind leaves into a finished book of any kind, including the sewing, gluing and casing-in operations associated with the creation of hardbound and paperback books and booklets, as well as the drilling, stapling, and inserting into binders associated with mechanical binding.

Bookburning: 1. Literally, the burning of proscribed books, as has happened on many occasions throughout the work, in modem times most spectacularly in Nazi Germany, but on some occasions also in

United States. 2. Loosely, the proscription of books by government or other institutions.

Book cloth: A series of treated cloths which, in the manufacture of book covers, are wrapped around the binder's board to form surfaces of the covers. Book cloths are made in several finishes, weights, and weaves; they, may be plastic-coated or filled with starch, or plastic, the former being most common. *Buckram,* which is a coarsely woven cotton cloth available in several weights, is very widely used, as well as some more closely woven and better quality fabrics. Common finishes include *linen; solid,* sometimes called *vellum;* and *natural,* in which the dyed cloth is seen without the textural effect called by filling, as filling is done after dyeing and from the side that will face the binding board rather than the surface of the cover.

Book club: A membership organization functioning as a vehicle for the sale and distribution of books to its members, by periodically, usually monthly, offering for sale books as main selections, which members may purchase or reject, and as alternate and special selections.

Book club rights: The rights to publish a book as a book club selection; one of a series of valuable property fights associated with book properties, and capable of being conveyed to others by the owner of the rights. Book club rights may be owned by an author; more commonly, they are owned by the book's publisher, as long as the book is kept in print and rights sold by author to publisher have not, reverted to the author under the terms of the author-publisher contract. When these fights are sold by a publisher to a book club, the author, normally receives a share—often 50%—of the proceeds, to be credit to the author's royalty account.

Book collector: One who actively acquires books for a personal library. Although some collectors acquire books for the use of the contents, most pay far more attention to the rarity, age, condition, an value of the books acquired.

Book collector's club: An organization composed of those who are actively engaged in book collection, in the study of books as physical objects, and in the development of the arts associated with book production: examples include New York's Grolier Club and London's Roxburghe Club.

Book dividend: A bonus book supplied by a book club to its members, sometimes without charge of any kind, sometimes accompanied only by postage and handling charges, and most often as part of a merchandising approach aimed at encouraging the purchase of books, by giving bonus book credit with other purchases.

Book face: Any typeface normally used in the composition of book body copy; usually a face tending toward considerable body and weight, rather than a very thin and light face but v of designer's choice.

Book fair: A trade fair, devoted to the display and sale of books; often accompanied by related promotional, educational, professional, and social activities, such as dinners, speeches, seminars, author appearances, and subsidiary rights sales activities.

Book feature: An article or series of articles in a periodical devoted to discussion of one or more books and their authors; often part of the promotional activities connected with the publication of a new book.

Booklet: A small softcovered publication, issued once rather than periodically.

Book life: 1. The length of time that a book may be sold before a new edition is necessary, whether for editorial or marketing reasons. 2. The length of time that a book exists in readily usable form, without significant deterioration, a period much decreased by the use of acidic papers, as in many modem books. Also called longevity.

Bookman: Traditionally, one who is deeply immersed in books, and usually describing someone who is immersed in some aspect of the book trade, as will. At this writing, the use of the term has diminished' sharply, due to connotations that are perceived as sexist by many women and men in the book trades, and it has not yet been replaced by an acceptably androgynous substitute.

Bookmark: A paperboard, plastic, or woven fabric card or piece of other material used to mark a reader's place in a book being read; popular as a promotional device, and often distributed carrying advertising messages.

Bookmobile: A traveling book display, bookstore, public library branch, or library distribution service, mounted in or on a bus, truck, or other vehicle.

Book paper: Any paper normally used in book and periodical contents, and traditionally implying paper of high enough quality to be used for the creation of durable books; but with the continuing deterioration in the quality of the paper used to produce many commercial books since the 1960's, many papers that would formerly have been considered unsuitable for books are now called book papers by their manufacturers and by those publishers using them, such as the short-lived acidic papers now often substituted for higher quality acid-free papers.

Bookplate: A label identifying the owner of a book, usually pasted on the book's inside front cover; bookplates from notable collections, especially when signed by the owner, can add substantially to the value of collectible books, and some bookplates are collected for their intrinsic artistic or historical worth.

Book producer: An individual or organization contracting with publishers to deliver a book package, consisting of at least camera-ready copy and often bound books, to the publisher's warehouse; usually one who does not actually write the book package delivered, but hires others to do so, treating the writing as one element of book package production. Often called a *packager* or *book packager;* the term *book producer is of* recent origin, developed by the practitioners themselves to enhance status and clarify functions performed.

Bookragger: A reviewer who is characteristically unkind to books reviewed, seeming to take pleasure in personal attacks upon authors, editors, and publishers.

Book rate: The United States Postal Service mailing rate for books; a preferential rate which recognizes the unique role played by books in the life of the nation.

Bookseller: One who retails books. Although publishers who operate bookstores and those who sell at list prices by mail are booksellers, the designation is generally applied to those whose primary book business is retail sales.

Book size: The physical, or trim, size of the pages of a book, in the United States measured approximately by the height of the page, and in England measured rather specifically by the height and width of the page, although there is no very great historical justification for either. Historically, page sizes were a function of the sizes of the sheets used for printing, and the standard descriptors of resulting book sizes are purely a function of how often the sheets used were folded after printing, and the number of pages therefore derived from each sheet. A sheet folded once, whatever its original size, was a *folio.* A sheet folded twice, to create four leaves, whatever their size, resulted in a size called *quarto,* for the four resulting leaves. A sheet folded three times was an octavo, after the eight resulting leaves. A sheet folded four times, is, similarly, a *Sixteenino, or 16 mo.* There are also many other classifications. such as *24 mo, 32 mo, 48 mo,* and *64 mo,* from further sheet foldings. The several American and British sizes a found throughout this book, in place, where they are defined and referred back to this entry for further clarification; some modem American references to book size refer to binding height, rather than page height, but the differences are minor as the page or book heights used are only approximate.

Book-tech stores: A store that is heavily involved in the sale of both books and computer-related materials.

Book trade: The business of selling books at retail, including new, used, and antiquarian books; sometimes used more widely to include those portions of the publishing industry concerned with the production and sale of books sold at retail.

Book welding: In bookbinding, the use of specially coated paper and very hot laser beam to weld together the paper to be bound.

Book with legs: A colloquialism describing a book so commercially successful that it "walks out of the store."

Bookworm: 1. One who incessantly reads and is immersed in the content of books. 2. The larva of any of several kinds of insects that devour the paper and bindings of books.

Bound books: Books that have been cased in, usuallv referring to books that have been sewn, glued, or stapled into permanent bindings rather than pages placed into looseleaf binders; but not necessarily meaning books that have been entirely finished and made ready for shipment as such operations as cover stamping and jacketing may not have been completed. Also called *bound copies,* although bound copies may also refer to copies of nonbook publications, such as magazines and booklets.

Brand name author: A very well known author, whose public virtually guarantees that his or her books will sell well.

Broadcasting: The transmission, by means of radio waves, of programmes of sound, vision and other services for general reception.

Broadcasting network: The interconnected installations necessary to provide a broadcasting service.

Broadcasting station: A centre comprising one or more transmitters and associated antenna systems, for providing a broadcast service.

Generation of modulating signals generally takes place at sites remote from the station.

Broadcast standard: In video practice, representing the highest quality of recording and reproduction, capable of meeting the stringent requirements of broadcasting organisations.

Brochure: A booklet devoted to advertising matter, often illustrated, printed on expensive paper, and using a good deal of display type Brochures vary widely in size and style, ranging from a small folded broadside to a substantial booklet virtually indistinguishable from a small book.

Bulldog edition: The earliest edition of a newspaper; sometimes an edition that is of limited size and is used for mailings to long-distance subscribers and for other special purposes.

Bullet: A heavy dot used before copy to set it off, if less heavy, sometimes called a *centered dot* and used as a raised decimal point.

C

Campus novel: A novel, usually comic or satirical, in which the action is set within the enclosed world of a university and highlights the follies of academic life. Many novels have presented nostalgic evocations of college days, but the campus novel in the usual modern sense dates from the 1950s: Mary McCarthy's *The Groves of Academe* and Kingsley Amis's *Lucky Jim* began a significant tradition in modern fiction including John Barth's *Giles Goat-Boy*. David Lodge's *Changing Places,* and Robertson Davies's *The Rebel Angels.*

Casebook: A book in content wholly or mainly composed of illustrative cases; a traditional American lawbook form, and more recently a textbook form adopted by business and other professional schools.

Catalog: To create a list; also the list so created, such as a publisher's list of books for sale, sometimes spelled catalogue.

Cataloguing in Publication (CIP): An arrangement whereby publishers May send information on a forthcoming work, usually including front matter describing the work and data on the author, to the Library of Congress, receiving in turn its completed catalog information in time for inclusion in the published work, usually on the copyright page.

Catalogue verse: Verse that records the names of several persons, places, or things in the form of a list. It is common in epic poetry, where the heroes involved in a battle are often enumerated. Other types of catalogue verse record genealogical or geographical information. Wait Whitman created a new kind of catalogue verse in his Song *of* Myself, which celebrates the huge variety of peoples, places, and occupations in the United States in the form of long lists.

Celebrity book: A book written about or by someone who has celebrity status; often thought by trade publishers to have substantial commercial possibilities.

Chapbook: The name given since the 19th century to a kind of small, cheaply printed book or pamphlet hawked by chapmen from the 16th century to the early 19th century, and containing ballads, fairytales, old romances, accounts of famous criminals and other popular entertainments. A kind of small, inexpensive, paperbound book containing a wide variety of contents, such as stories, brief biographies, poetry, and essays; much like a modem popular magazine, but usually without periodicity.

Chapel: A union association in a printing shop; a local union, part of a larger local.

Chapter: A self-contained, relatively small portion of a written work, often numbered, entitled, and introduced by large headings called *chapter headings;* the size of a chapter is a matter of authorial editorial choice.

Character: A specifiable pattern preparable on a visual display unit, monitor or printer, including letters, numbers and specific symbols. A personage in a narrative or dramatic work: also a kind of prose sketch briefly describing some recognizable type of person. As a minor literary genre, the character originates with the *Characters* of the Greek writer Theophrastus; it was revived in the 17th century, notably by Sir Thomas Overbury in his *Characters* and by La Bruyere in Les *Caractres.*

Character generator: Device to issue the sequence of signals needed to form the desired character on the cathode ray tube.

Characterization: The representation of persons in narrative and dramatic works. This may include direct methods like the attribution of qualities in description or commentary, and indirect methods inviting readers to infer qualities from characters' actions, speech, or appearance. Since E. M. Forster's *Aspects of the Novel* a distinction has often been made between 'flat' and 'two-dimensional' characters, which are simple and unchanging, and 'round' characters, which are complex, 'dynamic', and less predictable.

Cheap edition: A considerably less expensive edition of a book issued by its original publisher, but in the same basic form as the original issue; a less expensive hardbound edition of an originally hardbound book is a cheap edition, but a paperbound edition is not. The distinction may be significant for authors and publishers, as some publishing contracts call for different royalty schedules for hard-bound cheap and paperbound editions.

Checking copy: A copy of a publication containing advertising sent to advertisers or their representatives for review of accuracy, placement, and such matters as quality of reproduction of photos.

Chief editor: The top editorial executive of a publishing organization, and the individual directly responsible for leading that organization's editorial activities and supervising all editorial functions. A single publishing company may include many publishing organizations and suborganizations, and each may have a chief editor. Also called *editor-in-chief.*

Children's books: Books designed for an audience gene I rally of elementary school age; but in a publishing sense children's books and young adult books overlap, with no sharp boundaries between the two categories.

Choral character: A term sometimes applied to a character in a play who, while participating in the action to some degree, also provides the audience with an ironic commentary upon it, thus performing a function similar to that of the chorus in Greek tragedy. Two examples are Thersites in Shakespeare's *Troilus and Cressida* and Wong in Brecht's *The Good Woman of Setzuan.*

Choriamb or choriambus: A metrical unit combining one trochee and one iamb into a single foot of four syllables, with two stressed syllables enclosing two unstressed syllables, as in the word *hullabaloo.* It was used frequently in Greek dramatic choruses and lyrics, and by the Roman poet Horace, and later in some German verse. Usually, as in the Asclepiad, it is combined with other feet A rare English example of choriambic verse is Swinburne's 'Choriambics', in which the line consists of one trochee, three choriambs, and one iamb:

Chromakey: Video special effects technique in which areas of saturated blue in 'a foreground scene are substituted by a picture from another source, into which the foreground is 'keyed'. (= *colour separation overlay*)

Chromatic aberration: Defect of a lens or optical system causing light of different colours to be focused in different planes, usually apparent as coloured fringes around the image. A property of an optical lens, whereby the focal length differs over the range of spectral colours. Combinations of transparent materials with differing refractive indices can correct the effect, and such lenses are known as achromatic pairs.

Classicism: An attitude to literature that is guided by admiration of the qualities of formal balance, proportion, decorum, and restraint attributed to the major works of ancient Greek and Roman literature in preference to the irregularities of later vernacular literatures, and especially to the artistic liberties proclaimed by Romanticism. A classic is a work of the highest class, and has also been taken to mean a work suitable for study in school classes. During and since the Renaissance, these overlapping meanings came to be applied to the writings of major Greek and Roman authors from Homer to Juvenal, which were regarded as unsurpassed models of excellence.

The adjective classical, usually applied to this body of writings, has since been extended to outstandingly creative periods of other literatures: the 17th century may be regarded as the classical age of French literature and the 19th century the classical period of the Western novel, while the finest fiction of the United States in the mid-19th century from Cooper to Twain was referred to by D. H. Lawrence as Classic American literature. A classical style or approach to literary composition is usually one that imitates Greek or Roman models in subject-matter or in form or both. As a literary doctrine, classicism holds that the writer must be governed by rules, models, or conventions, rather than by wayward inspiration: in its most strictly codified form in the 17th and 18th centuries, it required the observance of rules derived from Aristotle's *Poetics* and Horace's *Ars Poetica*, principally those of decorum and the dramatic unities.

The dominant tendency of French literature in the 17th and 18th centuries, classicism in a weaker form also characterized the Augustan Age in England, the later German classicism of the late 18th and early 19th centuries was distinguished by its exclusive interest in Greek models, as opposed to the Roman bias of French and English classicisms. After the end of the 18th century, 'classical' came to be contrasted with 'romantic' in an opposition of increasingly generalized terms embracing moods and attitudes as well as characteristics of actual works. While partisans of Romanticism associated the classical with the rigidly artificial and the romantic with the freely creative, the classicists condemned romantic self-expression as eccentric self-indulgence, in the name of classical sanity and order.

The great German writer J. W. von Goethe summarized his conversion to classical principles by defining the classical as healthy, the romantic as sickly. Since then, literary classicism has often been less a matter of imitating Greek and Roman models than of resisting the claims of Romanticism and all that it may be thought to stand for the critical doctrines of Matthew Arnold and more especially of T. S.

Eliot are classicist in this sense of reacting against the Romantic principle of unrestrained self-expression.

Cinemascope: System of anamorphic wide-screen motion pictures making use of a horizontal compression/expansion factor of 2: 1. (Trade name)

Cinematography Recording and reproducing motion as a series of images on a strip of photographic film.

Circular: An advertising piece, circulated by any means of physical dissemination, as by mail or hand distribution.

Circular polarisation: In antennas and propagation, a radio wave in which the electric field polarisation rotates about the axis of propagation. Rotation can be clockwise or anti-clockwise. FM broad-casting sometimes takes place from transmitting antennas that generate a circularly polarised wave. The object is to provide a choice at the receiving point between the use of a vertical or horizontal antenna. The received signal power is divided between vertical and horizontal, and field strengths will be -3 dB compared with a radiated field in one plane only.

Circulation: The number of copies of an issue of a periodical that are in any way distributed. Circulation is often composed of paid copies and complimentary, or free, copies. The average number of copies distributed in a given period is a publication's *average circulation.*

Circulation guarantee: The number of copies of a periodical publication its publisher states as the current average circulation figure; often verified by an independent auditing organization. The publisher's circulation guarantee plays a major part in the development of their advertising rates.

Codex: A book consisting of ancient manuscripts. The study of codices is called codicology.

Colour separations: A set of monochrome photographic images recording colour information in limited spectral ranges, usually red, green and blue.

Comedy: A play written chiefly to amuse its audience by appealing to a sense of superiority over the characters depicted. A comedy will normally be closer to the representation of everyday life than a tragedy, and will explore common human failings rather than tragedy's disastrous crimes. Its ending will usually be happy for the leading characters. In another sense, the term was applied in the Middle Ages to narrative poems that end happily: the title of Dante's *Divine Comedy* carries this meaning. As a dramatic form, comedy in Europe dates back to the Greek playwright Aristophanes in the 5th century BC. His Old Comedy combines several kinds of mischief, including the satirical mockery of living politicians and writers. At the end of the next century, Menander established the fictional form known as New Comedy, in which young lovers went through misadventures among other stock characters; this tradition was later developed in the Roman comedy of Plautus and Terence, and eventually by Shakespeare in England and Lope de Vega in Spain.

The great period of European comedy, partly influenced by the *commedia dell' arte,* was the 17th century, when Shakespeare, de Vega, and Jonson were succeeded by Moliere and by the Restoration comedy of Congreve, Etheredge, and Wycherley. There are several kinds of comedy, including the romantic comedy of Shakespeare's *A Midsummer Night's Dream,* the satire in Jonson's *Volpone* or in Moliere's *Le Tartuffe,* the sophisticated verbal wit of the comedy of manners in Wilde's *The Importance of Being Earnest,* and the more topical 'comedy of ideas' in the plays of George Bernard Shaw. Among its less sophisticated forms are burlesque and farce.

Commonplace book: Not a dull or trite book, as the usual sense of' commonplace' would suggest, but a writer's notebook in which interesting ideas and quotations are collected for further reflection and possible future use. In this sense, a commonplace is a remark or written passage that is worth remembering or quoting. Notable examples of commonplace books that have been published include Ben Jonson's Timber and W. H. Auden's A Certain *World.*

Comparative literature: The combined study of similar literary works written in different languages, which stresses the points of connection between literary products of two or more cultures, as distinct from the sometimes narrow and exclusive perspective of Eng. Lit. or similar approaches based on one national canon. Advocates of comparative literature maintain that there is, despite the obvious disadvantages. much to be gained from studying literary works in translation.

Compiler: Complex computer program to convert source code (orientated around a high level language) into executable code for later use. The resulting 'object code' is usually, but not always, *machine code,* it can be P-code.

Complementary colours: Colours resulting from subtracting a given colour from white light, thus the complementary colour to red is 'minus red' which is cyan (blue-green).

Composite: A photographic montage of images, as in multi-screen also, several images on a single slide mount.

Composite video: A television signal with both picture and synchronising information.

Compound table: A device to provide and rotary movement used with a rostrum camera in animation and in the production of streak and other effects in slides.

Compressor: Device restricting the dynamic range of programme material to a predetermined narrower range. A system for reducing signal amplitude variations in a specified manner.

Computer: A electronic device designed to perform a wide range of tasks, utilising some form of flexible programming technique.

Computer graphics: Visuals originated or animated by computer.

Computer language: A specific vocabulary and way of using it designed for communication with a computer.

Conceit: An unusually far-fetched or elaborate metaphor or simile presenting a surprisingly apt parallel between two apparently dissimilar things or feelings: 'Griefe is a puddle, and reflects not cleare /Your beauties rayes'. Under Petrarchan influence, European poetry of the Renaissance cultivated fanciful comparisons and conceits to a high degree of ingenuity, either as the basis for whole poems or as an incidental decorative device. Poetic conceits are prominent in Elizabethan love sonnets, in metaphysical poetry, and in the French dramatic verse of Corneille and Racine. Conceits often employ the devices of hyperbole, paradox, and oxymoron.

Contact printing: Still or motion picture printing in which the processed film to be copied is held in contact with the raw stock at the time of exposure.

Continuous printing: Motion picture printing in which the processed film to be copied and the raw stock move continuously past the point of exposure.

Copy editing: This editing involves examining the minutest details of a typescript, it might be called is copy-editing, and the person who does the job is called a copy-editor. In some companies, copy editing is the responsibility of the production department rather than of the editorial department and is often done along with 'marking the typescript for press'. Copy preparation consists of marking on the typescript instructions to the typesetter regarding the manner and style in which it has to bet set in type. Copy editing and even macro editing are sometime entrusted to persons with the requisite knowledge and skill who are not regular employees of the publishing house. The following example shows reduced size sheets of a typescript after copy editing and marking-up for the press.

Couplet: A pair of rhyming verse lines, usually of the same length: one of the most widely used verse-forms in European poetry. Chaucer established the use of couplets in English, notably in the *Cantebury Tales*, using rhymed iambic pentameters later known as heroic couplets: a form revived in the 17th century by Ben Jonson, Dryden and others, partly as the equivalent in heroic drama of the alexandrine couplets which were the standard verse-form of French drama in that century. Alexander Pope followed Dryden's use of heroic couplets in non-dramatic verse to become the master of the form, notably in his use of closed couplets. The octosyllablic couplet is also commonly found in English verse. A couplet may also stand alone as an epigram, or form part of a larger stanza, or round off a sonnet or a dramatic scene.

Courtesy book: A book that gives advice to aspiring young courtiers in etiquette and other aspects of behaviour expected at royal or noble courts. This kind of work—sometimes written in verse—first became popular in various parts of Europe in the late Middle Ages. In the Renaissance, some important courtesy books expanded more philosophically on the nature of the ideal gentleman and his varied accomplishments. The most influential of these was Baldessare Castiglione's II *Libro del Cortegiano,* a sequence of dialogues on court life and platonic love. English examples include Henry Peacham's *The Compleat Gentleman.*

Crash editing: Switching a videotape recorder direct from playback mode to record; the new recording may not be in synchronisation with the earlier one.

Criticism: The reasoned discussion of literary works, an activity which may include some or all of the following procedures, in varying proportions: the defence of literature against moralists and censors, classification of a work according to its genre, interpretation of its meaning, analysis of its structure and style, judgement of its worth by comparison with other works, estimation of its likely effect on readers, and the establishment of general principles by which literary works can be evaluated and understood. Contrary to the everyday sense of criticism as 'fault-finding', much modern criticism assumes that the works it discusses are valuable, the functions of judgement and analysis having to some extent become divided between the market and the educational world.

The various kinds of criticism fall into several overlapping categories: theoretical, practical, impressionistic, affective, prescriptive, or descriptive. Criticism concerned with revealing the author's true motive or intention emerged from Romanticism to dominate much 19th- and 20th-century critical writing, but has tended to give way to 'objective' criticism, focusing on the work itself and to a shift of attention to the reader in reader-response criticism. Particular schools of criticism also seek to understand literature in terms of its relations to history, politics, gender, social class, mythology, linguistic theory, or psychology.

D

Database management: The handling of a computerized database by its human managers to collect, store, and use that data most effectively.

Database publishing: In the widest sense the generation of information-based Products, such as print, computer terminal screen, and videodisc texts, from the information stored in a database. In this sense, a group of publications generated from information stored in and retrieved from a computer memory, a group of publications generated from continually updated standing type, and a group of publications generated from a single major current events periodical are all database publications. In a more limited and more widely used sense, a group of publications generated from information stored in and retrieved from a computer memory.

Data processing: A general term for the processing of information in a systematic way. The major way of processing data in modem business is electronically, through computers, the descriptive terms being *electronic data processing* and *computer processing*.

Data reduction: The transformation of raw data into usable form.

Data transmission: The communication of information between two or more geographically separate points, as in the transmission of documents over telephone lines with input of the printed document at the sending point and printout of the document at the receiving point, or as in transmissions between computers in a network, using computer codes. Also the process of collecting data in remote locations and transmitting it to a central storage unit.

Decadence: A state of decay shown in either the inferior literary quality or the looser moral standards of any period's works compared with a preceding period, as with Hellenistic Greek or post—Augustan Latin literatures: or the 19th-century literary movement in Paris,

London, and Vienna that cultivated the exhausted refinement and artificiality it admired in the 'decadent' ages of Greek and Latin literature. Although the term has various unfavourable connotations ranging from simple inferiority to moral 'degeneracy', several writers in the late 19th century accepted the description proudly, thus implying a shocking parallel between their imperial societies and the decline of the Roman empire.

The Decadent movement, closely associated with the doctrines of Aestheticism, can be traced back to the writings of Theophile Gautier and Edgar Allan Poe in the 1830s, but became a significant presence only after the publication of Charles Baudelaire's influential collection of poems, *Les Fleurs du mal*, and culminated in the *fin-de-siecle* culture of the 1880s and 1890s. The basic principle of this decadence, expounded in the 1860s by Gautier and Baudelaire, was complete opposition to Nature: hence its systematic cultivation of drugs, cosmetics, Catholic ritual, supposedly 'unnatural' sexual practices, and sterility and artificiality in all things. A complete decadent way of life is portrayed in Joris-Karl Huysmans' novel *A Rebours,* upon which Oscar Wilde's *The Picture* of *Dorian Gray* is partly based. In France, decadence became almost synonymous with the work of the Symbolists, some of whom were associated in the *1880s* with the journal *Le Decadent.* In England, it emerged from the Pre-Raphaelite circle, in the poetry of D. G. Rossetti and in Swinburne's scandalous *Poems and Ballads,* leading to the work of Wilde, Ernest Dowson, and Arthur Symons in the 1890s. until Wilde's imprisonment in 1895 suddenly ended the decadent episode. Symons, in his essay 'The Decadent Movement in Literature', described the phenomenon as 'an interesting disease' typical of an over-luxurious civilization, characterized by 'an intense self-consciousness, a restless curiosity in research, an over-subtilizing refinement upon refinement, a spiritual and moral perversity'.

Deconstruction: A philosophically sceptical approach to the possibility of coherent meaning in language, initiated by the French philosopher Jacques Derrida in a series of works published in 1967, and adopted by several leading literary critics in the United States—notably at Yale University—from the early 1970s onwards. Derrida's claim is that the dominant Western tradition of thought has attempted to establish grounds of certainty and truth by repressing the limitless instability of language. This logocentric tradition sought some absolute source or guarantee of meaning which could centre or stabilize the uncertainties of signification, through a set of 'violent hierarchies' privileging a central term over a marginal one: nature over culture, male over female, and most importantly speech over writing. The 'phonocentric' suspicion of writing as a parasite upon the authenticity of speech is a crucial target of Derrida's subversive approach to Western philosophy, in which he inverts and dissolves conceptual hierarchies to show that the repressed or marginalized term has always already contaminated the privileged or central term. Thus, drawing on Saussure's theory of the sign, Derrida argues that the stable self-identity which we attribute to speech as the authentic source of meaning is illusory, since language operates as a self-contained system of internal differences rather than of positive terms or presences: writing, distrusted in the Western 'metaphysics of presence because it displays the absence of any authenticating voice, is in this sense logically prior to speech.

Derrida's central concept is presented in his coining of the term *differance,* a French portmanteau word combining 'difference' with 'deferral' to suggest that the differential nature of meanings in language caselessly defers or postpones any determinate meaning: language is an endless chain or play of differance which logocentric discourses try vainly to fix to some original or final term that can never be reached. Deconstructive readings track down within a text the aporia or internal contradiction that undermines its claims to coherent meaning; or they reveal how texts can be seen to deconstruct themselves. Derrida's difficult and paradoxical attitude to the metaphysical tradition seeks to subvert it while also claiming that there is no privileged vantage-point from which to do this from outside the instabilities of language. Deconstruction thus undermines its own radical scepticism by admitting that it leaves everything exactly as it was; it is an unashamedly self-contradictory effort to think the 'unthinkable', often by recourse to strange neologisms, puns, and other wordplay.

Although initially directed against the scientific pretensions of structuralism in the human sciences, it was welcomed enthusiastically into literary studies at Yale University and elsewhere in the English-speaking world, partly because it seemed to place literary problems of figurative language and interpretation above philosophers' and historians' claims to truth, and partly because it opened up limitless possibilities of interpretation. The writings of Paul de Man, Barbara Johnson, J. Hillis Miller, and Geoffrey Hartman in the 1970s and 1980s applied and extended Derrida's concepts to critical questions of interpretation, tending to challenge the status of the author's intention or of the external world as a source of meaning in texts, and questioning the boundary between criticism and literature. These and other deconstructionists came under fierce attack for dogmatic nihilism and wilful obscurity. For an extended introduction to this sometimes bewildering school of thought, consult Christopher Norris. Deconstruction: Theory and Practice.

Delivered price: A price quoted by a seller that includes the cost of shipping the goods sold to the buyer, as when a publisher absorbs the cost of shipping books to a bookseller. The price quoted may include the addition of the freight costs associated with a single sale, but more often will be a fixed price for delivery within an area or for delivery anywhere in the country.

Delivery: 1. The legal transfer of possession of real or personal property. The transfer of possession may be by means of physical delivery or by means of an instrument of control, such as a bill of sale or deed, it may be absolute or conditional, actual or constructive. 2. In commercial transactions, the actual physical delivery of purchased goods to their buyer, as specified by contract or common practice.

Deluxe edition: An edition more expensive, and sometimes more expensively made, than the regular edition of a work. Normally, the text of such an edition is identical with that of a regular edition, but it may be printed on more expensive paper and have more expensive binding than that of the regular edition. Sometimes an illustrated edition is called *deluxe* for marketing purposes, the term being used rather spongily.

Demography: The study of human population, focusing on such factors as population densities, growth rates, occupational trends, income levels of various strata, birth and death rates, and consumer behaviour. The consumer behaviour aspects of demography are the subject of considerable advertising and marketing research, and in that context are often called *demographics.*

Derivative works: 1. Works so closely resembling and dependent upon previous works by the same author that they are protected by the same copyright as the original work, and covered by the same author-publisher contract, in which copyright is passed from author to publisher; for example, excerpts and condensations. 2. Works depending heavily on research and thinking done by others; for example, an encyclopedia article using secondary, rather than primary sources; in this sense, the term characterizes much nonfiction, although it is sometimes used pejoratively.

Diacritic: A mark placed above or below a letter or syllable to specify its distinctive sound value. Diacritics commonly found are the acute accent, grave accent circumflex umlaut and cedilla Diacritical markings commonly used in scansion include the macron for long syllables, the breve for short syllables, the acute accent or the virgule for stressed syllables, and the symbol for unstressed syllables.

Diacritical marks: Marks such as dots and accents appearing above or below letters, thereby distinguishing those letters from others and often indicating different pronunciation or meaning.

Diaeresis or dieresis: A Greek word for 'division', used in three, different senses: (i) in classical prosody, the coincidence of a word ending with the end of a foot; (ii) the separation of two adjacent vowels into distinct sounds also the umlaut mark which indicates this; (iii) in rhetoric, a figure by which the parts or attributes of anything are enumerated.

Diagnostic routine: A computer program developed to find errors in existing programs and hardware.

Dialect: A variation of a 'standard' programming language. A distinctive variety of a language, spoken by members of an identifiable regional group, nation, or social class. Dialects differ from one another in pronunciation, vocabulary, and in grammar. Traditionally they have been regarded as variations from a 'standard' educated form of the language, but modern linguists point out that standard forms are themselves dialects which have come to predominate for social and political reasons.

Dialectic: (1) the art of formal reasoning, especially the procedure of seeking truth through debate or discussion: (2) the reasoning or logical structure that holds together a continuous argument or exposition: (3) the interplay of contradictory principles or opposed forces, as understood in the European tradition of philosophy influenced by G. W. F. Hegel and including Marx and Engels. Some schematic versions of dialectical philosophy speak of a unification of opposites in which the thesis is opposed by the antithesis but united with it in a higher synthesis.

Dialogue: Spoken exchanges between or among characters in a dramatic or narrative work, or a literary form in prose or verse based on a debate or discussion, usually between two speakers. Dialogue is clearly a major aspect of drama, and is usually a significant component of prose fictions and of some narrative poetry, as in the ballad. As a literary form, the dialogue was much favoured in ancient Greek and Latin literature for didactic and satirical purposes well as in pastoral poetry. The Socratic dialogues of Plato are the most influential ancient works in dialogue form; a modern counterpart is Wilde's *The Critic as Artist.* The *debat* and the flyting are special varieties of verse dialogue. In modern poetry. W. B. Yeats often used the dialogue form, as in 'Michael Robartes and the Dancer.

Dictionary: A body of defined words, terms, or phrases, appearing as an entire book; distinguished from a *glossary,* which is sometimes a book of definitions, but more often appears as only a portion of a work largely composed of narrative text. When such a body of definitions appears as part of a non-print work, such as a computerized database or videodisc, the terms *dictionary* and *glossary* are synonymous.

Dime novel: A paperback popular novel; a 19th and early 20th century forerunner of the modem mass market paperback novel.

Directory advertising: Advertising placed in such printed materials as trade association and telephone directories.

Direct platemaking: The creation of an image directly on the surface of a printing plate, without intermediary processes, as when a typewriter is used to strike impressions directly into a paper offset plate, or when laser beams are used to bum images into a printing plate.

Disc storage: The storage of computerized information on devices, each much like a pile of phonograph records, which can quickly be accessed when put into the computer. A widely used variant is the floppy *disc,* which is a single flexible disc, used for such storage and often containing its own programming.

Display: The characters and graphic shapes on the cathode ray tube screen of the visual display unit. 1. To exhibit goods or information in such a way as to get attention, as in an attractive arrangement of books in a bookstore window or at a book fair; also the arrangement itself, sometimes called an *exhibit.* 2. A visual presentation of information as on a cathode ray tube (CRT) at a computer terminal.

Distribution: The process of moving goods and services from manufacturer to consumer, including all physical and marketing steps, as when publications are moved from their publishers to consumers, Although marketing is sometimes used as a synonym, it is only part of the distribution process. In publishing, as in many other industries, small publishers often market their publications through larger distributing publishers.

Distribution arrangements: Contractual arrangements between publishers in which one agrees to distribute the published works of the other; many small publishers so distribute their publications through larger publishers, finding the costs of distribution prohibitive if carried alone.

Dos-a-dos binding: A single binding that contains two books bound together, with a single spine and two front covers, and with their back covers facing each other; sometimes neither book has a back cover, but the two sets of contents are bound as one, with two front covers.

Dual selection: A book or other membership club selection, offering two items as a single package to members.

Dubbing: (1) Combining two or more sound records into a single composite recording. (2) Transferring a sound recording from one medium to another, e.g. from magnetic tape to photo graphic film. (3) Making a copy, e.g. a show copy cassette from a reel-to-reel tape. (4) In motion picture production, the process of recording new dialogue to be substituted for the original version.

Duplex: A mode of data transmission where each station can send and receive simultaneously.

Duplicate: In general terms, an exact copy as distinct from an original record. (1) For slides and for audio and video tapes, a reproduction matching the original as closely as possible. (2) In motion pictures, duplicate refers to a copy negative matching the original exposed in the camera.

E

Edit: 1. To make or suggest changes in existing written or otherwise recorded material. For example, a writer may make changes in his or her own material; an editor may comment upon, revise, or copyedit material intended for publication; a word processor may revise composed material moving into composition or into a computer memory; and a filmmaker may edit cinema or video material. 2. In the widest sense, to write or find material for publication, acquire the right to publish it, and move it through the publishing process for publication.

Editing: The process of selecting from a large amount of recorded material that relevant to the purpose and assembling a programme by transposing or combining separate sequences.

Editing block: An aid to joining magnetic tape.

Editing terminal: A computer terminal used in composition and other word processing operations, which allows its operator to see and alter text displayed on a screen, thereby making editorial changes in the body of the text itself. Also called a *video display terminal (VDT).*

Edition: One or more printings of a work that is substantially the same in the several printings. Subsequent printings of an edition often carry corrected matter, but without major changes in the body of the work. *A new edition,* also called a *revised edition,* carries substantial changes, though not necessarily large amounts of resetting; for example, a computer-set directory may issue annually with as little as 10% of its type reset and be thereby so updated as to be clearly a new edition.

Editio princeps: The first printed edition of a work; Latin for "first edition." The term is normally used to describe first editions of very old books, antedating movable type, and originally published in manuscript.

Editorial: 1. Pertaining to editing functions. 2. A formal expression of opinion in print on the part of a newspaper or other periodical editor, often representing the views of the owners or managers of the publication. 3. Any expression of opinion, as distinct from fact on the part of a news writer; sometimes a separate article, but any straying from fact may be called editorializing.

Editorial assistant: One who assists others in the performance of editorial functions; as a practical matter, many editorial assistants work directly with copy and perform editorial and administrative functions, often considerably blurring the distinction between editor and editorial assistant.

Egotistical sublime: The phrase by which John Keats criticized what he felt to be the excessively self-centred quality of Wordsworth's poetry, in contrast with his own ideal of negative capability, which he found in the more anonymous imagination of Shakespeare.

Electronic Data Processing (EDP): The recording and processing of data by electronic means, using computers, and computer-related machines, materials, and techniques. EDP is by far the widest use to which computer are put. Also called automatic data processing.

Electronic editing: The selection and composition of video information, making a new recording by a transfer from a variety of original material.

Electronic news gathering: Recording of newsworthy subjects using lightweight, battery-powered television cameras and recorders. Picture quality may have to be slightly downgraded from studio, quality to achieve 'weight and Power reductions.

Electronic publishing: Images reproduced through television, video devices, discs, tapes, cassettes, closed-circuit broadcasts cable broadcasts and other electronic means. A general term, intended by its users to embrace all computerized and computer-assisted publishing forms, techniques, and instruments; used widely to include a variety of word processing, composition, printing, editing, information, and database functions.

Electrostatic printing: A printing process in which an electrically charged sheet attracts dry ink particles, which form an image on the sheet; widely used in xerography and other copying techniques, as well as in dry pressureless printing processes.

Elegy: An elaborately formal lyric poem lamenting the death of a friend or public figure, or reflecting seriously on a solemn subject. In

Greek and Latin verse, the term referred to the metre of a poem not to its mood or content: love poems were often included. Likewise, John Donne applied the term to his amorous and satirical poems in heroic couplets. But since Milton's 'Lycidas' the term in English has usually denoted a lament while the adjective 'elegiac' has come to refer to the mournful mood of such poems.

Two important English elegies that follow Milton in using pastoral conventions are Shelley's 'Adonais' on the death of Keats, and Arnold's 'Thyrsis'. This tradition of the pastoral elegy, derived from Greek poems by Theocritus and other Sicilian poets in the 3rd and 2nd centuries BC, evolved a very elaborate series of conventions by which the dead friend is represented as a shepherd mourned by the natural world; pastoral elegies usually include many mythological figures such as the nymphs who are supposed to have guarded the dead shepherd, and the muses invoked by the elegist.

Embossing: The stamping or printing of a raised design on a material, such as paper, cloth, or leather.

Emblem: A picture with a symbolic meaning, as in heraldry or visual allegory: or a simple kind of literary symbol with a fixed and relatively clear significance. In the 16th and 17th centuries the term was applied to a popular kind of woodcut or engraving accompanied by a motto and a short verse explanation of its meaning. The vogue for the emblem books in which these were found began with Andrea Alciato's *Emblemata* and culminated in England with the Emblems of Francis Quarles. Poets of this period often drew upon such works for their imagery. The term emblem poem is sometimes applied to pattern poems. *Adjective:* emblematic.

Encyclopedia: A substantial body of information, on many topics or in a single area of knowledge, organized so as to Provide ready access, with articles arranged alphabetically or thematically; often appearing in a multi-volume set, and in a very real sense providing an accessible database for its users, whether organized in traditional book form or in such newer forms as computerized databases or videodiscs.

Encyclopedistes: The group of writers and philosophers led by Denis Diderot and jean d'Alembert who contributed to the *Encyclopedie ou Dictionnaire raisonnee des sciences, des arts et des metiers* which began to appear in 1751 under Diderot's editorship, eventually running to 35 volumes including indexes. Other leading contributors were Condillac, Helvetius, Voltaire, and the, flacon d'Holbach, who played host to the meetings of this loose association. The Encyclopedistes were the leading spirits of the Enlightenment, hoping through this ambitious project to sweep away the superstitions of Church and State by offering a rational account of the universe.

Endpapers: Two heavy leaves of paper, one at the beginning and the other at the end of a bound book, connecting covers to contents. One half of each leaf is pasted to the front or back cover, the other half forming the first or last leaf of the book. Most endpapers do not carry printing, but some do, although the title page is normally carried on the front of the second leaf of the book.

Engraver's proof: A proof drawn from a halftone or line cut, to be checked for printing quality.

Expanded type: A wider-than-normal typeface of its kind; also called extended type.

Export: A publication originating in one country and shipped abroad, whether as finished goods or partially finished goods; for example, finished books may be shipped abroad and sold as is, or may be purchased in the United States as printed sheets and made into finished books abroad. Also the publication rights to a work originating in one country and sold for publication abroad, with the work wholly manufactured abroad.

F

Facilities for training in book publishing: There are in India a number of institutions running courses in journalism and a good training or experience in this field is an asset for anyone seeking a career as a book publishing editor. But this is certainly not essential; only a part of what is taught in a course in journalism would be of direct application in book publishing. A course in what is now termed 'communication' or 'mass communication' would certainly provide a very useful orientation for a person operating in book publishing-an orientation which will perhaps fit her to face more successfully than otherwise the impact of the growth of the electronic media on the book as we now know it and to adapt it or even radically alter its form to meet the developing situation.

Delhi University, at its College of Vocational Studies, offers a B.A. Pass course with Book Publishing as a major subject. This course is a rather general one and has yet, at the time of the revision undertaken for this second edition, to develop a satisfactory practical orientation. As at present taught, it provides only a broad acquaintance with what book publishing is, what it does, and how it does it.

Also at the College of Vocational Studies, Delhi University provides a two-year postgraduate diploma course in book publishing. All graduates, whatever their subjects for graduation, are entitled to be considered for admission to the course. A choice of specializations is offered: Editing, Production, and Promotion and Sales. The lectures for this course are held in the evening and it can therefore be taken by persons already working in publishing. It is such persons who will find this course most useful, as their place of work will provide the essential practical side of such training, for which, at the time of this revision, facilities are still not available in the college itself. The college, since 1984, has been housed in its own spacious grounds and premises, which should now (1996) enable it to make good this deficiency.

Facing page: Any page that forms a double spread with another, from the viewpoint of one discussing the other.

Facsimile: An exact copy. Examples include an exact copy of an original publication, such as an art book reproducing an old and rare book, called a *facsimile edition;* or an exact copy of a document, transmitted over a telephone line or other long-range communication device, in a procedure called *facsimile transmission.*

Fair trade: A concept that producers, distributors, and retailers should be allowed to set minimum prices on their goods. Formerly supported by a series of statutes in many states, setting minimum prices on a wide range of goods, it is now mainly prohibited since repeal of Federal laws that had barred application of the antitrust statutes to this form of collusive price fixing.

Fair use: The idea that some materials, otherwise protected by copyright, may be used by others in very limited fashion without that use constituting copyright infringement, as when an author quotes briefly from a copyrighted work without permission to do so, or copyrighted material is copied by others, using copying machines. This is an area of heavy and continuing litigation, with authors, publishers, librarians, and database developers in considerable disagreement; although many standards of "fair use" have been proposed, at this writing no single, unambiguous standard has been adopted by the interested parties or been imposed by law, either in the United States or internationally.

Fall off: Gradual reduction in illumination from centre of a screen to the edges and corners.

Fantastic, the: A mode of fiction in which the possible and the impossible are confounded so as to leave the reader with no consistent explanation for the story's strange events. Tzvetan Todorov in his *Introduction a la litterature fantastique,* argues that fantastic narratives involve an unresolved hesitation between the supernatural explanation available in marvellous tales and the natural or psychological explanation offered by tales of the uncanny. The literature of the fantastic flourished in 19th-century ghost stories and related fiction: Henry James's mysterious tale *The Turn of the Screw* is a classic example.

Fee work: Work for hire, in which an author writes for a specified fee and has no continuing proprietary interest, as is normally expressed by royalty arrangements, in the work.

Feedback: 1. Information sent back to its originator about any matter, whether in progress or recently completed; often used by the originator to modify and evaluate currently developing and recently completed projects and processes. 2. In computers systems, the transfer or energy back to input from output. A technique involving an amplifier system, whereby some fraction of the output power is fed back to the input. Feedback may be positive, tending to increase the overall amplification, or negative, which will reduce the amplification. Current or voltage feedback systems are used, the choice depending generally on effects resulting from feedback, such as changes in input or output impedance. The amount of feedback used is expressed generally as a percentage of the total load current or voltage.

Feedback is often unintentional, and may be due to coupling between output and input circuits or couplings external to the system, such as a common power supply impedance that may produce feedback effects over several stages.

Positive feedback is a requirement for oscillator systems. Energy is fed from the output of an amplifier to a tuned system, with a sufficient amount of positive feedback to offset the resistive losses in the tuned system. The combination of amplifier plus tuned system then becomes an AC generator having a frequency determined by the tuning elements. Unintentional positive feedback in an amplifier can result in instability. Negative feedback is extensively used in amplifier design. Its use minimises the effects of undesired couplings, improves the frequency/gain performance and also the frequency/phase response.

Electro-mechanical feedback systems are used. For example, the cutting stylus for disc recording, or the cone of a loudspeaker, may exhibit undesirable mechanical resonance effects over the frequency range of interest. A sensor attached to the stylus or cone can feed back resonance indications to a circuit controlling the gain of the driving amplifier.

Feedback, negative: Condition where a fraction of the output of a system is fed back to the input in antiphase, frequently used in electronic amplifiers. Input and output impedance, stability and linearity are affected.

Feedback, positive: Condition where the output of a system is fed back to the input in phase. There can be a build-up in amplitude leading to instability of the system, e.g. loudspeaker output fed back to the microphone input produces undesirable oscillations, 'how-round' or *threshold howl.*

Festschrift: a volume of essays written by the disciples of an eminent scholar or writer, to whom it is presented as a tribute on a special occsion such as a birthday or retirement. The custom and the term originated in German universities in the 19th century.

Feuilleton: A French term for the literary section of a daily newspaper: originally the lower part of the front page, devoted to drama criticism, but later a separate page or pages. The roman-feuilleton is a novel serialized in a newspaper: this form flourished in France in the 1840s, bringing great financial rewards to Balzac, George Sand, Dumas *pere* and other authors.

Fiction: 1. A work stemming wholly or mainly from the use of its author's imagination, whatever the extent to which the author may also use factual materials. 2. The body of such works, as a classification, including written plays, filmscripts, novels, novellas, and short stories. 3. Increasingly, in modem usage, whole visual works, such as cinema and video films, in which the script is an element of the work and itself a work of fiction, and the finished film a further developed work of fiction. The general term for invented stories, now usually applied to novels, short stories, novellas, romances, fables, and other narrative works in prose, even though most plays and narrative poems are also fictional. The adjective fictitious tends to carry the unfavourable sense of falsehood, whereas 'fictional' is more neutral, and the archaic adjective fictive, revived by the poet Wallace Stevens and others, has a more positive sense closer to 'imaginative' or 'inventive'. *Verb:* fictionalize.

Figure: A piece of nontext material in a publication such as a graph, chart, photograph, or other illustration; usually numbered sequentially and listed separately. An expression that departs from the accepted literal sense or from the normal order of words, or in which an emphasis is produced by patterns of sound. Such figurative language is an especially important resource of poetry, although not every poem will use it; it is also constantly present in all other kinds of speech and writing, even though it usually passes unnoticed. The ancient theory of rhetoric named and categorized dozens of figures, drawing a rough and often disputed distinction between those that extend the meaning of words, and those that merely affect their order or their impact upon an audience.

The most important tropes are metaphor, simile, metonymy, synecdoche, personification, and irony: others include hyperbole, litotes, and periphrasis. The minor rhetorical figures can emphasize or enliven a point in several different ways: by placing words in contrast with one another, by repeating words in various patterns, by changing the order of words, by missing out conjunctions by changing course or breaking off in midsentence or by assuming special modes of address or inquiry.

File (data): A named program or a collection of data. 1. A group of related records, whether held as information on paper in a file cabinet or on disc or tape in computer storage; also to store such records in a group. 2. To submit copy to a periodical publication, as when a correspondent or reporter files a story with a newspaper.

Filler: 1. In newspaper and other periodical publishing, material that, although it may be useful and interesting, is used primarily to fill a small empty space in the publication. 2. More generally, any published material used mainly to fill an empty space or add bulk to the contents of a publication, from five lines used to fill an empty space in a newspaper column to a useless hundred-page appendix in a reference book. 3. Substances such as starch or plastic used to smooth and strengthen the surface of book cloth materials or papers.

Filter (colour): Transparent material modifying the colour of the transmitted light by selective absorption of certain wavelengths.

Final manuscript: A manuscript on which all substantial pre-publication revisions have been completed, and which is therefore ready to go into copyediting.

First edition: 1. The entire original run of copies of a work from the same plates, which may be in one printing or in several printings, possibly with corrections in some printings. The original press run, or first printing, of the first edition is called the first issue or first *impression.* 2. A single copy of the first edition of a work, sometimes called simply a *first.*

Flexible binding: A binding in which the binder's boards are made of flexible material, and the resulting covers are flexible, rather than rigid. Also called *limp binding.*

Flexographic printing: A printing process that uses flexible rubber plates and liquid, fast-spreading ink to do high-speed printing on opaque materials, such as heavily-coated papers, coated cardboards, and plastics used in packaging.

Floppy disk: Digital memory using flexible magnetic disks.

Folio (F, f, fol; plural FF, ff, fols): 1. A number of a page in a book or manuscript. 2. A numbered leaf in a book. 3. A single sheet, folded once to create two leaves and four pages. 4. A group of American book sizes, 1350 inches high. The most common is the size called Folio (F)—13" — 15" high, but sometimes used to describe books up to 25" high. Other American folio sizes are *Atlas* Folio—approximately 25" high; *Elephant* Folio—23" — 25" high; and *Double Elephant* Folio—anything substantially over 25" high and up to 50" high. 5. A group of British book sizes, including Foolscap Folio 13½" by 10", *Crown* Folio—15" by 10", and Royal—20" by 12½. Also see book size. A large size of book in which the page size results from folding a standard printer's sheet of paper in half, forming two leaves. The collected editions of Shakespeare's plays published after his death, as distinct from the earlier unauthorized quarto editions, are often referred to as the Folios: the First Folio was published by his colleagues Heming and Condell in 1623, and three others followed in 1632, 1663, and 1685.

Folk song: A song of unknown authorship that has been passed on, preserved, and adapted in an oral tradition before later being written down or recorded. Folk songs usually have an easily remembered melody and a simple poetic form such as the quatrain. The most prominent categories are the narrative ballad and the lyric love-song, but the term also covers lullabies, carols, and various songs to accompany working, dancing, and drinking.

Folklore: A modern term for the body of traditional customs, superstitions, stories, dances, and songs that have been adopted and maintained within a given community by processes of repetition not reliant on the written word. Along with folk songs and folktales, this broad category of cultural forms embraces all kinds of legends, riddles. jokes, proverbs, games, charms, omens, spells, and rituals, especially those of preliterate societies or social classes. Those forms of verbal expression that are handed on from one generation or locality to the next by word of mouth are said to constitute an oral tradition. *Adjective:* folkloric.

Folktale: A story passed on by word of mouth rather than by writing, and thus partly modified by successive retellings before being written down or recorded. The category includes legends, fables, jokes, tall stories, and fairy tales or Marchen. Many folktales involve mythical creatures and magical transformations.

Follow copy: An instruction to compose copy exactly as it appears in manuscript form, without any alterations, even though such alterations may appear to compositors to be merely minor corrections.

Font: Originally, a set of printers' type of uniform style and size ('fount'); by extension, a uniform style of alphanumeric characters available for selection in a video graphics system. A complete set of type of one size and style, including all letters, numbers, and marks. The term originally referred to metal type; but with the advent of photocomposition, many type styles and sizes are carried simultaneously in photocomposition systems, and the number of sizes and number of styles, multiplied by each other, characterize the number of fonts in a single system. Also called a *fount.*

Foolscap: A sheet of paper in the 12" by 15" to 13" by 17" range.

Footnote: 1. A note at the bottom of a page, keyed to material in the main page contents, usually citing authorities or references, and some_ times further explaining main text materials. Sometimes notes containing such matter are carried at the ends of chapters, or in back matter. These are also sometimes called footnotes, but are more often and less confusingly called *chapter notes.* 2. In financial statements, comments keyed to financial items, to explain such items more fully to those reading the statements.

Footprint: The area of coverage of a satellite transmitter on the surface of the Earth.

Foreign editor: A newspaper or other periodical editor who is responsible for a publication's coverage *of* events and trends abroad.

Foreign rights: A group of subsidiary rights, consisting of the rights to 4 publish a work originating in one country in all other countries, and 4 including the rights to translate the work into other languages; a matter covered by specific clauses in author-publisher contracts. Sales of such rights range from the right to publish in a single country to the right to publish worldwide outside the country of origin.

Foreword: Introductory comments about a book and its author, often written by another person, such as a celebrity or expert whose endorsement is thought to enhance the book's appeal. Sometimes used synonymously *with preface,* although some books include both; part of the front matter *of a* book, before or after the table of contents. In propagation, a form of scattering in which the scattered waves tend to follow the direction of the incident wave.

Format: (1) The style or method of presentation of an image or its physical dimensions. (2) The configuration of information for display, transmission, storage or retrieval. The physical appearance of a publication, including all design factors, such as paper, binding, type choices, and page layouts. The term is used rather generally and may describe an entire publication, a page, or a single design element.

Formatting: 1. The process of designing a publication. 2. The process of instructing mechanical compositors as to the design elements involved in composing a specific publication, often as part of computerized composition operations.

Forwarding: In bookbinding, all operations following sewing and preceding finishing.

Free head: A recording head without electronics, provided on an audio cassette recorder for use with tape-slide control equipment.

Freelance: Describing one who sells services as an independent contractor; usually applied to skilled creative people, such as writers, graphic artists, and some consultants, although many consultants function as full-scale business organizations rather than as small individual operators.

G

Geneva school: A group of critics associated with the University of Geneva at various times since the 1940s. Its most prominent figure has been the Belgian critic Georges Poulet. while in the USA J. Hillis Miller was a significant practitioner of the school's methods before he adopted those of deconstruction, others include jean Rousset. jean Starobinski, and JeanPierre Richard. Drawing on the philosophical tradition of phenomenology, these 'critics of consciousness' saw the critic's task as one of identifying and fully identifying *with,* the unique mode of consciousness pervading a given author's works. Thus an author's particular sense of time and space would be seen as the unifying source of his or her entire *oeuvre,* regardless of the differences between individual works. Although related to some of the assumptions of biographical criticism, the 'phenomenological' approach of the Geneva critics differs in that it works back from the texts to the mind behind them, not from the life to the texts. An impressive example of this approach at work in English is J. Hillis Miller's *Charles Dickens: The World of his Novels*.

Genre publishing: Publishing that specializes in genre fiction; applied to publishers specializing in one or more genres, whatever their other publishing activities.

Gentlemen's agreement: An agreement in which the parties sign no document and produce no other evidence of the agreement they have reached. Such agreements are often tacit, very often extra-legal; they have no legal force, and rely only on custom and the verbal assurances of the parties involved.

Georgian poetry: A body of English verse published in the first half of George V's reign in five anthologies edited by Edward Marsh as *Georgian Poetry*. The group of poets represented here included Rupert Brooke, Walter de la Mare, John Drinkwater James Elroy Flecker, John

Masefield, and J. C. Squire. They are now usually regarded as minor poets, quietly traditional in form and devoted to what Robert Graves called 'un-controversial subjects' of rural and domestic life. The term Georgianism is sometimes used in a slightly extended sense to embrace this group along with other more or less traditional poets of' the time in contrast with the contemporary movement of modernism in English verse. The term Georgian is only rarely applied to the literature of the period of the first four Georges.

Georgic: A didactic poem giving instruction on farming, husbandry, or some comparable pursuit, often involving praise of rural life. The earliest Greek example is Hesiod's *Works and Days*, but the most influential work was the *Georgics* of the Roman poet Virgil, which includes advice on bee-keeping and vines. Several English poets in the 18th century produced banal georgics in imitation of Virgil, including John Dyer in *The Fleece* and James Grainger in *The Sugar Cane*. Apart from its didactic intention, the georgic is distinguished from the pastoral in that it regards nature in terms of necessary labour, not of harmonious idleness.

Ghost writer: One who writes works attributed to others, as when a professional writer writes a book that is published under a celebrity's name.

Glassine paper: Dirtresistant, smooth, and often transparent paper used in packaging; it is sometimes placed over book covers and jackets for protective purposes.

Gloss: An explanation or translation of a difficult word or phrase, usually added to a text by a later copyist or editor, as in many modern editions of Chaucer. When placed between the lines of a text, it is known as an 'interlinear gloss', but it may appear in the margin, or as a footnote, or in an appendix, and may form an extended commentary. A rare example of a poem that includes the author's own marginal glosses is Coleridge's 'The Rime of the Ancient Mariner'. A glossary is a list of difficult words and phrases with accompanying explanations.

Glossary: 1. Describing a highly Polished paper, with strongly light-reflective qualities. 2. A photograph on glossy paper.

Gothic type: A group of modem typefaces, similar to and descended from the old black-letter typefaces which also *black-letter type*.

Graphic equaliser: A multi-section frequency selective filter providing instant adjustment of the 'shape' of the frequency response characteristic.

Graphic arts: 1. In the widest sense, all those visual arts stemming from the application of drawings or writings to surfaces. 2. In a more commonly used sense, those visual arts stemming from the creation of artistic works meant to be reproduced on flat surfaces, and the multiple works so reproduced, such as printed pages, lithographs, etchings, and engravings.

Graphics: 1. In the widest sense, all the print elements in published work, including text, illustration, and print design factors. 2. The illustrative elements in printed work, excluding text and overall design; a sense more commonly used in publishing and printing. 3. Artwork, captions, lettering, photographs, etc. used in programmes. 4. Output presented in graphical form on a visual display unit.

Graphic equaliser: In audio frequency, an equaliser, often included in a signal path to vary the gain or loss of selected parts of the frequency range. The controls are usually arranged as vertical slider controls, side by side on a display panel. Thus, the position of the controls gives a visual indication of the overall equalisation that is being effected.

H

Handbook: A substantial book composed of many articles on a single theme or subject; usually organized thematically rather than alphabetically, and often containing articles written by many authors on professional themes.

As a practical matter, any book can be called a handbook, and man books that might just as easily be described as small encyclopedias or professional and reference books are called handbooks by their publishers for marketing purposes.

Hand composition: The process of setting metal type by hand, rather than by machine, using a composing stick; sometimes, but rarely, also used to describe page makeup operations connected with hot metal composition using typesetting machines.

Handmade paper: Paper literally made by hand, sheet by sheet, as was all paper until the advent of the Fourdrinier papermaking machine in the early 19th century.

Hanging indent: A body of composed type in which the first line of each paragraph is set full measure—that is, full width margin to margin—and subsequent lines are indented one or more ems and set Hush left under the second line in the paragraph.

Hard copy: A printed, thermally or electrically produced print-out as opposed to the image on a visual display unit.

Hardcover: A book bound with stiff covers, or boards; also called a *hardbound* or *clothbound book,* although it may be a bound book with limp but expensive covers, as in some leatherbound books. In modem usage, the term is used more to describe the publishing status of the book than its physical being, as a hardcover book has traditionally been the main vehicle through which authors bring their works to the public, and the right to publish in hardcover has been the main subject of author-publisher contracts, with all other publishing rights thought of as secondary or subsidiary; even when the primary contractual arrangement between author and publisher is for a trade paperback or mass market paperback sale, with the hardcover rights being subsidiary, the hardcover book has more "status."

Hardware: Term used in a computer context, to describe equipment, as distinct from software. The physical components, integrated circuits, etc. which, with the software program, together make a computer system. The term is also used to refer to picture and sound equipment used for presentation, as opposed to the programme software. 1. In computer technology, the machinery, consisting of the computers themselves and other associated physical devices, in contrast to software, or programming components. 2. Any machinery or other physical tools for doing a job; in this sense, a printing press is hardware.

Heading: The top caption of a body of copy, such as a page, chapter, group of chapters, table of contents, or subsection of a chapter; usually set in type different from that used in the body of the copy, and often larger and bolder than that copy. Often called a *head.*

Headline: A large, bold caption set above an article or story in, a newspaper or other periodical.

Head margin: The top margin on a page, above any printing on the page.

Head out: Film or tape wound on a reel so that it is at the start, ready for immediate projection.

Hellenistic: The term designating a period of Greek literature and learning from the death of Alexander the Great to that of Cleopatra, when the Centre of Greek culture had shifted to the settlements of the eastern Mediterranean, notably the great library of Alexandria. This period includes the poetry of Callimachus and Theocritus. the philosophy of Epicurus and the Stoics, and the scientific achievements of Aristarchus, Archimedes, and Euclid. A Hellenist is a student or admirer of Greek civilization, or, in a special sense promoted by Matthew Arnold in *Culture and Anarchy*, a devotee of Hellenism, which Arnold contrasted with Hebraism in his sketch of the two contending ideals within Western culture. Phrases or constructions derived from the Greek language are also called Hellenisms.

Heroic poetry: The kind of verse line used for epic poetry in a given language is known as the heroic line: the dactylic hexameter in Greek and Latin, the iambic pentameter in English, the alexandrine in French, the hendecasyllabic line in Italian. The heroic quatrain or heroic stanza is not used for epics, but is so named because it employs the English heroic line: it consists of four pentameters rhyming abab, as in Gray's 'Elegy written in a Country Churchyard', or *aabb*.

How-to book: A nonfiction book focusing on practical instruction on how to accomplish specific tasks, such as home and automobile maintenance and repairs.

Hurt books: Books that are somehow damaged and sold at reduced prices.

Hyphen (-): A horizontal printed line, usually one en long, used between the parts of some compound words, or at the end of the first part of a broken word, such as one begun on one line and continued on the next; a handling problem for some computerized composition programs.

I

Illocutionary act: An utterance that accomplishes something in the act of speaking. In the speech act theory proposed by J. L. Austin in How to *Do Things with Words*, an utterance involves not only the simple locutionary' act of producing a grammatical sentence, but also an 'illocutionary force' of effectiveness either as an affirmation or as a promise, a threat, a warning, a command, etc. The most explicit illocutionary acts are the performatives, which accomplish the very deed to which they refer, when uttered by authorized speakers in certain conditions: 'I arrest you in the name of the law', 'I hereby renounce the Devil and all his works', 'I promise to defend and uphold the constitution.'

Imagery: A rather vague critical term covering those uses of language in a literary work that evoke sense-impressions by literal or figurative reference to perceptible or 'concrete' objects, scenes, actions, or states, as distinct from the language of abstract argument or exposition. The imagery of a literary work thus comprises the set of images that it uses: these need not be mental 'pictures', but may appeal to senses other than sight. The term has often been applied particularly to the figurative language used in a work, especially to its metaphors and similes. Images suggesting further meanings and associations in ways that go beyond the fairly simple identifications of metaphor and simile are often called Symbols.

The critical emphasis on imagery in the mid-20th century, both in New Criticism and in some influential studies of Shakespeare, tended to glorify the supposed concreteness of literary works by ignoring matters of structure, convention, and abstract argument: thus Shakespeare's plays were read as clusters or patterns of 'thematic imagery' according to the predominance of particular kinds of image, without reference to the action or to the dramatic meaning of characters' speeches.

Imagination: The mind's capacity to generate images of objects, states, or actions that have not been felt or experienced by the senses.

In the discussion of psychology and art prior to Romanticism, imagination was usually synonymous with fancy, and commonly opposed to the faculty of reason, either as complementary to it or as contrary to it. S. T. Coleridge's famous distinction between fancy and imagination in his *Biographia Literaria* emphasized the imagination's vitally creative power of dissolving and uniting images into new forms, and of reconciling opposed qualities into a new unity. This freely creative and transforming power of the imagination was a central principle of Romanticism.

Implied author: a term coined by Wayne C. Booth in *The Rhetoric of Fiction* to designate that source of a work's design and meaning which is inferred by readers from the text, and imagined as a personality standing behind the work. As an imaginary entity, it is to be distinguished clearly from the real author, who may well have written other works implying different kind of persona or implied author behind them. The implied author is also to be distinguished from the narrator, since the implied author stands at a remove from the narrative voice, as the personage assumed to be responsible for deciding what kind of narrator will be presented to the reader, in many works this distinction produces an effect of irony at the narrator's expense.

Implied reader: A term used by Wolfgang Iser and some other theorists of reader-response criticism to denote the hypothetical figure of the reader to whom a given work is designed to address itself. Any text may be said to presuppose an 'ideal' reader who has the particular attitudes appropriate to that text in order for it to achieve its full effect. This implied reader is to be distinguished from *actual* readers, who may be unable or unwilling to occupy the position of the implied reader: thus, most religious poetry presupposes a godfearing implied reader, but many actual readers today are atheists. The implied reader is also not the same thing as the narratee, who is a figure imagined within the text as listening to—or receiving a written narration from—the narrator.

Import: A publication originating abroad, and shipped into the buying country, whether a, finished goods or partially finished goods; for example, finished books may be shipped into the United States and sold as is, or may be purchased as printed sheets abroad and made into books in the United States.

Also the publication rights to work originating abroad and sold for publication in the buying country, with the work wholly manufactured in the buying country.

Imposition: The ordering of materials to be printed, so that they will fall into proper sequence once folded and trimmed, as in the pages of a signature.

Impression: 1. All the copies of a work printed in a press run, even though the run in may be interrupted and then resumed. The first run of a work is called a *first impression.*

2. A single printed piece; for example, a single sheet imprinted on one side due to the impact of a single printing plate.

3. A measure of the force of impact of a printing device upon the material being printed upon.

Impressionism: In the literary sense borrowed from French painting, a rather vague term applied to works or passages that concentrate on the description of transitory mental impressions as felt by an observer, rather than on the explanation of their external causes.

Impressionism in literature is thus neither a school nor a movement but a kind of subjective tendency manifested in descriptive techniques. It is found in Symbolist and Imagist poetry, and in much modern verse, but also in many works of prose fiction since the late 19th century, as in the novels of Joseph Conrad and Virginia Woolf.

Impressionistic criticism is the kind of criticism that restricts itself to describing the critic's own subjective response to a literary work, rather than ascribing intrinsic qualities to it in the light of general principles. Walter Pater's defence of such criticism, in the Preface to his *Studies in the History of the Renaissance,* was that 'in aesthetic criticism the first step towards seeing one's object as it really is, is to know one's own impression as it really is, to discriminate it, to realise it distinctly'.

The most common kind of impressionistic criticism is found in theatre and book reviews: 'I laughed all night'; 'I couldn't put it down'.

Imprimatur: A license to publish, issued by those having the fight to, stop publication, as when state or church has licensing and censorship powers. In some places and at some times, that license must be printed, in authorized published work; but where freedom to publish does not exist, and official bodies control all publication, the license is implicit in the act of publishing, for Prior censorship effectively prohibits other publications.

Imprint: 1. A publishing identification carried in a published work, whether that of the publisher, an affiliate or subsidiary of the publisher, or a trade name identifying a group of publications.

2. A statement in a published work identifying its printer.

3. An additional printing on already printed matter, as when a publisher prepares a newsletter, sells it in bulk to many customers, and "customizes" the newsletter by placing each customer's name on the copies purchased.

4. A publishing arrangement, in which a publisher acquires publishing properties through one or more editors who operate as a separate entity, with its own imprint or trade name, but without a corporate life of its own; used by some publishers as a means of stimulating editorial independence, entrepreneurial contribution, and financial responsibility, as compensation arrangements tend to favour heavily those imprint editors who make money for the publisher.

Independent Distributor (ID): A wholesale distributor of printed materials, including periodicals and mass market paperbacks, to retail outlets other than bookstores; wholesalers distributing to bookstores are usually called *jobbers.*

Indeterminacy: (1) in reader-response criticism, any element of a text that requires the reader to decide on its meaning; *(2)* in deconstruction, a principle of uncertainty invoked to deny the existence of any final or determinate meaning that could bring to an end the play of meanings between the elements of a text. *To* proclaim the ultimate indeterminacy of meaning need not mean that no decisions can be made about the meaning of anything, only that there is no final arbiter of such decisions. Some deconstructionists, however, have the habit of calling the meanings of literary works undecidable'.

Index: 1. Any finding device functioning as a guide to the content of a body of information such as a book or computerized database

2. An A-Z list of references to the body of a printed publication; usually carried in the back matter of the publication, but in many reference publications part of front matter.

3. A symbol used in printing, to draw the reader's attention to a section of print; also called fist, *hand,* or *index* mark, after the pointing

index finger. In the semiotics of the American philosopher C. S. Peirce, a sign that is connected to its object by a concrete relationship, usually of cause and effect. A finger or signpost pointing to an object or place is indexal; so, in more clearly causal ways, are many kinds of symptom, mark, or trace: scars, footprints, crumpled bedclothes etc. Thus smoke may be seen as an index of fire. Peirce distinguished the index from two other kinds of sign: the icon and the symbol.

Information: In communications, general term for electrical signals which, transmitted from a source to a recipient, will convey an intelligent message when they are decoded and/or transduced into sound and/or vision. An addition to this definition is the transmission and reception of signals intended to provide an alarm or control function.

Information bits: In data transmission, those bits generated from the data; not including any bits used for control or other functions.

Information explosion: The worldwide expansion of data and new knowledge in all business science, and technical areas in this century and especially in the period since the end of World War II.

Information Industry Association: A national association of American publishers, database suppliers, database networks, other software and hardware suppliers, and information products users, engaged in such trade association activities as legislative representation, new technology information supply, and professional and industry development.

Information storage: The entry of information and holding of an accumulated body of information in any kind of database; usually referring to the development of a body of information stored in computer-readable form and capable of being retrieved by computer.

In-house: Functions performed inside a publishing house; normally used to describe functions which might be performed either by a publisher's employees or by outside contractors, such as composition, printing, artwork, advertising, and editing.

Inking: In computer graphics, using an input to sketch freehand with a stylus.

Inlaid binding: A decorative binding into which materials other than the main material used in the binding have been inserted; for example, a leather binding inset with precious metals, gemstones, ivory miniatures, or other leathers or fabrics. When the ratio of inlay to basic binding material is high, a mosaic effect may be achieved, and the binding may then be called a *mosaic binding.*

In press: Work in production, from the beginning of composition to the delivery of finished works to the warehouse, but not including work being warehoused and shipped.

In print: Describing a work being currently stocked and supplied by a publisher; often refers to a specific edition rather than to the work itself, which may be out of print in other editions, countries, or forms; for example, a book may be in print in hardcover in England and out of print in the United States, or may be in print only in mass market paperback in the United States, but out of print in hardcover or paperback in England and in hardcover in the United States.

Input: The data or signals entering a computer or microcomputer; more generally, the signal applied to any electronic device or system.

Insert: In video editing, any material replacing a section within an existing recording. In film, it is usually a scene photographed separately and added during editing, such as a close-up shot of a letter or a newspaper. 1. An addition to manuscript made by an author or editor.

2. An addition to the contents of a work, made during binding, usually consisting of maps, foldouts, and other material not primed as part of the signatures making up the main body of the work's text.

3. An addition of new material to a mechanically bound publication, as when additional loose pages are added to a looseleaf publication.

Inside covers: The second and third covers of a publication, which are the Insides of the front and back covers respectively; often preferred advertising positions in periodicals.

Inspection copy: A sample copy of a publication, sent by a publisher to a prospective purchaser, such as a faculty member, who may recommend multiple student purchases of the hook, if it is adopted for instructional use. Although such copies are theoretically meant to be returned to publishers after inspection, as a practical matter they very seldom are returned; publishers classify them as complimentary copies, and charge them off as one of the costs of doing business. Also called an examination copy.

Instant book: A book, often paperback, published within days or weeks of an event of great public interest, such as an assassination or striking military victory, rather than appearing months later at the end of the normal publishing process. Also called a *quickie* or an extra.

Institutional advertising: Advertising that seeks to enhance the image of the organization advertising rather than to sell specific products directly, though it is often aimed at aiding the sale of the company's products in general, as when a company under attack for damaging the environment buys advertising stressing its social responsibility and public interest contributions.

Intaglio printing: Printing from a plate into which an image has been cut, rather than raised, as in *relief printing.* As the image has been cut below the surface of the plate, when the plate is inked, the ink flows into the cuts; then, when the excess ink is cleaned off the surface of the plate, the ink remaining in the cuts prints on paper in contact with the plate. Also called *gravure printing.* When done on a rotary press, it is called *rotogravure;* when printing photos, it is called pho*togravure.*

Integrated data processing (IDP): Data processing that is treated as a total system from the acquisition of data to its end uses.

Interface: A circuit that converts the output of one system or subsystem to a form. suitable for the next system or subsystem. The facing and touching boundaries of two or more systems. Although originally used in business as a computer term, the term is now widely used to refer to the meeting place of any two or more contiguous systems, such as the government business interface or the military industrial interface.

Term for the point of inter-connection of items of equipment performing separate functions. For example, an RF tuner has performed its function when it has developed an AF output from an RF signal. Its connection to the input of an AF amplifier would be the interface, requiring certain technical requirements to be met, such as impedance.

Interior monologue: The written representation of a character's inner thoughts, impressions, and memories as if directly 'overheard' without the apparent intervention of a summarizing and selecting narrator. The term is often loosely used as a synonym for stream of consciousness. However, some confusion arises about the relationship between these two terms when critics distinguish them: some take 'stream of consciousness' as the larger category, embracing all representations of intermingled thoughts and perceptions, within which interior monologue is a special case of 'direct' presentation; others take interior monologue as the larger category, within which stream of consciousness is a special technique emphasizing continuous 'flow' by abandoning strict logic, syntax, and punctuation.

The second of these alternatives permits us to apply the term 'interior monologue' to that large class of modem poems representing a character's unspoken thoughts and impressions, as distinct from the spoken thoughts imagined in the dramatic monologue: Browning's 'Soliloquy of the Spanish Cloister' is an early example.

More often, though, the term refers to prose passages employing stream-of-consciousness techniques: the most celebrated instance in English is the final chapter of James Joyce's *Ulysses*. Joyce acknowledged Edouard Dujardin's novel *Les Lauriers sont coupees* as a precedent in the use of interior monologue.

Interlude: A short play, of a kind believed to have been performed by small companies of professional actors in the intervals of banquets and other entertainments before the emergence of the London theatres. This rather loose category includes several types of play that are regarded as transitional between the morality play and Elizabethan comedy: some resemble the morality plays in didactic intent and are sometimes called 'moral interludes', while others are closer to farce.

Interludes flourished in England from the end of the I 5th century to the late 16th century. An early example is Henry Medwall's *Fulgens and Lucres.* The foremost author of interludes was John Heywood, who wrote *The Play of the Weather* among other works.

International Standard Book Number (ISBN): An identifying number system for printed books, set up by international agreement, used in many parts of the world, and by the overwhelming majority of book publishers in the English-speaking countries. The system provides that each edition of each book published be assigned a unique identifying number, which is clearly printed in the book, usually on the verso, which is the back of the title page, as well as on the book jacket.

In the ten-digit number, the first digit identifies the country or group of countries of origin, the next four are the publisher prefix, the next four are the title number, and the last is a check digit, by which computers can check the accuracy of the number.

International Standard Serial Number (ISSN): An identifying number system for serial publications, set up by international agreement; used by many, but far from all publishers of serials. The system provides that each periodical published be assigned a unique identifying number, which is clearly printed on each issue of the material.

International Telecommunications Satellite Consortium (INTEL-SAT): The international organization governing the development of the world communications system, involving joint use of communications satellites.

Intertextuality: A term coined by Julia Kristeva to designate the various relationships that a given text may have with other texts.

These intertextual relationships include anagram, allusion, adaptation, translation, parody, pastiche, imitation, and other kinds of transformation.

In the literary theories of structuralism and post-structuralism, texts are seen to refer to other texts rather than to an external reality. The term intertext has been used variously for a text drawing on other texts, for a text thus drawn upon, and for the relationship between both.

J

Jacket: An outer cover placed over the binding of a hardcover book, which provides space for visual display and promotional copy, called *jacket copy,* as well as title and author information. Usually designed to be eye-catching, whether seen face-out or spine-out in a bookstore display; with promotional copy under the title on the front cover, on both inner flaps, and on the back cover. Used for most trade hardcover books, but omitted for many scholarly, educational, and professional publications. Also called *dust Jacket, dust cover, dust wrapper,* and *book jacker*

Jacket band: A printed band, wrapping around and enclosing a jacketed book, carrying promotional copy designed to enhance sales of the book.

Japan paper: A high quality and expensive paper, sometimes used for art printing, particularly for printing etchings and engravings.

Jet printing: A highspeed printing process, using ink sprayed from nozzles on paper passing before it; widely used in highspeed computer printout devices.

job: 1. A specific order, as when a printer contracts with a publisher to produce a specific number of copies of a particular book. 2. To sell joint authorship to others in quantity lots, usually for resale by them to others in units to function as a wholesaler or jobber.

Job lot: A body of merchandise sold as a single lot, usually at a discount, consisting of several kinds of goods grouped together in small quantities, which would normally be sold in larger lots by kind of goods

Job press: A press that is normally used for running a miscellany of small printing jobs, rather than for long runs better suited to other kinds of presses.

Job shop: A firm that primarily fulfills specific orders, rather than long term contracts; for example, a small commercial printing shop the works mainly on specific orders, called *job work.*

Joint authorship: The writing of a work by two or more authors; a legal and contractual status, it must be recognized by author-publisher contract and publication credit. A book partially or wholly written by a ghostwriter, for example, is a collaboration in fact, but is considered as joint authorship only if that status is indicated by contact and public recognition.

Joint contract: A contractual obligation undertaken in common by two or more parties, as when two authors contract jointly with a publisher to write a book; each author is completely responsible for the writing of the book should the other author withdraw or otherwise become unable to complete the book.

Jouissance: The French word for 'enjoyment', employed by the critic Roland Barthes in his *Le* Plaisir du *texte* to suggest a kind of response to literary works that is different from ordinary plaisir. Whereas plaisir is comfortable and reassuring, confirming our values and expectations, jouissance—usually translated as 'bliss' to retain its erotic sense—is unsettling and destabilizing. The distinction seems to stand in parallel with Barthes's preference for those fragmentary or dislocated texts which he called *Scriptible rather* than lisible, that is, those that challenge the reader to participate in creating them rather than just consume them.

Journal: 1. A synonym for *newspaper;* in modem usage, normally, encountered as part of a newspaper's title. 2. A periodical covering a, single subject area, such as many professional publications. 3. A synonym for *diary.*

journalism: The gathering and publication of news and news-related material, in such publications as newspapers, magazines, newsletters,; looseleaf reporters, books, and computerized databases.

journalist: One involved in the practice of journalism; usually applied to one working with material appearing in or derived from newspapers and magazines.

journeyman: A skilled crafts-person who does professionally competent work; in some trades, one who is so certified by a standard setting group.

Juvenalian: Characteristic of or written in the manner of the Roman poet Juvenal, whose sixteen verse satires are fierce denunciations of his fellow-Romans in general and of women in particular for their mercenary lives. Juvenalian satire is the kind of satire that bitterly condemns human vice and folly, in contrast with the milder and more indulgent kind known as Horatian satire. In English, Samuel Johnson's poems London and The Vanity of Human Wishes are both imitations of Juvenal, but the satires of Jonathan Swift come closer to Juvenal's uncompromisingly disgusted tone.

Juvenilia: The collective term for those works written during an author's youth. Use of the term commonly implies that the faults of such writings are to be excused as the products of immaturity or lack of experience.

K

Keep standing: An instruction from publisher or customer to printer to hold composed matter in type or in computer storage after printing has been completed, in anticipation of a possible return of the job to press. Some matter is held in composed form in anticipation of partial resetting, as when directory or other current-information database material is periodically updated and reprinted.

Key: An identifying code; for example, a list of numbers or letters carried on illustrative matter correlated with a set of notes explaining the content of that matter, or a group of numbers printed on an advertisement or mail order solicitation, identifying the publication in which an ad was placed or the list from which a sale was made. Also called *keycode* or *legend*.

Keyboarding: The process of printing or otnerwise entering information through use of a set of keys, which when struck or pressed enter the information; used alike for all kinds of such devices, including typewriters, calculators, and computer systems.

Keyed advertising: Advertising that carries a code identifying the media in which it is placed, and therefore identifies the source of returns from that placement, as when a coupon-carrying advertisement in the Chicago Tribune carries "CT" somewhere on the coupo indicating on coupon return that this was from the advertiseme carried in the Chicago Tribune.

key-word access: Describing a mode of access to computerized databases through the use of words and phrases that lead users to desired material held in that database; in essence, a synonym for access through indexes, for keyword access materials are in fact indexes to information stored in databases.

Kitsch: Rubbishy or tasteless pseudoart of any kind. It is most easily recognizable in the products of the souvenir trade, especially those attempting to capitalize on 'high' art or on religion and is found in many forms of popular entertainment—the films of Cecil B. De Mille, much 'Easy Listening' music. It is harder to identify in written works, but the sentimental doggerel found in greetings cards is one obvious example, while the trashier end of the science-fiction and sword-and-sorcery fiction markets provide many more pretentious cases.

Knittelvers: A German verse form consisting of four-stress lines rhymed as couplets. Found in the popular poetry of the 15th and 16th centuries either in accentual metre or in regular octosyllabic fines, it was rejected by 17th-century poets as too clumsy, but was revived in the 18th century by Gottsched, Schiller, and Goethe.

L

LAN (n): *Local area network,* a computer network, usually confined to a single office that allows for the sharing of files and other resources among several users and makes interoperability among various systems possible.

LAN adapter: A card installed into a PC to attach it to a LAN.

Land Information System: A computer system (hardware and software) which is used to analyse land management information, for example, the distribution of natural resources, land usage patterns, property ownership, rateable values etc. A Lan Information System (abbreviation LIS) is not necessarily an online system. It draws data from external, primary and secondary, sources and its tasks may include cartography, statistics and databases.

LAN Workplace: Novell's TCP/IP client software for Macintosh and DOS computers.

Landing Zone: An area on a hard disk platter reserved for 64 parking" the read/write head. Early designs of hard disk required a manual "parking" command but this is now included as the last action in the dying moments of power availability. The landing zone is a non-data storage area, and is often the highest numbered track/cylinder on the disk.

Landmark: A proprietary hardware/software evaluation system developed in America.

Landscape: This refers to the hard copy images. Landscape indicates that the job was printed across the long side of the page rather than the vertical orientation which is far more common.

LapTop Computer: A PC specifically designed to be easily portable (light and compact) and to be easily usable on a person's lap. LapTop computers started out as very basic machines but many now have very powerful processing capabilities.

Laser Printer: A high resolution printer, typically 300 dpi, which uses electrostatic techniques and laser beams to produce images. The printer uses laser beams to create an electrostatic charge on selected parts of the image surface which is then transferred to the print surface. Dry powder ink, usually referred to as "toner", is attracted to the charged area and forms the appropriate image. Laser printers are frequently used with PCs, to provide high quality output. Print speeds are in the range 5-10 pages per minute for text, much slower for graphics. Many mainframe computers use a laser printer as an output device for hard copy. Output of these machines is often measured in metres of paper per minute or boxes of paper per hour.

Latency: The amount of time required, on average, for the required data to appear under the read\write head of a disk drive. If the required data has just passed under the read\write head at the time of data request then the latency period will be close to the maximum possible. A full revolution of the disk platter is necessary before the data again appears under the read\write head. On a hard disk spinning at 3600 revolutions per minute this will be approximately 16 milliseconds.

Latinate: Derived from or imitating the Latin language. Latinate diction in English is the use of words derived from Latin rather than those originating in Old English, e.g. *suspend* rather than *hang. A* Latinate style may also be marked by prominent syntactic inversion, especially the delaying of the main verb: while the normal English word-order is subject-verb-object, Milton frequently uses the Latin order object-subject-verb in his poem *Paradise Lost*, as in the line.

Law book: A book in content concerned with the law, including statutes, regulations, cases, interpretation, application, and application, and related mat directed mainly at an audience composed of lawyers and law students.

Layout: The design plans of a body of printed material, whether that material be a page or an entire book, with specifications and markings to guide those involved in composition. Composition and makeup of pages both proceed from layout design.

Led: The UNIX ftp command to change the local directory (as opposed to the working directory at the ftp host site).

Leading: The spacing between lines of text measured in points. The leading or a given point size would always be greater than the point size of the font. Leading and font point sizes are often quoted together to give an impression, to the trained mind, of how the finished product would look on paper. The text in this book is set in 11/12 Times Roman, indicating an 11 point typeface with 12 points ot leading.

Leaf: 1. In network architecture, a computer that receives a signal from a more central computer but does not pass a signal along to a more remote computer, 2. *In (audio* cassette) tape trees, a participant who receives a copy of the tape being distributed but does not make copies of the tape for anyone else.

Leaf site: A Usenet computer that receives a newsfeed from another site but does not distribute news to any other computers.

League for Programming Freedom: A group that opposes software patents and copyrights; information available via anonymous FTP at prep.ai.mit. edu in the pub/lpf directory or by e-mail at league@prep.ai.mit. edu.

Learning curve: A graph showing the relationship between continued practice at a given task and the resulting gains in proficiency, speed and accuracy. Sometimes called an experience curve. Software users may talk of "an easy learning curve" or "a long learning curve".

Leased line: A telephone line leased from the telephone company to provide a permanent connection from a LAN to an Internet service provider or to a WAN.

Leavisites: The name given to followers of the English literary critic F. R. Leavis, who achieved an extensive influence in mid-20th century British culture as coeditor of the journal *Scrutiny,* as a teacher in Cambridge, and as the author of *New Bearings in English Poetry. Revaluation, The Great Tradition,* and several other books. Leavis's attitude to literature and society, strongly influenced by his wife Q. D. Leavis's book *Fiction and the Reading Public,* was marked by an intense moral seriousness and a militant hostility both to Marxism and to the utilitarian values of modem 'commercialisam. He saw the critic's task as one of preserving the values of the best literature—identified with those of 'Life'—against the hostile cultural environment of 'mass' society. His harshly exclusive literary judgements were influenced partly by T. S. Eliot's rejection of 19th-century poetry in favour of the metaphysical poets and partly by admiration for the work of D. H. Lawrence. Many of his pronouncements on the decline of English culture followed Eliot's hypothesis of the dissociation of sensibility and invoked the supposed merits of the organic community' of the rural past.

The Leavisite influence on the teaching of English literature was strong in Britain during the 1950s and 1960s, and produced a detailed version of English literary history in *The Pelican Guide to English Literature*, but it has declined sharply since Leavis's death in 1978. The Leavisites are sometimes referred to as 'Scrutineers', after the name of their journal. The adjective Leavisian is applied more neutrally to ideas characteristic of Leavis's work.

Legend: A story or group of stories handed down through popular oral tradition, usually consisting of an exaggerated or unreliable account of some actually or possibly historical person—often a saint, monarch, or popular hero. Legends are sometimes distinguished from myths in that they concern human beings rather than gods, and sometimes in that they have some sort of historical basis whereas myths do not; but these distinctions are difficult to maintain consistently. The term was originally applied to accounts of saints' lives, but is now applied chiefly to fanciful tales of warriors, criminals, and other sinners; or more recently to those bodies of biographical rumour and embroidered anecdote surrounding dead film stars and rock musicians. *Adjective:* legendary.

Letterbomb: An e-mail message containing either escape characters that can lock up certain types or terminals, or harmful commands to be interpreted by the user's shell.

Lexis/Nexis: A proprietary system of searchable databases of legal briefs (Lexis) and newspaper and magazine articles (Nexis)

Lharc: A file compression program for DOS.

.lhz A file extension that indicates lharc compression.

Library: A collection of pre-written, pre-tested program modules that can be called upon to form part of a new program. Libraries are usually stored on disk and are made available during compile-time and run-time as required.

Library catalogues: Most university and library catalogs are available via telnet. Hytelnet index of library catalogs.

Library of Congress: The main repository of information of the U. S. government, available by telnet at locis. loc.gov.

Light emitting diode: An electronic device that emits light when a voltage is applied to it. They are often used as a "Power On" indicator on computers and computer hardware.

Light pen: A hand held device, connected to a computer, that can read bar-codes. They are commonly used in super-markets and other retail stores. Light pens can also be used as a pointing device in conjunction with a computer monitor. The pen is pointed at an object, for example, a menu choice, on the monitor screen in order to make a selection.

Light verse: The general term for various kinds of verse that have no serious purpose and no solemnity of tone. They may deal with trivial subjects, or bring a light-hearted attitude to more serious ones. Light verse is often characterized by a display of technical accomplishment in the handling of difficult rhymes, metres, and stanza forms. The many forms of light verse include Anacreontics, clerihews, epigrarns jingles, limericks, mock epics, nonsense verse, parodies, and *vers de societe*

LIM-EMS: Abbreviation for Lotus Intel Microsoft Expanded Memory Specification.

Line: A generic term for a transmission medium. It may actually be a line, as in a cable, but increasingly it is likely to be a microwave or optical fibre link.

Line cater: A bug in older versions of Usenet newsreader software for UNIX that caused certain lines at the beginning of posts to vanish. To appease the line cater, posters would include lines of spurious text to be sacrificed instead of the actual contents of the message.

Line feed: A character that moves the cursor down one line (ASCII 10) usually starting a new line in combination with a carriage return character.

Line graph: A type of graph that links, or attempts to link, all of the data points of a dataset. A Line Graph may be used to demonstrate trends in a dataset over a period of time.

Line length: The number of characters that fit on a line—fixed on some systems, settable on others. The standard, line length on the Internet is 80 characters: e-mail or Usenet posts produced with software using longer line lengths will wrap irregularly and appear awkward to users with 80-character lines.

Line noise: Static or interference on a wire that corrupts the signal. On a character-based modern connection, for example, line noise might result in random gibberish and escape characters polated with the intended text.

Line-oriented (adj): Said of applications and interfaces that display text one line at a time, rather than making an entire screenful of text available at once.

Link (n): 1. In UNIX, a reference to a directory or file contained elsewhere that appears in directory listings just as if the remote directory or file were in the current, directory; 2. On Web pages, a hypertext connection, a button or high-lighted bit of text that, when selected, jumps the reader to another page.

Linear programming: A mathematical procedure used to determine the best combination of limited resources and activities necessary to fulfil a specific objective. Although termed "Linear Programming" this technique predates "programming" in its modem sense.

Line Printer: A fast moving printer, used on mainframe and minicomputers only. Line printers are also known as "Line-at-a-time-Printers" as they assemble the characters on a line by line basis, not on a character basis as do most other printers. Output of line printers is often measured in metres of paper per minute or boxes of paper per hour! Types of line printer include a Band Printer, a Chain Printer and a Drum Printer. See separate entries for each of these.

Link Access Protocol (LAP): A data link layer protocol for AppleTalk that specifies the interface to network hardware.

Linker: A software application that links object files, library routines, procedures and variables into a, form ready for execution as a program. Some compilers are also linkers, they take source code and produce an executable file, by passing a separate linking process.

Linotronic: A proprietary brand of typesetting equipment, developed and manufactured by Linotype Corporation. Linotronic typesetters provide very high resolution (1200-2500dpi) and are commonly used at commercial printing premises.

Linux *(line-ux)*: An implementation of UNIX for IBM PC-compatibles. It has been developed as a collaborative effort by widespread Internet users and is distributed for free.

Liquid crystal display: This is a type of monitor which uses an alternative to cathode ray technology and is particularly useful where power supplies are limited. A Liquid Crystal Display (abbreviation

LCD) uses aromatic hydrocarbons, for example, quinones, which polarize when a voltage is applied to them. This enables the quinones to either pass or block light. Background lighting falling on a LCD screen is normally reflected, however where the quinones allow light to pass through, the image of the appropriate character is formed. LCD technology depends on background lighting, in the absence of this the LCD display is useless. Many manufacturers have overcome this by providing "back-ground" lighting.

LISP: A high level language designed in the late 1950s at Massachusetts Institute of Technology (USA). LISP is used for Artificial Intelligence and other complex applications.

List (v): 1. To view the names of files in a directory; *2. To* display the contents of a file.

Listserv: A type of automated mailing list software that runs on IBM mainframes and originated on the BITNET network.

Little-endian (adj): A storage format in which the most significant byte has the highest address, as opposed to big-endian.

Local (adj): Said of a computer to which a user is connected directly or of a device (such as a printer) or process under the user's direct control, as contrasted with remote hosts, devices, and processes.

Local Area Network: A computer network whose participants are located close together often within the same building. Local Area Networks have the advantage that they can utilise very high data transmission speeds and the terminals, which are often personal computers, can share expensive resources such as laser printers and software.

Local Area Transport (LAT): Digital (DEC) architecture for connecting terminal servers on Ethernet networks to host computers.

Local echo: 1. A copy of the data being sent (usually typed) over a communications device (such as a modem) displayed in a terminal window so that the sender can monitor the process; *2. A* terminal mode in some communications programs, specifying half duplex transmission, in which the communications program displays the user's input on the screen, instead of relaying an echo from the host.

Localhost (n): Also local host, the host computer a user is currently logged in to. The *address of* any user's current localhost is always 127.0.0.1.

Local node: The computer on a network to which a user is connected directly.

LocalTalk: Shielded, twisted-pair wiring and connectors for using the Macintosh's built-in AppleTalk network hardware.

Local Variable: A variable whose value is controlled by a program module, such as a subroutine. The variable may or may not be accessible to the main program and/or other modules, however only the module containing the "local variable" can alter its value. This is a useful programming technique as it allows compartmentalisation, and therefore safe-guarding, of different program variables.

Locative domain name: A two-letter geographical domain name, such as us for the United States, *uk* for the United Kingdom, *de* for Germany, and so on.

LOCIS: The *Library of Congress Information Service,* available by telnet at locis.loc.gov or on the Web at http://www,loc,gov/.

lock up (v): To freeze, as when certain sequences of characters, freeze a keyboard, preventing the user from typing.

Log book: Nautical jargon borrowed by the computer profession. A log book is often used to keep a record of computer staff on duty and the processing tasks performed. It may also be used to keep a record of hardware maintenance schedules and breakdowns.

Logical: Said of a computer address or device, identified by a numerical reference, which may or may not correspond to a physical address or device.

Logic error: A program fault that does not necessarily prevent the program running but produces an output error. Programs with logic errors invariably run through from first to last statement but produce the wrong answer or output.

logical conjunction: A word that joins two or more key words by specifying a logical relationship between them.

Logical drive: Part of a physical storage medium (for example, a hard disk) that has been separated by the operating system into distinct storage locations.

The hard disk may have a storage capacity of 42MB, but for operational reasons (users preference or operating system restrictions) it may be necessary to divide the 42MB into two logical drives". Under

MS-DOS the two locations may be designated as the C and D drives (A and B are usually reserved for floppy disk drives).

In this case the C and D drives share a common physical storage medium.

Logic gate: A flip-flop, or collection of flip-flops, that will 1 and respond to varying input conditions. Widely used in a CPU and in registers.

Logical Link Control (LLC): The Institute of Electrical and Electronic Engineering 802 standard that specifies a uniform user interface.

Logical tree: Any logical arrangement of devices, files, data, and so on in which all relationships stem from a root; child branches are subordinate to parent branches, and an element without any children is called a leaf.

Log in (v): To connect to a network or computer, identify oneself as a user, supply a password, and start a session.

Login (n): 1. A username, the *handle a* user logs in with, corresponding to an account; 2. An instance of logging in.

Login script: A prerecorded sequence of login steps that can play back automatically to connect a user to a computer or network. Login scripts can breach security if they automate the process of supplying a password, thereby allowing anyone who runs the script to log in.

Log-on: The process of gaining access to computer facilities. This may include entering a password.

Log out (v): To end a session and disconnect from a computer or network.

Longitudinal redundancy check: An error checking technique, used in data communications, in which the parity check character is applied to each column of bits within a data block.

Loopback (n): A test in which a signal is sent from a source to an intermediate point and 'hen back to the original source to evaluate the accuracy of the transmission.

Loopback address: The Internet address (127.0, 0.1) that always points back to the localhost.

Low-bandwidth: Said of a connection that can only manage a slow connect speed or of a resource on the Internet that a user with a slow connection will still find useful.

Low level format: The basic installation of a hard disk, usually only performed once in the lifetime of a hard disk. A low level format is also known as a pre-format and can be performed by many disk management utilities.

Low level language: A programming language that is fairly close to the machine code used by the processor. Low level languages are often hardware specific and are not necessarily portable between computers.

LSI: Abbreviation for Large Scale Integration, the manufacture of integrated circuits where many thousands of electronic circuits are placed on one silicon chip.

Lurk: To read a mailing list or newsgroup without posting to it. Every new user should lurk for a while before posting to get a feel for what the group is all about and how others in the group behave.

M

Mailing list: A list of mailing addresses, compiled by interest or activity, such as a customers' list, a subscribers' list, or a list compiled by a firm in the business of renting lists to others.

Most mailing lists are available for rent or purchase to selling organizations, with those listed becoming prospective purchasers of goods, services, or ideas advertised by mail.

Management: 1. In the widest sense, the operation and control of any function or organization, including the management of one's own time, a household, or the provisioning of an ocean liner. 2. The operation and control of business organizations, aiming at attaining the overall goals of those organizations at minimum cost and maximum profit. Management may participate in overall goal setting and may in fact exercise many other ownership functions. 3. Those who are responsible for the operation and control of business organizations.

Management consultant: One who is professionally engaged in advising management as to the most effective ways of achieving management's goals. Most such consultants are independent contractors, whose value to management lies primarily in their independence and broad business experience.

Management Information System (MIS): A computer-based information system aimed at providing management with an ongoing flow of operating and financial data that will help provide the basis for consistently informed decision making.

Managing editor: That editor designated as primarily responsible for the production of a publication and who supervises all the production processes involved.

Mannerism: A vague term for the self-conscious cultivation of peculiarities of style—usually elaborate, ingenious, and ornate—in literary works of any period. Like the baroque, with which it often overlaps, mannerism is a concept more clearly defined in art history than in literary studies: art historians have marked out a Mannerist period between the High Renaissance and the Baroque, characterized by distortions of figure and perspective. Clear equivalents in English literature of this period would be the *mannered* style of euphuism, and the elaborate conceits of the Elizabethan sonnet. But mannered styles can be found in many later periods, from the Latinate style of Milton to the far-fetched similes of Raymond Chandler. A common indicator of literary mannerism is that the elaborate manner is maintained, whatever the nature of the matter treated.

Manual: An instructional publication, usually in the form of book or booklet, carrying step-by-step and detailed instructions about how to accomplish stated tasks or goals; for example, instructions on machine repair and maintenance.

Manuscript (ms, MS, or Ms; plural mss, MSS, or Mss): 1. Any piece of written work, whatever the instrument used for writing and whatever the material written upon; originally referred only to a hand written work, but in modem times has broadened to include typescripts, or material in typewriter type, and material written using computer equipment.

2. A piece of written work ready to begin the manufacturing processes, starting with composition, that will make into a publication.

Marginal costing: A costing technique that assigns only a marginal or incremental cost factor, rather than assigning a full shares of all costs being incurred; often used in evaluating new product, results.

Marginal revenue: The revenue resulting from a single additional sale. If revenue per sale remains constant, each additional unit sold yields as much as each previous unit, but if price decreases as units sold increase, revenue for each additional unit sold is less than a full unit price. For example, 5 units sold at $5 each yield $25. If 6 units are sold at $4.50 each, the yield is $27, which is only $2 more than $25. The marginal revenue is $2.

Market potential: The sales possibilities for a product, in both present and future; a key assessment to be made by those developing new products.

Marketing: In the widest sense, the distribution function, including buying, selling, transporting, financing, and collecting. In modem business organizations, however, the term describes a group of selling and sales-related functions including advertising, promotion, and direct selling.

Marketing manager: One who is Professionally engaged in developing marketing activities on behalf of a product or group of products.

Markup: 1. The amount added to the cost of a product to cover additional costs and profits; for example, the amount added by a bookseller to the price paid a publisher for a book, to cover operating expenses, other selling costs, and profit. Often used as a synonym for *discount,* but that is appropriate only when both markup and discount are expressed in currency, rather than in percentages. If a book lists at $10, and the bookseller buys it from the publisher at $6 and sells it to the public at the list price of $10, then both markup and discount are $4. But in percentage terms, the book listed at $10 and sold for $6 is discounted 40%, while the book bought for $6 and sold for $10 the same book, but seen differently—is marked up $4 on $6, and therefore the markup is 66 2/3%.

2. A raising of a retail price; literally the marking of a higher price on an item sold at retail, as when a publisher, jobber, or retailer places a $15.95 sticker over the $13.95 price shown on a book.

Married print: A motion picture print with both picture and sound on the same strip of film correctly synchronised for projection.

Marrying-up: Preparing picture and sound negatives in the laboratory for making *married prints.*

Martianpoets: The term applied in the 1980s to a small group of poets in Britain whose work is marked by the prominence of surprising visual metaphors, similes, and conceits. The leading figures are Christopher Reid and Craig Raine, who both published important collections in 1979: Reid's *Arcadia* and Raine's *A Martian Sends a Postcard Home* both transform everyday objects, in a playful kind of defamiliarization. The term comes from the title poem of Raine's book in which we are shown familiar earthly sights through the inexperienced eyes of a visiting Martian. Similar effects are achieved by David Sweetman in *Looking Into the Deep End* and by Oliver Reynolds in *Skevington's Daughter*

Masque or mask: A spectacular kind of indoor performance combining poetic drama, music, dance, song, lavish costume, and costly stage effects, which was favoured by European royalty in the 16th and early 17th centuries. Members of the court would enter disguised, taking the parts of mythological persons, and enact a simple allegorical plot, concluding with the removal of masks and a dance joined by members of the audience.

Shakespeare included a short masque scene in *The Tempest*, and Milton's play *Comus* is loosely related to the masque; these are now the best-known examples, but at the courts of James I and Charles I the highest form of the masque proper was represented by the quarrelsome collaboration of Ben Jonson with the designer Inigo Jones from 1605 to 1631 in the hugely expensive *Oberon* and other works. The parliamentary Revolution of the 1640s brought this form of extravagance to an abrupt end.

Masking (audio): Psychoacoustic effect whereby a sound suppresses the subjective effect of noise in the adjacent frequency band.

Masking (colour): In colour photography, a method of correcting unwanted absorption in the dye components by the use of complementary colour images, which may be integral to the material or separate from it.

Masking: The indication of the unwanted areas of an illustration, either by means of an opaque cut-out overlay or by lines marked on a transparency, or on the back of an illustration.

Masking (projection): Limitation of a projected picture by combination of the aperture in the projector and black borders surrounding the screen.

Masking (contrast control): Combination of a normal photographic record with a low density image of inverse tonal values to reduce its effective contrast in printing or projection.

masking: The ability to adjust the colour balance by matrixing the *RGB* signals. Used to match colour film primaries to the television standard.

Masking: Covering part of an illustration with opaque material, thereby removing it from the illustration when it is reproduced.

Mass communication: The process of disseminating information, ideas, and entertainment via such mass media as television and radio broadcasting, newspapers, and large-circulation magazines.

Mass marketing Marketing geared to the distribution of goods and services to very large numbers of consumers, through the employment of substantial marketing resources, including such vehicles as chain, department, and discount stores; catalogue selling; and mass media advertising.

Mass market paperback: A paperback designed for the widest possible distribution, in tens of thousands of locations, rather than for limited distribution in some thousands of bookstore locations, as are most hardcover books and trade paperbacks, and therefore produced in a smaller format and sold for a relatively low price.

To some extent, the distinction between mass market and trade paperbacks has blurred, with price and format becoming less important than the means of distribution achieved, and some books achieving mass market distribution with trade paperback formats and prices.

Mass media: The vehicles through which mass communications are disseminated, 'such as television and radio broadcasting, newspapers, and large-circulation magazines.

Master proofs: The set of proofs that is sent to the compositor as the single guide to be used in making corrections and changes in composed material; contains corrections from authors and proofreaders, with all inconsistencies resolved and queries answered. Other duplicate proofs are then regarded as foul matter.

Masking: (1) In audio, an effect whereby a sound may apparently be suppressed by another which may be louder, or on a different frequency range, or both.

(2) In colour television.

Matrix printer: A text and graphic printer using an electromagnetically operated matrix of needles, usually 7 x 9, producing characters or graphics as a pattern of dots.

Matte: An opaque mask limiting the area of a picture which is exposed in special effects.

It may be a cut-out aperture or a high density image on film, while in video it may be electronically generated to blank off the appropriate signal.

Matte finish: A dull finish, as distinguished from a glossy finish.

Matte print: A photographic print with a dull finish, as distinguished from a glossy finish.

Media: A group of forms through which things are done, as in communications media, artistic media, and media of exchange. In business, the term usually describes the means of mass communication, including television and radio broadcasting and newspaper and magazine publishing.

Medievalism or mediaevalism: Enthusiasm for or imitation of the arts and customs of Europe during the Middle Ages—that is, from about the 8th century to the I5th. In literature, this may manifest itself in the use of archaisms, in the choice of medieval settings for narrative works, or more broadly in an ideological attachment to values associated with medieval societies. Antiquarian interest in ballads and other aspects of medieval art grew in the late 18th century, influencing the Gothic novel and the strongly medievalist nostalgia of Romanticism.

Medievalism is a significant current in 19th-century literature from Walter Scott's novel *Ivanhoe* and Keats's poem 'The Eve of St Agnes' to the prose and verse romances of William Morris. Important works of Victorian social criticism, notably Thomas Carlyle's Past *and Present* and John Ruskin's *The Stones* of *Venke,* contrasted medieval social conditions favourably with those of the modern industrial city.

A medievalist is usually a scholar studying some aspect of medieval history or culture.

Metalanguage: Any use of language about language, as for instance in glosses, definitions or arguments about the usage or meaning of words. Linguistics sometimes describes itself as a metalanguage because it is a 'language' about language; and so on the same assumption criticism is a metalanguage about literature.

Some theorists of structuralism have spoken of meta-languages as if they were clearly separate from or standing above the 'object-language they describe, but this claim is denied by post-structuralism, which points out that linguistics, criticism etc.. are still within the same general language, albeit as specialized uses with their own terminologies.

Thus there is in principle no absolute distinction between criticism and literature.

Roman Jakobson in his listing of linguistic functions describes the metalingual' function as that by which speakers check that they understand one another.

In a wider sense literary works often have a metalinguistic aspect in which they highlight uses of language a very clear case of this is Shaw's Pygmalion. It is also possible to have a *meta-metalanguage,* i.e. a 'third-level' discourse such as an analysis of linguistics, or a work of metacriticism.

Multi-media: Describes a body of communications materials designed to operate as a unified whole while appearing in more than one medium of communication; for example, an instructional kit containing printed booklets, an audio record, and a slidefilm; or a marketing plan that combines print, radio, and television promotion

Multiprocessing: In computer processing, the joint operation of multiple processing units sharing a common memory, under the direction of one executive central processing unit; allows for time-sharing of computer equipment by many users at once.

N

Narrowcasting: A synonym for special interest marketing, which is the development of products and marketing approaches directed at relatively narrow special markets rather than at mass markets; a term currently in vogue in computer product marketing and in the development and marketing of computer-based publishing products.

Narration: The process of relating a sequence of events; or another term for a narrative. In the first sense, narration is often distinguished from other kinds of writing which may be included in a narrative; it is also distinguished from the events recounted, i.e. from the story, and from the narrative itself *Verb:* narrate.

Narrative: A telling of some true or fictitious event or connected sequence of events, recounted by a narrator to a narratee. Narratives are to be distinguished from descriptions of qualities, states, or situations, and also from dramatic enactments of events. A narrative will consist of a set of events recounted in a process of narration, in which the events are selected and arranged in a particular order.

The category of narratives includes both the shortest accounts of events and the longest historical or biographical works, diaries, travelogues, etc., as well as novels, ballads, epics, short stories, and other fictional forms. In the study of fiction, it is usual to divide novels and shorter stories into first-person narratives and third person narratives. As an adjective, 'narrative' means 'characterized by or relating to storytelling' thus *narrative technique* is the method of telling stories, and narrative poetry is the class of poems that tell stories, as distinct from dramatic and lyric poetry. Some theorists of narratology have attempted to isolate the quality or set of properties that distinguishes narratives from non-narrative writings this is called narrativity.

National Association of College Stores (NACS): A trade association' serving bookstores affiliated with American institutions of higher education, and representing its members in trade, educational and legislative activities of mutual concern.

National Book Critics Circle: A professional organization of American book critics, representing its members in matters *of* mutual interest and offering a series of annual book awards.

Negative impedance converter: An *active network* in which an impedance, connected to one pair of terminals, is converted to an impedance of negative value at another pair of terminals.

Negritude: The slogan of a cultural movement launched by black students in Paris in 1932, subsequently influencing many black writers, especially in the French speaking world. The movement aimed to reassert traditional African cultural values against the French colonial policy of assimilating blacks into white culture. Its two most important figures were the Senegalese poet and politician Leopold Sedar Senghor and the Martiniquam poet and politician Aime Cesaire, and its literary masterpiece is Cksaire's Cahier d'un retowr au pays natal.

Senghor defined nigritude very broadly as 'the sum total of the values of the civilization of the African world,' understood intermi of intuitive reasons and 'cosmic rhythm'. The influentli;ll joumal Prisence Afficaine, founded in 1947, promoted this ideal. A later, more politically radical generation of black writers. however, questioned the movement's limited aims: as Wole Soyinka wrote, 'the tiger does not proclaim his tigritude—pounces'.

Newspaper: A periodical that carries both news and advertisements, usually on newsprint, self-covered and unbound in large sheets, and generally issuing at least once a week.

Newsprint: A relatively inexpensive grade of paper, used mainly for newspaper printing,

Newsworthy: Material of such nature and currency as to cause some of those gathering and reporting the news to include it in their reports.

Nonbook: 1. A term of derogation, aimed at books accused of serving wholly as objects of conspicuous consumption, rather than as reading materials or works of art; for example, relatively expensive books containing mostly illustrations of little artistic or literary merit, intended to be given at Christmas time and displayed on coffee tables by their recipients. 2. Printed materials that are not in book or periodical form, such as audiovisual materials, or pamphlets; in this context, a term used less and less as new publishing forms blur the distinction between the different forms in which materials are published.

Nonfiction: All writings other than works avowedly of the imagination Commonly used to distinguish between published works of fiction a all other published works.

Nonfiction novel: A novel based upon real events and real people, which openly uses these events and people in an imaginative fashion attempt to create a work of art, without significantly altering or abstracting from reality; also called *documentary novel* or *fact novel.*

Non-impact printing: Any printing method in which printing is accomplished without the impact of an image-bearing surface, such as a typewriter key or a printing plate, upon the surface to be printed; for example, jet printing.

O

Off-line edit: Editing video material using low-cost equipment to produce a *rough cut* prior to using expensive broadcast standard equipment for the final work.

Off-line: 1. In electronic data processing, machines that are not directly controlled by the central processing unit.

2. In print production, machines that are not directly linked with the main printing machines during the printing process.

Offprint: A printing that is physically derived from a previously printed work; for example, a magazine article reprinted as a booklet.

Offset paper: Any paper suitable for offset printing; before offset printing became the most common method of printing publications, this term referred to papers specially designed and treated for offset printing, but most book papers are now manufactured suitable for offset printing.

Offset press: Any press designed to print using the offset printing method; a generic term.

Old English type: One of the group of Northern European black-letter, or gothic, type faces.

Omniscient narrator: An 'all-knowing' kind of narrator' very commonly found in works of fiction written as third-Person narratives, The omniscient narrator has a full knowledge of the story's events and of the motives and unspoken thoughts of the various characters. He or she will also be capable of describing events happening simultaneously in different places—a capacity not normally available to the limited Point of view of first-person narratives.

One colour job: A printing job using one ink colour; usually black ink on white paper, but may be any colour ink on any colour paper.

One-price policy: A pricing policy by which the seller sets a fixed price on a specified kind of merchandise and will not negotiate the price of that merchandise; often a stated intention and a tendency rather than a hard fact, as large customers tend to have considerable ?,41 bargaining power.

One-time rate: The charge for an advertisement placed only once, higher rate than that charged per ad for multiple placements.

On demand: 1. Describing the retrieval of single pieces or related bodies of information from computerized databases, whenever and in then whatever order desired, whether on screen alone or on screen and then in printed or hard, copy. 2. Describing a book of which only one copy is printed to specifications provided by its purchaser; generally a scholarly work or book composed of such modular units as articles stored on microfilm. Also called on *demand printing* and *demand printing.*

On-line: In electronic data processing, machines that are part of or are directly in contact with a computer system, whether controlled by the central processing unit or in remote contact with that unit, as when data is retrieved directly from a computerized database. 2. In printing production, machines that are directly linked with the main printing machines during, the printing process.

On-line search: The process of looking for and directly accessing material stored in a computerized database, usually involving the use of indexes, also known as *keyword* access devices.

Optical character recognition (OCR): In computer systems the machine reading and input into the system of printed materials by scanning light patterns, bypassing punched cards and other intermediate steps; in contrast to magnetic ink character recognition (MICR).

Optical printing: A method of photographic printing which an image of the original is formed on the print stock by a copy lens.

Oral tradition: The passing on from one generation to another of songs, chants, proverbs, and other verbal compositions within and between non-literate cultures; or the accumulated stock of works thus transmitted by word of mouth. Ballads, folktales and other works emerging from an oral tradition will often be found in several different versions, because each performance is a fresh improvisation based around a 'core' of narrative incidents and formulaic phrases. The state of dependence on the spoken word in oral cultures is known as orality.

Oratory: The art of Public speaking; or the exercise of this art in orations—formal speeches for public occasions. A literary style resembling public speech and its formal devices may be called oratorical.

Outdoor advertising: Display advertising placed in outside locations, such as billboards and other kinds of signs.

Out of Print (OP): Describing a work currently unavailable from its publisher, often refers to a specific edition, rather than to the work itself, which may be in print in other editions, countries, or forms.

Out of Stock (OS): A book still in print but temporarily from the publisher.

Overlap: Extending the sound track into the next scene for smooth continuity.

Overmatter: More composed matter than is required for a specific publication or portion of a publication, as when a periodical sets more than it needs for a particular issue; overmatter may be held and kept live, or may be killed.

P

Page break: The end of a printed page and the beginning of the next page, where text continues to a new page.

Page proofs: A set of proofs of fully composed and laid out pages, assembled for a final set of checking operations before a publication is printed.

Page-turner: Slang for a well-written popular work that will thoroughly engage its readers.

Pagination: The process of numbering the pages of a work, and the numbers indicated.

Paid circulation: The number of copies of a publication actually sold, as of the date of a given issue, including both subscription and individual copies sold, as well as subscriptions purchased but not yet paid for; but not including unpaid circulation resulting from subscriptions and single copies given away.

Palaeography: The study and deciphering of old manuscripts.

Palimpsest: A manuscript written on a surface from which an earlier text has been partly or wholly erased. Palimpsests were common in the Middle Ages before paper became available, because of the high cost of parchment and vellum.

Pamphlet: A relatively small, bound or unbound, paper-covered work of nonfiction; in practice used inter-changeably with booklet, but implying a somewhat larger work than a small booklet.

Paper: A material derived from wood, cloth, grass, or any other cellulose material which can be separated into its constituent fibers, turned into pulp,, and manufactured in thin sheets, for such end-use purposes as printing, writing, and wrapping.

Paperback: A book bound in paper, rather than cloth; generally also identified by distribution method, as either mass *market paperbacks* or *trade,* also called *quality, paperbacks.* Although periodicals are not generally described as paperbacks, the distinction between periodicals and paperback books sometimes blurs; as when a periodical issues a yearly buying guide issue, which is also sold separately as a paperback book.

Paperback original: A book first published in either mass market or trade paperback, rather than in hardcover.

Paperback rights: The right to publish a book in paperback, treated as subsidiary when the book has been contracted first as a hardcover book, and primary if the book has been contracted first as a paperback.

Parable: A brief tale intended to be understood as an allegory illustrating some lesson or moral. The forty parables attributed to Jesus of Nazareth in Christian literature have had a lasting influence upon the Western tradition of didactic allegory. A modem instance is Wilfred Owen's poem 'The Parable of the Old Man and the Young', which adapts a biblical story to the 1914-18 war, a longer prose parable is John Steinbeck's *The Pearl* . *Adjective.* parabolic.

Paraliterature: The category of written works relegated to the margins of recognized literature and often dismissed as subliterary despite evident resemblances to the respectable literature of the official canon. Paraliterature thus includes many modem forms of popular fiction and drama: children's adventure stories, most detective and spy thrillers, most science fiction and fantasy writing, pornography and women's romances, along with much television and radio drama.

Parallel communication: A multi-wire or bus system of communication.

Parametric equaliser: Equaliser that allows control of frequency and bandwidth.

Paraliterature: The category of written works relegated to the margins of recognized literature and often dismissed as subliterary despite evident resemblances to the respectable literature of the official canon. Paraliterature thus includes many modem forms of popular fiction and drama children's adventure stories, most detective and spy thrillers, most science fiction and fantasy writing, pornography and women's romances, along with much television and radio drama.

Paraphrase: A restatement of a text's meaning in different words, usually in order to clarify the sense of the original. Paraphrase Involves the separation or abstraction of content from form, and so has been resisted strongly by New Criticism and other schools of modem critical opinion.

Paraphrasable: This is a necessary theoretical warning, since the particular form and diction of a poem give it meanings that are not reducible to simple statements and that do not survive the subititutibn of synonyms; but the practice of paraphrase' can help to establish this very fact, and is an analytic procedure too useful to be outlawed. Adjective *paraphrastic.*

Parody: A mocking imitation of the style of a literary work or works. ridiculing the stylistic habits of an author or school by exaggerated mimicry. Parody is related to burlesque in its application of serious styles to ridiculous subjects, to satire in its punishment of eccentricities. and even to criticism in its analysis of style. The Greek dramatist Aristophanes parodied the styles of Aeschylus and Euripides in *The Frogs*, while Cervantes parodied chivahic romances in *Don Quixote.* In English, two of the leading parodists are Henry Fielding and James Joyce. Poets in the 19th century, especially William Wordsworth and Robert Browning. suffered numerous parodies of their works.

Partnership: The association of two or more people for the purpose of doing business together for profit. The main form is that of the general partnership, carrying with it unlimited liability, as well as the ability to bind and be bound by the commitments of individual partners, and needing no formal written agreements between the parties to be recognized in law as valid.

Pastiche: A literary work composed from elements borrowed either from various other writers or from a particular earlier author. The term can be used in a derogatory sense to indicate lack of originality, or more neutrally to refer to works that involve a deliberate and playfully imitative tribute to other writers. Pastiche differs from parody in using imitation as a form of flattery rather than mockery, and froin plagiarism in its lack of deceptive intent. A wellknown modern example is John Fowles's novel The French Lieutenant's Woman, which is partly a pastiche of the great Victorian novelists. The frequent resort to pastiche has been cited as a characteristic feature of post-modernism. A writer of pastiches is sometimes called a oasticheur. Verb: pastiche.

Patent pending: A statement by government that a patent has been, applied for; usually printed or otherwise affixed to a product or process,: for which patent has been applied for and not yet granted, to serve as a warning to others against patent infringement, because patent protection will be considered in effect retroactively since registration, when and if granted.

Penalty copy: Manuscript material in such a messy or nonstandard form that the compositor charges an extra amount, or *penalty,* often a percentage of the total composition charge, for setting it; for example, single-spaced copy, handwritten or illegibly corrected material, and pages that are undersized, oversized, or contain copy on both sides.

Pencil art: Drawings executed in pencil, rather than ink, often reproducing as well as ink when offset printing is used.

Pencil beam: In antennas, a very narrow beam with a cross-section which is approximately circular.

Periodic sentence: A long sentence in which the completion of the syntax and sense is delayed until the end, usually after a sequence of balanced subordinate ciauses. The effect is a kind of suspense, as the reader's attention is propelled forward to the end, as in this sentence from Ann Radcliffe's *Romance* *of the Forest.* describing the heroine's response to an unwelcome sexual advance

While he was declaring the ardour of his passion In such terms, as but too often make vehemence pass for sincerity, Adeline, to whom this declaration, if honourable, was distressing. and if dishonourable, was shocking, interrupted him and thanked him for the offer of a distinction, which, with a modest. but determined air. she said she must refuse.

Perfect binding: A binding process in which signatures are trimmed into loose sheets, which are then glued together by means of an adhesive applied to the spine of the book; then the binding itself is glued directly to the spine of the book. The result is a book that is glued, rather than sewn together; widely used in paperback books and sometimes used in hardcover books.

Perfecting press: Any press that prints both sides of a sheet at the same time, whatever the printing method used.

Performative: a kind of utterance that performs with language the deed to which it refers, instead of describing some state of affairs. The term was coined by the philosopher J. L. Austin in *How to Do Things with Words* as part of his speech act theory. Austin distinguishes 'constative'

utterances, which state that something is or is not the case, from performatives, which are verbal actions rather than true or false statements; however, he goes on to argue that constatives are also implicitly performative, in that they perform the act of asserting something.

Perforation: The process of cutting rows of very small holes in stock, so it may later be easily separated into pieces defined by the perforation, as when a coupon included as part of a mailing piece is perforated to make it easy to send back with an order.

Periodical: In the widest sense, any publication that issues from time to time, whether regularly or irregularly, and is intended to continue in issuance, including newspapers, magazines, looseleaf publications, newsletters, and other serials, but generally not including annuals. In somewhat narrower senses, the term is often used so as to exclude newspapers, and sometimes to exclude irregular serials.

Permission: A copyright owner's authorization for another to use copyrighted material, whether text or illustrations, in published form; copyright owners often charge for such use and may refuse permission in some cases, as when literary or historical materials are restricted for a period of time or when the proposed use would be in direct competition with the work from which material, was drawn.

Philistine: A person devoted narrow-mindedly to material prosperity at the expense of intellectual and artistic awareness; or ignorantly uninterested in culture and ideas. This sense of the term comes from the insulting label *Philister* applied by German students to their non-academic neighbours in university towns, likening them to the enemies of the chosen people in the Hebrew scripturm it was given wide currency in English by the poet and critic Matthew Arnold in his book *Culture and Anarchy*, which attacks the philistinism of the British middle class. Arnold usually applied the term 'the Philistines' to the prosperous bourgeoisie, especially to its nonconformist Liberal representatives.

Phonology: The branch of linguistics concerned with the analysis of soundsystems as they function in languages. The term is sometimes also applied to the soundsystem itself. in a given language: the 'phonology of English' is the system of distinctions and rules governing the speech of this language. The founding concept of phonology is that of the phoneme.

Photocomposition: A broad term covering all means of producing composed copy by use of photography, rather than by use of any kind of hot or cold type; in general, as a compositor types at the keyboard, images of the characters are formed on film or paper through a process, the result being composed copy.

Photocopying mill: A pejorative term for a photocopying establishment that makes something of a speciality of illegally copying and often distributing the copyrighted material of others without permission or payment for the use of that material.

Photogrammetry: A map-making technique, which produces maps from aerial photographs.

Photojournalism: That branch of photography that concerns itself with photographs that depict the news, with or without the help of written reportage.

Photo-conductive camera tube: In television, a camera tube in which the photosensitive feature is photoresistive.

Photo-electric emission: Emission of electrons from a surface, due to incident radiation.

Photo-emissive camera tube: In television, a camera tube in which the photosensitive feature is photoemissive.

Physical inventory: An actual count of all items held in inventory, and the resulting inventory listing.

Pica: A unit of measurement equal to about 1/6 of an inch. In printing, it is used as a unit of both vertical and horizontal measure; when used as a vertical measure, one pica is 12 points high.

Pica rule: A ruler, indicating picas; often indicating other units of measurement, as well.

Pica type: A common typewriter type, running approximately ten characters to the inch horizontally; somewhat larger than *elite* type.',' writer type, which runs approximately twelve characters to the inch horizontally.

Picture monitor: In television, a high-quality apparatus for display of a picture. Used for checking and assessment of picture quality. Picture monitors generally include many features not found in normal television receivers, such as direct red, green and blue drive for the display tube, and various calibration facilities.

Picture book: A book composed largely of illustrations, in which main focus of the author is upon the illustrations, rather than the text which is often thought of and described as "accompanying text."

Picture research: Research directed at the finding and supplying of appropriate illustrations for forthcoming publications. Picture researchers identify and search through sources, provide camera-ready illustrations, obtain any necessary permissions, and handle the payment of any required fees to copyright owners.

Plate: 1. An illustration; the use of the term implies a high quality art illustration, often printed on special paper and separately bound into a publication. 2. A printing surface used in any contact printing process.

Platemaking: The generation of images on a plate or cylinder that will be used in printing, by whatever means those images are created, including direct impact, chemical treatment, or laser beams.

Pornography: Published work, usually of considerable sexual content which may legally be proscribed because of alleged obscenity; the' subject of a considerable þody of litigation. Hard, *core pornography* is I often described in law and general usage as work of explicit sexual, content, and *soft core pornography* as sexually suggestive work. Beyond the shifting definitions of pornography developed by legal process, pornography is very much in the eye of the beholder; what is pornography in one place at one time is art in another place and me no matter how explicitly sexual the work may be.

Prepress: A general term describing all operations between the finishing of manuscript and the placement of printing plates on the press ready to run. When manuscript is keyboarded directly into a compositor, the distinction between manuscript preparation and prepress operations is blurred.

Preprint: 1. To print material in bulk, on which other printing or writing will later be placed, as when a logo or masthead is printed on newspaper stock which will be used for many issues of the newspaper, or a letterhead is printed on company stationery. 2. To print material such as a logo, Which will be used as part of original artwork in creating reproduction copy.

Prepublication (prepub): Describing those promotional activities that occur before the announced publication date of a work, such as supply of bound galleys to reviewers and potential book club rights purchasers, and advance advertising and publicity.

Prepublication offer: Any kind of discounting arrangement offered by publishers to others that terminates at or near official publication date, as when publishers offer booksellers special discounts or retail purchasers special prices for purchases made before a specified publication date.

Prepublication orders: Sales made before the official publication date of a new publication, such as sales made to mail order purchasers, jobbers, libraries, and others who are solicited for purchase before publication. Also called *advance orders.*

prepublication review: 1. A review of a forthcoming book, carried in a reviewing medium in advance of official publication, usually prepared either from early copies of the finished book after manufacture but before official publication date some weeks later, or from bound galleys of the work supplied to reviewers prior to the production of finished books. 2. The study of a forthcoming work before publication by a potential censor, as when the Central Intelligence Agency (CIA) reviews the manuscript of a forthcoming work written by one of its former employees, with possible censorship in mind.

Press binder: A mechanical binder, in which sheets trimmed into loose leaves are bound into a binder that contains a strong set of springs in its backbone, the springs closing on the book's contents to hold them; used in books requiring periodic updating or removal of leaves for use.

Press proof: A proof drawn from a corrected and completed form, just before the press run begins.

Press release: A public statement issued to the press, in either printed or verbal form, by an individual or organization.

Press run: The entire number of satisfactory copies of a publication in a single printing; this number includes overs to allow for spoilage in later steps in the manufacturing process, but does not include spoilage experienced during the run itself.

Presswork: All operations involved in printing; traditionally does not include composition and bindery operations, but as some modem presses include bindery operations, such as folding, as integral parts of their operations, the distinction between press-work and some aspects of bindery has blurred in some instances.

Preview book: A booklet containing excerpts or condensations of material from a forthcoming book; used as a prepublication sales tool by publishers.

Print: Photographic copy of a film, usually with a positive image.

Print through: Unwanted transfer of the signal on a magnetic tape record to adjacent layers of the tape with which it is in contact when wound on a spool.

printer: 1. One who runs a machine that prints; usually describing one who runs a printing press. 2. Any machine that prints, other than a printing press or a typewriter. As developing technology causes many kinds of printing machines to appear, the distinction between printing presses, copiers, typewriters, word processors, computer printers, and other kinds of printing machines are blurring.

printer's devil: An apprentice; a term rapidly becoming archaic.

printer's error (PE): An error in composition, attributable to the compositor rather than to the author or editor. Most author-publisher contracts specify limits beyond which costs of author's alterations will be home by authors, and printers charge publishers for all alterations other than those caused by printer's errors, so the attribution of errors is a source of constant discussion and negotiation between printers, publishers, and authors.

Printing: The process of applying images to surfaces, by hand or machine, whatever the surface used; also the resulting image. The main printing methods are relief printing, planographic printing, and intaglio printing, with others including screen-process printing, ink jet printing, and electrostatic printing.

Printing press: A machine used to press an image onto a surface, by contact between a printing plate and the surface being printed.

Print order: A purchase order from customer to printer, containing the specifics of the printing job, including all printing, binding, and delivery specifications; functions as a conditional contract between purchaser and printer, with printer's satisfactory fulfillment of the conditions of the order creating an obligation on the part of purchaser to pay for the work done.

Printout: Printed material issuing from computed or stored material, as when a computer prints the results of its computations or retrieves data stored in a computer memory, a calculator prints the result of calculations, or a microform reader printer prints out material stored on microforms.

Print run: The number of copies of a single work to be produced, whether interrupted or in a single uninterrupted period; sometimes used to indicate only the number of copies to be produced in a single period, uninterrupted except by minor machine service and repair needs.

Printed circuit: A pattern of copper connections on a substrate, forming a complete circuit. For example, a helical spiral can form an inductor and, using copper on each face of the substrate, capacitors can be formed.

Printed wiring: A system of copper connections on a substrate board, inter-connecting a number of components separately secured to the board.

Prototype L-section: A reactance network forming a basic unit for an image-parameter filter. Series and shunt arms are inverse impedance.

Production editor: An editor responsible for seeing a manuscript through the production process, from composition through printing and binding to finished publications, acting throughout as liaison between editorial and production personnel.

Professional and reference publishing: That branch of publishing concerned with the publication of nonfiction specialist publications for the professions and of reference books of all kinds, other than works of popular reference.

Proof press: A press mainly functioning to run press proofs before the start of a print run; usually a hand operated press.

Proofreader: One who reads composed copy for the purpose of identifying and correcting errors in that copy, usually read side by side with the original of that copy. Proofreaders sometimes work in two-person teams, with one person, called the *copyholder*, reading original copy aloud and the other, who is the *proofreader*, correcting the composed copy.

Proofreader's marks: A relatively standard set of correction marks placed in composed copy by proofreaders.

Proofs: Test images of composed matter, drawn from that matter at any of several stages of the printing process, as from galleys, composed forms, or composed forms ready to print, and therefore variously called *galley, page, foundry, stone,* and *press* proofs; sometimes also identified by the usage intended, as in *author's proofs* or *reader's* Proofs.

Publication: 1. The process of preparing and making available to the public material in print or electronic media.

2. Any printed work made available for sale or distribution to the general public, with no explicit or implicit restrictions regarding disclosure of the contents.

Publish: To prepare and make available written material for We or distribution to the general public; while the term often refers to printed material, new technology allows work to be published without being formally composed or printed, as when a work is photocopied from typescript and distributed or to be published without words ever appearing on paper, as when a work is composed and available solely on electronic networks. More narrowly, to release written work to the general public.

Publisher: 1. An organization that publishes, such as a commercial publisher, an academic press, or a government publishing organization. 2. An individual who undertakes overall entrepreneurial responsibility for the publication of works, whether financing the publication of those works or as an employee of a publishing organization.

Publisher's representative: One who sells for a publisher, whether books to booksellers or advertising space to advertisers.

Publishing: 1. As a process, the securing, physical preparation, manufacture, and distribution of publications, and all related business functions. 2. As an industry, the aggregate of all publishers.

Publishing house: A synonym for publisher, usually describing a commercial book publishing organization.

Q

Quantizing: Process in converting an analogue signal to digital form, in which it is sampled at regular intervals and the instantaneous amplitude expressed as one of a defined number of discrete levels, which can then be assigned a digital value.

Quantizing error: The error caused by the limited number of discrete steps into which the input signal has been analysed.

Qwerty: The standard English typewriter keyboard layout, named from the first six characters of the top row of letters.

R

Rack: A display device for books and other publications; often a portable or revolving device with many shelves used to display paperbacks for sale in bookstores and other sales outlets.

Racking: Another term for *framing*.

Rack jobber: A middleman who supplies retailers with goods and usually the racks and other display devices from which those goods arc sold.

Rack-over: Movement to bring the viewfinder of a camera into line with its objective lens system.

Radar: The use of reflected or retransmitted radio waves to observe, with suitable receivers, positional and other characteristics of distant still or moving objects.

Radiation: The emission of energy from a radiating system, in the form of *electromagnetic waves*.

Radiation intensity: In antennas, in a given direction in the *far field*. The power radiated per unit solid angle, expressed in watts/steradian.

Radiation pattern: (1) Of antenna systems, a graphical representation of the dire-ctional radiating properties of an antenna. The pattern may be in polar or Cartesian coordinates. In polar form, the pattern is often termed a polar diagram. (2) In audio, a graphical representation of the directional response of a microphone or the radiation characteristics of a *loudspeaker* system, in an *anechoic* environment.

Radiation resistance: Of antenna systems, at any point on the system, a value of resistance which, multiplied by the mean square value of the current flowing at the point, gives a value for the power in the system. The usual reference point is the feed point of the system. The radiation resistance is shown in the equivalent circuits, as the total resistance.

Radiation resistance is not a quantity that can be measured with an ohmmeter. It is the value of an equivalent resistance that, connected to the feed system in place of the antenna, would dissipate the same power as the antenna would radiate, for the same current flowing.

Radio beacon: A radio transmitter, radiating a coded identification signal, which can be used for position finding by a mobile vehicle having a suitable receiving system.

Radio broadcasting: The use of radio waves for the dissemination of sound and television entertainment programmes and other services.

Radio communication: Communication by means of radio waves without any constraints other than those imposed by the propagation conditions prevailing over the propagation path through space.

Radio frequency: Any frequency that can be used for communication by means of *electromagnetic waves.* It is becoming increasingly difficult to assign frequency boundaries to this definition. At the low-frequency end, radio frequencies now extend down to a few Hertz. At the higher frequencies, an arbitrary limit of about 300 GHz exists, but radio-frequency techniques are used well into the infrared and visible light frequency ranges. With the increasing use of lasers, *glass-fibre transmission* lines and infrared control systems, the upper frequency limit requires redefinition

Radio frequency interference: Interference introduced into electronic circuits by radio transmitters or other sources of electro-magnetic radiation.

Radio horizon distance: Of tropospheric propagation. The distance to a point approximately 4/3 times the optical horizon distance.

Radio link: In a communication system, a radio system, generally two-way, forming part or whole of a complete communication circuit.

Radio microphone: A microphone connected to a very small portable radio transmitter, the radiation from which is picked up by a local receiver, thus avoiding trailing wires.

Radio receiver: An assembly of devices, equipment and components used for processing signals developed in an antenna system and presented at the input, and delivering the processed information at the output.

Radio relay broadcast station: A transmitting station that receives its input signals by radio from a parent station, for re-broadcasting.

Radio station: An installation comprising antenna system(s), radio receiver(s), and/or radio transmitter(s).

Radio telemetry: A radio communication system intended for the transmission of measurable quantities in a suitable coded form, to a remote receiving point.

Radio transmitter: Apparatus for the generation of radio-frequency carrier energy, and means for its modulation. For radiation, the transmitter requires to be connected suitably to an antenna system.

Rag content: The cloth content of paper made wholly or partly from rugs, as when a paper made 75% *of* wood pulp and 25% of rags is described as having a 25% rag content.

Raised cosine pulse: Another term for the sin' pulse used for many tests in television systems.

Raised printing: A printed image that is raised from the surface On which it is printed, creating a textured effect; used for special purposes such as embossing or *Braille printing,* in which raised dots represent characters.

RAM: Random Access Memory. Memory that can have any byte of its data written in, or read out in any order.

Ramp generator: A generator of a repetitive signal waveform in which the current or voltage rises linearly with time during each cycle. An example of a ramp generator is the circuit that provides a linear scan for a *cathode-ray tube* display.

Random access: The ability to store and retrieve specific data in computer storage without reading through all stored data in sequence, as is necessary in sequential access; also called *direct access*

Random noise: Noise, or an electrical signal, that is random in its amplitude, frequency and phase characteristics.

Random numbers: Numbers not related to each other in any way.

Rare books: Scarce, prized, and valuable books; usually antiquarian books that are seldom available for acquisition, and that when available sell for high prices.

Raster: In television, a pattern of *scanning lines* traced on the face of a display tube, to cover a prescribed area. The term is often applied to a television tube display of an unsyncronised line and field scan, without picture modulation.

Raster graphics: A method of presenting graphical data as a display comprising groupings of pixels on the raster of a cathode ray tube. (cf. *vector graphics)*

Raster unit: The distance between the midpoints of two adjacent *pixels.*

Rate card: A card or sheet indicating the prices charged by a publication for advertising space.

Ratio defector: A type of demodulator for frequency or phase modulated trans-missions, in which the output is proportional to the *deviation.*

Raw data: Data that has only been collected, but not yet in any way processed, whether by machines or people.

Raw stock: Unexposed and undeveloped photographic film.

Ray: In propagation, the path along which a wave will travel.

Ray diversity: One system for *diversity* reception, used when it is possible to discriminate between different rays, as with the *MUSA antenna* system.

RC: A Resistor/Capacitor combination. Often referred to as a time-constant expressed in seconds, the time-constant being the capacitance in farads multiplied by the resistance in ohms.

Reach: An estimate of how many people are in any significant way affected by a publication; always a rather imprecise estimate, as the estimate includes those who buy the publication, those additional people thought to read it, and those influenced by such readers.

Reactance device: A reverse-biased semiconductor *diode* behaves as a capacitance, the value of which is determined by the magnitude of the biasing voltage. In suitable circuits, transistors can be used to simulate capacitors or inductors.

Read: To put information into a computer from a store, memory, disk or tape.

Readability: The ease with which a piece of written work may be comprehended by its audience, often as measured by one or more standard readability tests, which attempt to quantify readability in terms of such factors as syllable counts or length of sentences; of some importance in educational or general materials aimed at people who read at less than high school levels. More generally, how well a piece of work is written, in terns of clarity of exposition.

Reader: 1. An elementary textbook. 2. One who reads and evaluates manuscripts for a publisher. 3. A machine that reads magnetic tape and translates it into instructions that run machines, such as compositors; widely used in industry for many such applications. 4. One who habitually reads books; connotes identification as part of a bookreading audience.

Reader-printer: A machine used to read microforms, which is capable of producing a printed copy of the microform displayed on the viewing screen of the reads. Sometimes used to describe any machine capable of reading stored material on a screen and producing a printed copy of that material, including machines that can read and print from computer memories and videodiscs.

Reader-response criticism: A general term for those kinds of modern criticism and literary theory that focus on the responses of readers to literary works, rather than on the works themselves considered as selfcontained entities. It is not a single agreed theory so much as a shared concern with a set of problems involving the extent and nature of readers' contribution to the meanings of literary works, approached from various positions including those of structuralism. psychoanalysis, phenomenology, and henn-eiieutics. The common factor is a shift from the description of texts in terms of their inherent properties to a discussion of the production of meanings within the reading process. Important contributions to this debate include Wolfgang Iser's *The Act of Readinq*, which sees readers as 'actualizing' texts by filling in their 'gap or indeterminacies of meaning, and Stanley Fish's *Is There a Text in this Class?*, which gives the reader an even more active role as the text's true producer.

Readership: An estimate of all those who read a publication, usually an that referring to the readership of some sort of periodical, rather than that of a book; sometimes used more loosely as a synonym for audience.

Reader's proofs: A set of proofs to be corrected by proofreaders.

Read-only access: Programmed access that allows data in a computer system to be read but not altered.

Real: In computer practice, a type of *variable* which is a precision number and may have a fractional or decimal component, e.g. TOTAL = 159.34 Also termed floating *point number*.

Real cost of borrowing: The net of true interest minus the rate of inflation, without allowing for hidden inflation, which does not show up in government figures indicating the current rate of inflation.

Real time: In computer processing, the operation of the system quickly enough to control ongoing processes, such as in controlling traffic or monitoring supply and distribution of commodities on a current basis.

Real time programming: Programming a *tapeslide* show while, the tape is running at its normal speed.

Realism: A mode of writing that gives the impression of recording or 'reflecting' faithfully an actual way of life. The term refers, sometimes confusingly, both to a literary method based on detailed accuracy of description and to a more general attitude that rejects idealization, escapism, and other extravagant qualities of romance in favour of recognizing soberly the actual problems of life. Modern criticism frequently insists that realism is not a direct or simple reproduction of reality but a system of conventions producing a lifelike illusion of some 'real' world outside the text, by processes of selection, exclusion, description, and manners of addressing the reader. In its methods and attitudes, realism may be found as an element in many kinds of writing prior to the 19th century but as a dominant literary trend it is associated chiefly with the 19th-century novel of middle or lower-class life, in which the problems of ordinary people in unremarkable circumstances are rendered with close attention to the details of physical setting and to the complexities of social life.

The outstanding works of realism in 19th-century fiction include Honore de Balzac's *Illusions perdues*. Gustave Flaubert's *Madame Bovary*, and George Eliot's *Middlemarch*. In France, a self-consciously realist school announced itself in 1857 with the publication of Champfleury's Le *Realisme,* but the term normally refers to the general convention rather than to this barely significant group. in the work of some novelists, realism passes over into the movement of naturalism, in which sociological investi-gation and determinist views of human behaviour predominate. Realism also established itself as an important tradition in the theatre in the late 19th and early 20th centuries in the work of Henrik Ibsen, George Bernard Shaw, and others; and it remains a standard convention of film and television drama. Despite the radical attempts of modernism to displace the realist emphasis on external reality realism survived as a major current within 20th-century fiction, sometimes under the label of neo-realism.

Ream: A quantity of paper, usually consisting of 500 sheets of paper, but for some papers, 480 sheets.

Rear feed: In microwave antennas, a primary radiator feed to a mirror reflector, which passes through the rear of the mirror.

Rebacking: The process of replacing an old book spine or back with a new back.

Rebinding: The process of replacing the old binding of a book with a completely new binding; if the old binding is removed, repaired and reaffixed, the process is called *recasing*.

Re-broadcast link: A receiver and antenna system, sited at a radio relay broadcast station, for reception of broadcast signals from a parent station to serve as the main feed for the relay station.

Receiver: A device which receives data, particularly radio or television equipment which receives a modulated radio frequency and provides a demodulated output.

Receiver lead: In cabled distribution systems, the lead that connects a system outlet to a receiver.

Receiver noise: Noise signals appearing at the output of a receiver, originating within the receiver.

Receiver radiation: Electro-magnetic radiation from a receiver, due to signals generated in the receiver. Radiation, due generally to the receiver local oscillator, can become a source of interference to other communication systems, and can take place from the receiver chassis itself. Close attention to circuit layout, screening and earthing where possible can minimise direct radiation. A second and more serious aspect of receiver radiation occurs if such radiation finds its way to the input antenna connection. In this case, the antenna system can radiate a disturbing field over a considerable area.

A third path for receiver radiation is via the power-supply leads, where the radiation can find its way into other receivers which are using the same power supply mains. An RF filter in the power supply leads to the receiver can minimise the effects of such radiation.

Rear projection: Presentation of an image on a translucent screen by a projector placed on the far side from the viewer.

Recasing: The process of rebinding a book in its old covers; a very substantial set of repairs rather than replacement with a new binding.

Receipt: 1. A written acknowledgment that something has been received, capable of being used as legal evidence of such receipt; for example, a warehouse receipt for goods delivered to that warehouse or a store receipt for goods purchased from that store. 2. The act of receiving Sash or any other assets to he recorded on books of account.

Receivables: 1. That which is now or will be collectible, in the forrns of accounts and notes receivable. 2. In accounting, a statement of the total of all accounts and notes receivable.

Reception theory: A branch of modem literary studies concerned with the ways in which literary works are received by readers. The term has sometimes been used to refer to reader-response criticism in general but it is associated more particularly with the 'reception a esthetics *outlined* in 1970 by the German literary historian Hans Robert Jauss. Drawing on philosophical herme-neutics, Jauss argued that literary works are received against an existing horizon of expectations consisting of readers current knowledge and presuppositions about literature, and that the meanings of works change as such horizons shift. Unlike most varieties of reader-response theory, then, reception theory is interested more in historical changes affecting the reading public than in the solitary reader.

Recension: A version of a literary work arrived at by a process of revision or textual criticism; or the process of reconstructing the most reliable readings from variant versions of a text.

Recessive accent: A stress placed on the first syllable of a two-syllable word that is normally pronounced with the stress on its second syllable. This sometimes occurs in English verse when such a word is followed by a stressed syllable: for the sake of conformity to the metre, the stress is shifted to the initial position, as in John Donne's line

But extreme sense hath made them desperate

The recessive accent is thus a specific type of 'wrenched accent'.

Reciprocity failure: Divergence from the photographic *reciprocity law* which may occur at extremely high or low values of light intensity or time

Reciprocity law: In photography the relation which states that constant exposure will be obtained if greater intensity of light is compensated by proportionally shorter time and vice versa.

Reciprocity theorem: In a network, if an EMF e at a point in a network produces a current *i* at a second point, then the same voltage at the second point will produce the same current *i* at the first point. In antennas, an extension of this theorem proves to be very useful. If an antenna system is fed with RF power, the antenna will exhibit such characteristics as radiation resistance, band-width, directivity, beam-width etc. and, at a distance *d*, will develop an EMF in another antenna. If the antennas are identical and the rates of radiating and receiving are exchanged, it is found that the former receiving antenna will exhibit all the characteristics of the original radiator, and will develop the same EMF in the other antenna.

The value of the theorem, when considering antennas, lies in the fact that we can consider an antenna behaviour as a radiator, and any conclusions such as directivity, radiation resi-stance, beam-width, etc. can all be applied to the use of the antenna for reception. Similarly, an antenna can be considered as a receiving antenna and, again, any conclusions as to its properties can be applied directly to its use as a radiator. Depending on expediency, it is convenient to consider the behaviour of an antenna in the most easily-understood manner, either as a radiator or as a receiver, knowing that the theorem permits conclusions to be applied to either use. In general considerations of antenna behaviour, as in this volume, the antenna is considered to be a radiator.

Recit: The French word for an 'account' or narrative of events. As used in modem French narratology, the term refers to the actual narrative text itself, as opposed both to the story and to its narration.

Reconditioned carrier reception: A method of reception used with reduced carrier transmission. Most audio and video recording takes place using magnetic tape or disc. Plastic discs used for audio reproduction are made from master recordings on magnetic tape. *Video* recording uses three basic methods. Magnetic recording requires a high relative transport speed of the tape past the head, and two methods are used to achieve this end. One uses a 2 in wide tape and an assembly of four heads traversing successively across the tape width as the tape moves along its length. The other magnetic system wraps the tape round a drum in, effectively, one turn, and the head(s) rotate with the drum thus tracing a long angled track across the width of the tape. The third system of video recording uses a modulated *laser* beam to indent a plastic disc to provide the recording. The recording is played-back by using a low-power laser beam as a light source directed at the recorded track, the reflection from the track being collected by a photocell.

Record: 1. Any written or otherwise stored information, usually in sequential form for multiple items examples include accounting information stored in books of record and legal proceedings, often referred to in the law as "the record." 2. To place information in storage, or in storable form. 3. In computers, a single kind of information, one of many like it; for example, the record of a purchase in a store is computerized business handling system. 4. The best, most, worst, or least, as in a record snowfall.

Recovery time: Time taken for a device to return to normal after a signal above the processing threshold has been removed.

Rectifier: A component in an electrical circuit which will pass electrical current in one direction but not in the other, hence a device which converts an alternating current into a direct current.

Rectification: A process for obtaining a unidirectional current from an alternating voltage source by means of a rectifier.

Recto: The front side of a printed sheet; thus the right-hand page in a book, as opposed to the *verso,* which is the left-hand, even-numbered page on the other side.

Recursive filtering: Method of reducing video noise and random defects by the comparison of two or more adjacent frames, non-repeating items being eliminated.

Redaction: The editing or revising of a work for publication; or a new edition of a work. An editor is sometimes called a redactor. *Verb:* redact.

Reduction: Process of mixing signals f rom multi-track master tapes to produce a master tape for production.

Reductionism: The tendency to explain away the complexities of a literary work as the products of a single, much simpler cause. A reductive interpretation of a work reduces or'collapses' its actual complexity into a reassuring simplicity, seeing it as the direct expression of some originating element such as a personal motive, a psychological defect, a national or social identity, or a mythic archetype.

Reduction printing: Optically printing motion picture film to produce an image smaller than the original, usually on film of narrower gauge.

Reel: (1) A flanged hub on which film or tape is wound. (UK film usage is spool). (2) A roll of film, the unit in which a programme or part of a programme is usually handled, either as the assembled negative or corresponding positive print.

Reel-to-reel: Film or tape path with separate feed and take-up reels in a camera, projector or tape recorder/reproducer, in contrast to the enclosed cassette or cartridge.

Reference book: A work containing a considerable body of information, which is primarily intended to be accessed selectively as needed for information, rather than to be read from beginning to end; for example, an encyclopedia or dictionary. Many reference works are in book form, but are actually periodicals; for example, looseleaf reporters and periodically issued catalogues. In the widest sense, computerized databases are also reference works. Works intended for purchase by large popular audiences are often described as works of *popular reference,* to distinguish them from reference works intended mainly for professional and library use.

Reference marks: A group of symbols used to mark copy, including the asterisk (*), double asterisks (**), dagger (t), and double dagger (+,), used generally in that order, to key text matter to footnotes and chapter notes.

References: Citations to supporting authorities, keyed from text to footnotes or chapter notes. Also called citations.

Reference white: In television, a white surface, sometimes used for the alignment and adjustment of cameras, monitors, etc.

Reflection coefficient: (1) In propagation, at a surface, for a wave of specified direction and polarisatlon, the ratio of the reflected field to the incident field. This is of particular significance where a wave is incident on the earth's surface, from which it will partly be reflected to a degree dependent on the reflection coefficient, with a phase angle dependent on the *dielectric constant.* The reflection coefficient and phase angle vertically-polarised waves incident on an average earth at two frequencies. It is seen that at shallow angles, considerable changes in reflection coefficient can take place between near unity and near zero. (2) In transmission lines, an indication of the degree of mismatch between two impedances. (3) In television, most of the light reaching the camera tube is that reflected from the various objects comprising the scene, thus the reflection coefficient of the scene details and the intensity of the overall illumination are closely related.

Reflectionism: A term sometimes used to refer to the common assumption that literary works reflect a preexisting reality. This view is often challenged in modem literary theory, on the grounds that it denies the active nature of language and of the writer's transforming work.

Reflectometer: An instrument for measurement of the *reflection coefficient* at a discontinuity in a signal path.

Reflector: (1) In antennas, a secondary radiator, energised generally by the induction field of a primary radiator, so spa as to increase the forward radiation and reduce radiation from the rear of the array. (2) Repeller (US), in some electron tub, an electrode whose function is to reverse the direction of electron flow.

Reflex camera: A camera in which the image in the viewfinder is obtained through the main objective lens, so that parallax error is eliminated.

Reflex projection: A special effects process in which foreground action is photographed against a background image projected along the axis of the camera lens on to a highly reflective beaded surface. Also called *front axial projection.*

Refraction: In propagation, a radio wave directed into the *ionosphere* can experience refraction whereby the pro-pagation path will be deflected away from a region of maximum *ionisation* density. The degree of refraction will depend on the frequency and the density of the ionisation, and a *refractive index* can be determined. The use of the HF band relies on this means of propagation and 'multiple hops', involving successive refractions from the iono-sphere and reflections from the ground back to the iono-sphere, provide for long-distance paths.

Refractive index: In propagation, a radio wave experiencing refraction functions in a similar manner to a light ray passing through a boundary between one medium and another with a different index. It is seen that, if the frequency is high enough, no refraction will be experienced. On average, this takes place for frequencies higher than about 30 MHz, where the wave will pass through the ionised regions, and not be returned to ground. This upper limit will vary with ionisation density and, particularly, during the sunspot cycle.

Refrain: A line, group of fines, or part of a line repeated at regular or irregular intervals in a poem, usually at the end of each stanza. It may recur in exactly the same form, or may be subject to slight variations. It may form part of a stanza, as in the ballade or villanelle: or it may appear separately, as in many songs and ballads, in which case it may be called a burden, and, if intended for group singing, a chorus.

Refresh: (1) To recharge regularly the cells of a *volatile* digital memory so that their contents are not lost. (2) In computer graphics, the process in which the electron gun repeatedly draws a display on the surface of a *refresh tube.*

Refresh tube: A cathode ray tube in which the electron gun must be activated repeatedly to maintain the display.

Regional advertising: Advertising so placed as to cover a substantial geographical region, such as the Northeast or Southwest, as when advertisements are placed in the regional editions of national magazines.

Register: The accurate positioning of printing on a page, so that each page image will exactly back up the page image on the other side of a sheet, and so that successive colour impressions will exactly match on a page. When such positioning are inaccurate, the images and impressions are described as out of register or *off register.*

Registration: In colour television, adjustment of colour signal timing so that, on the receiver display tube, all colour and luminance signals are co-incident at any one colour cell. Registration involves many factors along the transmitter-receiver chain and depends on optical, electrical and mechanical features.

Register bar: A locating device consisting of a metal strip with two or more upstanding pegs, used to ensure accurate placing of material to be photographed or copies. The drawing or cel is edge perforated to match the pins.

Register mount: A slide mount containing locating pegs for precise location of the film by means of its perforations.

Register pegs: Pegs on a light box or rostrum, on which cels can be placed and kept in register.

Register pins: Locating pegs accurately shaped to fit into the edge perforations of film, paper or transparent sheet. In a camera, register pins precisely locate the film by means of its perforations.

Registration: (1) The precise location of successive images in a sequence so that unintentional movement is not introduced. (2) The correct positioning of three-colour component images to be coincident without overlapping or fringing.

Reinstatement: Restoration of a periodical subscription which had previously lapsed.

Reissue: The republication of a work that has either been out of print or in print but little promoted, usually with a new cover and tide page, but from a previous composition essentially as is; sometimes such a republication takes a new form, as in the issue in trade paperback of a work previously done in hardcover.

Rejection slip: A notice from publisher to author or agent, declining to publish a proffered manuscript.

Rejector: Term used formerly for a parallel tuned circuit, when used in a signal path to present a high impedance at one frequency.

Rekeying: Any rekeyboarding, as in the retyping of a manuscript; most often used to describe the rekeyboarding of material into a computer memory.

Relaxation oscillator: A generator of oscillations generally involving the charge/discharge cycle of a capacitor through a resistor.

Relay: (1) In communication, a system of message transmission to a receiving point, where the message is either retransmitted to a final destination or stored for later transmission. (2) In electrical circuits, an electrically-operated switching device for opening or closing a circuit path, or changing circuit characteristics.

Release: 1. To clear material for general publication; in that sense, sometimes synonymous with *publish. Also* material so placed in general circulation, such as a publicity release or a *press release.* 2. To give up a legal claim or possible legal claim upon another; also the document evidencing the renunciation of such a claim.

Release print: A motion picture positive print of picture and sound made for general distribution and exhibition.

Relief printing: Printing accomplished by direct contact between a printing plate carrying a raised image and the surface to be printed, as in letterpress, flexograph, and multigraph printing. The letterpress method of printing, involving composed metal type set as a mirror image on the image to be imprinted, was the main printing method used throughout the world between the invention of movable type and the middle years of the 20th century, when it gave way to offset, a form of planographic printing.

Relocatable: In a computer, when *machine code* will execute correctly even if it is moved to a different address location.

Remainder: To sell books previously manufactured, but still unsold in a publisher's warehouse, to wholesalers and other booksellers who will then resell them at deeply discounted prices to retailers and at retail; books so discounted are called *remainders*.

Remanence: The residual magnetism of a ferromagnetic substance when, after being magnetised to saturation, the magnetising field is removed.

Remote: That which is located at some distance, often far away; in business, often used to describe that which is any distance from a machine which it controls or works with. For example, a television set may be controlled from a distance of a few feet and be described as being remotely controlled; a computer may be reached by telephone line from thousands of miles away and be described as being remotely accessed.

Remote access: The ability to reach and work with a computer from some distance away; usually moving input and output through terminals or some other computer.

Remote control: Control of a device at a location remote from the, device, by cable, radio, infra-red or other means.

Renaissance, the 'rebirth' of literature, art, and learning that progressively transformed European culture from the mid-14th century in Italy to the mid-17th century in England, strongly influenced by the rediscovery of classical Greek and Latin literature, and accelerated by the development of printing. The Renaissance is commonly held to mark the close of the Middle Ages and the beginning of the modern Western world, although the problems of dating this process have caused much debate: the existence of a significant renaissance of European learning in the 12th century is now accepted while the 18th-century Enlightenment is a direct continuation of the Renaissance's intellectual tendencies.

The term normally refers to the combined intellectual and artistic transformations of the 15th and 16th centuries, including the emergence of humanism, Protestant individualism, Copernican astronomy, and the discovery of America. In literary terms, the Renaissance may be seen as a new tradition running from Petrarch and Boccaccio in Italy to Jonson and Milton in England, embracing the work of the French *Pleiade* and of Sidney, Spenser, and Shakespeare; it is marked by a new self-confidence in vernacular literatures, a flourishing of lyric poetry, and a revival of such classical forms as epic and pastoral literature. The term 'Renaissance' has also been extended to various literary revivals in specific times and places:

Renewal: The continuation of a subscription contract for a new subscription period.

Rental library: A library that rents publications, recordings, or films to the public for a fee. Although some public libraries charge fees for some services, such as computerized research services, this term is applied only to private libraries.

Reorder: Any additional order for goods that were previously ordered, as when a bookseller reorders more copies of a book previously stocked.

Repartee, a rapid and witty response in conversation, especially one that turns an insult back on its originator, or a succession of such replies in a dialogue between characters. The term may also be applied to a person's talent for making witty replies.

Repetend, a word, phrase, or fine that recurs in a poem. As distinct from a refrain, a repetend is repeated only partially or only at irregular intervals.

Replica: A copy that resembles an original work so closely as to make it difficult to distinguish between original and copy without expert knowledge, and sometimes without the use of sophisticated tests.

Report: To supply others with information and analysis, orally or in writing; also the information so supplied.

Reporter: 1. One who gathers and conveys the news. 2. A publication supplying current information and analysis; a term often encountered in the titles and subtitles of looseleaf publications and newsletters.

Report program generator (RPG): In computer processing, a method of programming that allows production of a wide variety of reports of tabulated data.

Reprint: 1. An additional printing of a book, sub-stantially unchanged from and in the same form as a previous printing, although often with minor corrections made. 2. A new printing of a book in another form when a hardcover book is reprinted as a trade or mass market paperback.

Reprint house: 1. A publisher primarily in the business of reprinting previously published works, generally works that are out of print in their original form and often those that have passed into the public domain. Such houses usually reprint in hardcover, but sometimes in softcover. 2. A paperback house, reprinting recently issued hardcover books in paperback; a disappearing use of the term, as paperback houses continue to extend their publishing activities to original publications.

Reproduction copy: Copy, including both text, and illustrative material, that is ready to be photographed and made into plates for offset printing purposes. Also called *cameraready copy, repro copy,* and *repro.*

Reproduction proof: A cameraready copy or proof of material to be printed. Also called *repro proof* and *repro.*

Reprographics: A diverse group of image reproduction processes, all capable of producing short runs, whether by copying or printing, from machines normally found in-house and used for internal needs, including many kinds of office copiers and short-run printing processes. Originally referring to photocopying machines, the term's use has broadened as the distinction between printing and copying has faded.

Requisition: 1. A direction issued by a college teacher to a purchasing organization, such as a college bookstore, to buy a quantity of a book to be used in a course, for resale to students taking that course. 2. A written intra-organization request for goods or services; for example, for books from a company warehouse.

Research and development (R and D): Investigation aimed at developing new products and processes, whether directly through applications research or indirectly through basic research.

Reseau: A network or mosaic of small elements, as used in some forms of colour reproduction process.

Reset: To compose previously composed type again, as for corrections and design changes.

Residual rights: 1. Those publication rights owned by a copyright originator that have not been sold or leased to another, or which have been sold or leased to another but will revert to the originator on occurrence of stated conditions, such as a work being declared out of print by a publisher, or by the passage of time as specified by copyright laws. 2. Compensation rights, held by performing artists and others in the arts, covering payments to be made to them when screened and recorded work, such as movies, videodiscs, and audio records, are played or sold, as provided by individual contracts or union contracts. Often called *residuals.*

Resolution: (1) In television cameras, resolution is considered in terms of a standard pattern of vertical alternate black and white bars of equal width. Each voltage change during a one-line·scan is termed a 'line', and resolution is given as the ratio of the voltage amplitude generated for a 400-line pattern, to that of a coarse pattern such as 40 lines, expressed as a percentage.

(2) In a television system, the ability of a system to resolve fine. Part of a pattern consisting of alternate black and white squares, being scanned by a spot equal in diameter to the line width. At (b) is shown the resulting signal output, which has an AC waveform, the' frequency of which corresponds to the highest modulation frequency that will be generated at maximum amplitude. A smaller spot diameter will resolve smaller detail, but there will be gaps between the lines. A larger spot will cover more than one square and thus will not resolve the detail at maximum voltage or definition.

Resolution chart: In televisıuıı, a chart or slide carrying a pattern designed for assessment of the overall system resolution.

resonant antenna: A *standing-wave antenna* operating atone of its resonance frequencies.

Resonant line: An open or closed transmission line of such a length that it can be used as a parallel or series resonant system.

Resonance: Sympathetic oscillation of a mechanical or electrical system at its own natural frequency.

Response curve: Term for a graphical plot relating a function such as frequency, to an output voltage, current or power.

Restoration comedy, a kind of English comedy, usually in the form of the comedy of manners, that flourished during the Restoration period in England, when actresses were first employed on the London stage. Appealing to a fairly narrow audience of aristocrats in the recently reopened theatres, Resto-ration comedy relied upon sophisticated repartee and a knowledge of the exclusive code of manners in high society, the plots being based on the complex intrigues of the marriage-market. The characters can often be divided between the young aristocrats who can understand and manipulate the rules of the social game, and the middle-class upstarts who wish to be thought fashionable and witty but expose their ignorance in a series of blunders. The frequently cynical approach to marriage and sexual infidelity in Restoration comedy invited accusations of immorality.

Reticle: Ground glass in a camera viewfinder engraved with exact size and position of camera gate, centre cross lines, etc. See *graticule.*

Reticulation: Distortion of a photographic emulsion surface into a pattern of small cracks and wrinkles, usually caused by severe temperature differences in the processing solutions.

Retouching: To alter or clean a photograph or other artwork by painting out or painting over some of its details, as when a negative is so altered to eliminate unwanted marks or to enhance the image it carries

Retrace: In television and *cathode-ray oscilloscopes,* an alternative term for *flyback.*

Retrieve: To read or recover stored data.

Retriggerable: Describes a *monostable,* which can additionally be triggered to remain in its unstable (or abnormal) state for a further time period.

Retrofocus lens: An Inverted telephoto lens design providing a long back-focus distance.

Return loss In transmission lines and matched systems where some mismatch is experienced, the modulus of the reciprocal of the *reflection coefficient.*

Return privilege: The right of a bookseller to return unsold books to publishers for credit.

Returns: Unsold books returned to publishers by booksellers for credit.

Returns level: The rate at which booksellers return for full credit books sold to them by publishers but unsold by booksellers; normally expressed as a percentage of books originally sold. For example, if a bookseller returns 40 of 100 books originally purchased, the publisher's returns level is 40%. Also called *rate of returns.*

Return to zero: A method of digital magnetic recording in which the tape or disk is saturated in a positive direction for a 1 and in a negative direction for a 0, with a return to zero or no magnetising condition in between.

Revenge tragedy, a kind of tragedy popular in England from the 1590S to the 1630s. following the success of Thomas Kyd's sensational play *The Spanish Tragedy*. Its action is typically centred upon a leading character's attempt to avenge the murder of a loved one, sometimes at the prompting of the victim's ghost; it involves complex intrigues and disguises, and usually some exploration of the morality of revenge. Drawing partly on precedents in Senecan tragedy, the English revenge tragedy is far more bloodthirsty in its explicit presentation of premeditated violence, and so the more gruesome examples such as Shakespeare's Titus Andronicus are sometimes called 'tragedies of blood'. Notable examples of plays that are fully or partly within the revenge tradition are Christopher Marlowe's *The Jew of* Malta, Cyril Tourneur's *The Revenger's Tragedy, John* Webster's *The Duchess of Malfi,* and John Ford's 'Tis Pity *She's* a *Whore.*

Reverberation: In *audio frequencies,* of an enclosed chamber, the persistence of a sound generated in the enclosure, after the sound stimulus has ceased.

Reverberation time: The time taken for the echoes of a sound to drop 60 decibels in amplitude after the termination of the direct sound (60 dB is one millionth of its original value).

Reverdie: A kind of medieval French dancing song celebrating the arrival of spring. The term is sometimes extended to include any poem or poetic passage that welcomes spring's return.

Reversal film: A film which after processing yields an image whose tonal distribution matches that to which it was exposed, e.g. a camera film giving a positive image, or a duplicating stock giving a negative image from a negative.

Reverse: To step back one slide with a slide projector or back one image with a dissolve pair.

Reverse compatibility: In television, the property of a colour television system whereby a black-and-white transmission will be reproduced by a colour receiver, in black-and-white.

Reverse plate: A plate in which white and black are reversed, the background being dark and the image white; therefore a plate that prints a white on black image, called a *dropped* out or *reversed out* image.

Reversionary interest: An interest that reverts to its owner after an interest granted to another has ended, for whatever reason; for example, publication rights granted by author to publisher, which may under the terms of an author-publisher contract revert to the author if the publisher allows the book to become out of print. Such reversion of rights is also called *repossession of rights.*

Review: To develop a critical evaluation of a work; also the resulting evaluation. May be a private evaluation of a proposed work or a work in progress, including suggestions for its development, or may be a published critical examination of a published or broadcast work.

Review copy: A free copy of a work, sent to reviewers in hope of securing the publicity generated by reviews, or to those purchasing or influencing the purchase of books in quantity, such as college professors who might recommend adoption of books as course materials, or premium buyers or training directors, who might buy quantities directly.

Reviewer: One who prepares a critical evaluation of a work, in the form of a review. A reviewer who primarily focuses on literature and the performing arts is sometimes also called a *critic.*

Review list: A list of reviewers to whom a publisher will send copies of new work in hope of securing published reviews and the publicity generated by such notices.

Review space: The amount of space allotted for reviews in a publication.

Revise: A new version of an existing piece of work; in publishing, often describing a proof carrying alterations from any previous proof of the same material.

Revision: 1. The process of altering a body of written work; for example, alterations made in a manuscript by its author at any stage of manuscript preparation, alterations made in a published work in preparation for issuance of a new edition, or alterations made in a contract being negotiated. 2. A new edition of a previously published work, containing alterations amounting to more than corrections; often including updating materials, as in a textbook or annual. Also called a *revised edition.*

Revision cycle: The time between successive editions of a work; for example, an annual is on a yearly revision cycle, a dictionary may be on a revision cycle measured in decades, and some portions of a looseleaf reporter, or computerized database my be revised weekly.

Revolve: A turntable system.

Revue: A theatrical entertain-ment consisting of a series of songs, dances, and comic sketches. It is often devoted to topical satire, although another kind of revue concentrates on spectacular costumes and dancing.

Rewind: To transport a film or tape in the reverse direction, back onto its original hub or spool.

Rewrite editor: A newspaper editor who edits and often substantially rewrites written, material received from reporters and other material intended for publication.

RF cues: In motion picture printing, cues applied to the edge of the negative in the form of small metal patches which are sensed by a radio-frequency detector.

RGB: (1) Red Green Blue, the primary colours of an additive system in photographic or video colour reproduction. (2) Hence, a method of signal connecting giving direct access to the primary colours on a monitor or visual display unit.

Rhapsody: In the modem sense, a Work or passage expressing ecstatic or uncontrolled emotion, often in a loosely structured fashion. In ancient Greece, a rhapsody was a selection of epic poetry sung by a rhapsode or rhapsodist-literally a 'stitcher' who combined memorized passages with his own improvisations, although this kind of minstrel was later required chiefly to recite Homer's Iliad and *Odyssey* in their established versions.

Rhetoric: The deliberate exploitation of eloquence for the most persuasive effect in public speaking or in writing. It was cultivated as an important art and science in antiquity, and was an essential element of medieval university education, involving the elaborate categorizing of figures of speech together with the arts of memory, arrangement, and oratorical delivery. The emphasis on sincerity in the culture of Romanticism helped to discredit rhetoric, so that the usual modern sense of the term implies empty and ineffectual grandness in public speech. Modem, critics sometimes refer to the rhetorical dimension of a literary work, meaning those aspects of the work that persuade or otherwise guide the responses of readers. A practitioner or theorist of rhetoric is called a rhetorician.

Rhombic antenna: A directional *travelling wave antenna,* consisting of four conductors forming the sides of a rhombus, fed at one corner and usually terminated at the remote corner. The sides are generally several wavelengths long. Each side has a four-lobed radiation pattern, and the angles between the sides of the rhombus are arranged so that lobes are coincident along the major length of the rhombus. A change of frequency results in little change in lobe angle, and the rhombic is thus characterised by substantially aperiodic operation over a wide frequency range. Termination at the end remote from the feed point renders the system unidirectional, and the coincident lobes radiate in the direction of the termination. With no termination, the rhombic is bi-directional.

Rhyme: The identity of sound between syllables or paired groups of syllables, usually at the ends of verse lines: also a poem employing this device. Normally the last stressed vowel in the line and all sounds following it make up the rhyming element: this may be a monosyllable, or two syllables, or even three syllables. Where a rhyming element in a feminine or triple rhyme uses more than one word, this is known as a 'mosaic rhyme'.

The rhyming pairs illustrated so far are all examples of 'full rhyme' ; departures from this norm take three main forms: (i) rime *riche,* in which the consonants preceding the rhyming elements are also identical, even if the spellings and meanings of the words differ: *(ii)* eye rhyme, in which the spellings of the rhyming elements match, but the sounds do not; (iii) half-rhyrne or 'slant rhyme', where the vowel sounds do not match. Half-rhyme is known by several other names: 'imperfect rhyme'. 'near rhyme'. 'pararhyme'. etc. Although rhyme is most often used at the ends of verse lines, internal rhyme between syllables within the same line is also found. Rhyme is not essential to poetry: many languages rarely use it, and in English it finally replaced alliteration as the usual patterning device of verse only in the late 14th century. A writer of rhyming verse may sometimes be referred to disparagingly as a rhymester or rhymer.

Rhyme royal: A stanza form consisting of seven 5-stress lines rhyming, first used by Chaucer and thus also known as the Chaucerian stanza. Following Chaucer's use of rhyme royal in his Troilus and Criseyde, The Parlement *of* Fowles, and some of the Canterbury Tales it continued to be an important form of English verse in the 15th and 16th centuries, being used by Dunbar, Henryson. Spenser, and Shakespeare; William Morris's The Earthly Paradise is a rare example of its use in later periods. The name of this stanza seems to come from its use in The Kingis Quair, a poem uncertainly attributed to King James I of Scotland.

Rhyme scheme: The pattern in which the rhymed line-endings are arranged in a poem or stanza. This may be expressed as a sequence of recurrences in which each line ending on the same rhyme. Rhyme schemes may follow a fixed pattern, as in the sonnet and several other forms, or they may be arranged freely according to the poet's requirements. The simplest rhyme schemes are those of rhyming couplets and of the common quatrain forms, while those of ottava rima, rhyme royal, the Spenserian stanza, and the French fixed forms are far more intricate.

Rhythm: The pattern of sounds perceived as the recurrence of equivalent 'beats' at more or less equal intervals. In most English poetry, an underlying rhythm is manifested in a metrical pattern—a sequence of measured beats and 'offbeats' arranged in verse lines and governing the alternation of stressed and unstressed syllables. While metre involves the recurrence of measured sound units, rhythm is a less clearly structured principle: one can refer to the unmeasured rhythms of everyday speech, or of prose, and to the rhythms or cadences of non-metrical verse.

RIAA curve: Recording Industries Association of America recommended audio reproduce/equalisation characteristic, now universally adopted.

Ribbon, copy: The original of a typed manuscript; with the advent of copying machines capable of producing copies as clear as, and some times even better than, such originals, the term has lost its practical significance, and is falling into disuse.

Ribbon microphone: A microphone in which the electrical output is developed between the ends of a thin metal ribbon suspended in a strong magnetic field. The ribbon is exposed to the air and, with both faces exposed, acts as a pressure-gradient transducer with one face exposed, it behaves as a pressure type.

Riddle: A puzzlingly indirect description of some thing, person, or idea, framed in such a way as to challenge the reader to identify it. Riddles, usually in verse, are found as a popular literary form in most cultures and periods. An important Old English collection is preserved in the 10th-century Exeter Book.

Rider: A provision added by the parties to a basic contract, such as an author-publisher contract, which takes up some special questions; such a provision may be signed at the time the contract is originally made or added later by the parties.

Rifle microphone: A highly directional microphone which can be aimed at its sound source.

Rigging: The setting up of lights, loudspeakers or projectors on a set, stage or venue.

Right of privacy: The right of an individual or organization to withhold itself from public view and examination, and to avoid intrusion upon its life, to the extent that law and public policy permit; often in somewhat shifting and uneasy balance with some First Amendment rights.

Rights: In publishing, the body of ownership interests created by copyright law in the originator of copyrighted material, which may be held or sold or leased to others, as when an author sells or leases publications rights to a publisher, including hardcover, paperback, book club, first and second serialization, condensation and adaption, foreign, translation, movie, television, radio, videodisc, computerized database, microform, dramatization, and any kind of reproduction or adaptation rights. The first fights sold or leased—usually hardcover, but sometimes paperback, rights—are the *primary sale;* all other rights sold then become *subsidiary rights,* as they are preceded by the contract for the primary fights sale. Within a publishing house, the primary sale is generally handled by the acquiring editor or publisher, but subsidiary rights are more often handled by specialists, such as a *subsidiary rights manager* or *foreign rights manager.* All such fights that are not specifically transferred to others continue to belong to the originator-owner of the copyright.

Rime riche: A kind of rhyme in which the rhyming elements include matching consonants before the stressed vowel sounds. Often this means the rhyming of two words with the same sound and sometimes the same spelling but different meanings, e.g, seen/scene. The term also covers word-endings where the consonant preceding the stressed vowel sound is the same, compare/ despair. An even more excessive land of rhyme is rime tres riche. 'in' which not only the preceding consonant but also the vowel sound before that remains the same: allowed/aloud. Usually avoided in English, rimes riches are found far more often in French verse.

Ring binder: A mechanical binder, used to hold contents consisting of holepunched loose leaves: often used in publications requiring periodic updating or the removal of leaves for use.

Ringing: A damped oscillatory response at the beginning or end of a *pulse* signal. In a video display, it appears as closely spaced light and dark bands of decreasing intensity at the edge of an image where a marked change of brightness occurs.

Ring modulator: Device requiring two inputs to produce an output consisting of sum and difference frequencies between the signals.

Ripple: (l) Unwanted AC signal superimposed on a DC supply. (2) A rapid succession of cuts or dissolves across a series of screen areas of a *multi-screen* presentation. (3) A *mix* effect in which 95 the outgoing and incoming scenes are distorted behind rippling lines.

Rise time: The time taken for the leading edge of a pulse to rise from 10% to 90% of its maximum amplitude.

Ringing: In television and pulse systems, a damped oscillatory response following a step change in voltage. In television display, a pulse change in luminance is followed by closely-spaced light and dark bands of decreasing intensity.

Ring modulator: A modulator used for generation of a suppressed carrier modulated output, i.e. sidebands only

Ripple: Term for a residual AC component imposed on a DC supply which has been derived from an AC power source.

Ripple finish: A paper design carrying textured wavelike lines in the surface of the paper; rolled or calendared into the paper during the papermaking process.

Rise-time: The time taken for a rising pulse voltage to change from 10% to 90% of its final value. Every practical communications system has a finite bandwidth and, hence, a rectangular pulse waveform. The start and finish of the voltage change are difficult to determine, but the 10% and 90% values are readily established from a cathoderay display. The falltime is imilarly defined as the time required for the voltage to fall from 90% to 10% of its final value.

Rising rhythm: A rhythmic effect often found in metrical verse in which the unstressed syllables are perceived as being linked with the succeeding stressed syllables rather than with those preceding them. In terms of classical prosody, lines composed of iambs or anapaests may show this rising rhythm, although this is not inevitable. Rising rhythm in English verse is far more common than its opposite, falling rhythm.

River: A vertical stream of white space, on a printed page appearing either because spaces on several lines in a row happen to fall, under each other, or because of too-wide spacing in several succeeding lines.

Roan: A sheepskin leather binding material; a relatively inexpensive leather, often used in partial leather bindings, and more for selling purposes than because of its binding qualities.

Rococo: An 18th-century style of architecture and furnishing characterized by elaborately playful decoration, and regarded by stern classical purists as 'effeminate' or tastelessly pretty. As applied to literature, the term is unhelpfully vague, but usually suggests a cheerful lightness and intimacy of tone, and an elegant playfulness: Pope's The Rape *of* the *Lock* and Sterne's Tristram Shandy have been cited as English examples.

Rodomontade: A blusteringly boastful speech, or any arrogantly inflated manner of speaking or writing.

Rolling revision: A continuous revision process, in which portions of a work are always in revision; for example a six-volume encyclopedia may issue one revised volume each year, continuously working on a six-year revision cycle.

Roman a clef: The French term for a kind of novel in which the well-informed reader will recognise identifiable persons from real life thinly disguised as fictional characters. A significant English example is Thomas Love Peacock's satirical novel *Nightmare Abbey,* in which 'Mr Flosky' is clearly the poet Samuel Taylor Coleridge, 'Mr Cypress' is Lord Byron, and' Scythrop' is Percy Bysshe Shelley. Very many novels based upon their authors' own lives are to some degree romans a clef.

RO: Receive Only, a tele-printer term.

Roam: In a graphic display, to move the *window* through which a portion of the image is accessed and observed.

Rock and roll: The ability to move a video tape or synchronised picture and sound films backwards and forwards at varying speeds, to decide an edit point or for convenience in dubbing and mixing.

Roll: To start the camera(s), audio or video tape reco-rder(s).

Roll feed: Device to feed a roll of material into or across a machine. Specifically, the attachment to an overhead projector to feed the transparency material across the platen.

Rolling title: A series of titles of captions moving upwards across the picture area. (= *creeping title)*

ROM: Read-Only Memory, used for storing non-varying data or instructions, e.g. *operating systems.*

Roman a these: The French term for a 'thesis novel' that is, a didactic novel that puts forward an argument or proposes a solution to some problem of politics, morality or philosophy, The most celebrated example in English is Harriet Beecher Stowe's *Uncle Tom's* Cabin, which powerfully urged the abolition of slavery. A more philosophical kind of thesis novel is jean-Paul Sartre's *La Nausee*, which embodies many of the principles of his existentialism.

Roman a tiroirs: The French term for an episodic novel, such as Alain-Rene Lesage's Gil Blas—a tiroir being a drawer in a desk or chest.

Romance: A fictional story in verse or prose that relates improbable adventures of idealized characters in some remote or enchanted setting; or, more generally, a tendency in fiction opposite to that of realism. The term now embraces many forms of fiction from the Gothic novel and the popular escapist love story to the 'scientific romances' of H. G. Wells, but it usually refers to the tales of King Artheir's knights written in the late Middle Ages by Chrdtien de Troyes Sir Thomas Malory, and many others.'Medieval romance is distinguished from epic by its concentration on courtly love rather than warlike heroism.

Long, elaborate romances were written during the Renaissance, including Ludovico Ariosto's *Orlando Furioso*, Edmund Spenser's *The Faerie Queene*, and Sir Philip Sidney's prose romance *Arcadia*, but Cervantes's parody of romances in *Don Quixote* helped to undermine this tradition. Later prose romances differ from novels in their preference for allegory and psychological exploration rather than realistic social observation, especially in American works like Nathaniel Hawthorne's *The Blithedale Romance*. Several modern literary genres, from science fiction to the detective story, can be regarded as variants of the romance. In modern criticism of Shakespeare, the term is also applied to four of his last *plays—Pericles, Cymbeline, The Winter's Tale*, and *The Tempest*—which are distinguished by their daring use of magical illusion and improbable reunions. The Romance languages are those languages originating in southern Europe that are derived from Latin: the most important of these are Spanish, French, Italian, and Portuguese. In Spanish literature, the term has a special I sense, the *romance* being a ballad composed in octosyllabic lines.

Roman—fleuve: A continuous sequence of novels through which are traced the fortunes of the same character or group of characters; literally a 'river-novel' that flows through from one book to the next. The most celebrated example is Marcel Proust's seven-novel sequence *A la recherche du temps perdu*. In English, significant examples are Anthony Trollope's five Barsetshire novels. Anthony Powell's *A Dance to the Music of Time*, and Doris Lessing's *Children of Violence* sequence.

Roman numerals: The numbering system used in the Roman Empire, rather than the Arabic numerals used today; the main symbols used in the Roman system, and their Arabic numeral equivalent, are: I = 1; V 51 X = 10; L = 50; C = 100; D = 500; M = 1,000.

Romantic comedy: A general term for comedies that deal mainly with the follies and misunderstandings of young lovers, in a light-hearted and happily concluded manner which usually avoids serious satire. The best-known examples are Shakespeare's comedies of the late *1590s. A Midsummer Night's Dream, Twelfth Night,* and *As You Like It* being the most purely romantic, while *Much Ado About Nothing* approaches the comedy of manners and *The Merchant of Venice is* closer to tragicomedy.

Roman type: Any of many typefaces designed in the old Roman style, featuring straight, vertical letters rather than slanted letters, as in the contrasting italic typefaces. Bodoni is an example of a modem Roman type.

Romantic Irony: A kind of literary self-consciousness in which an author signals his or her freedom from the limits of a given work by puncturing its fictional illusion and exposing its process of composition as a Matter of authorial whim This is often a kind of protective self-mockery involving a playful-attitude towards the conventions of the genre. Byron's narrative poem *Don Juan* is a sustained exercise in romantic irony, as is Laurence Sterne's novel *Tristram Shandy,* but the effect may also be found in Chaucer and many other authors of different periods.

Romanticism: A sweeping but indispensable modern term applied to the profound shift in Western attitudes to art and human creativity that dominated much of European culture in the first half of the 19th century, and that has shaped most subsequent developments in literature—even those reacting against it. In its most coherent early form, as it emerged in the 1790s in Germany and Britain and in the 1820s in France and elsewhere, it is known as the Romantic Movement or Romantic Revival. Its chief emphasis was upon freedom of individual self-expression: sincerity, spontaneity, and originality became the new standards in literature, replacing the decorous imitation of classical models favoured by 18th-century neoclassicism. Rejecting the ordered rationality of the Enlightenment as mechanical, impersonal, and artificial the Romantics turned to the emotional directness of personal experience and to the boundlessness of individual imagination and aspiration. Increasingly independent of the declining system of aristocratic patronage, they saw themselves as free spirits expressing their own imaginative truths, several found admirers ready to hero-worship the artist as a genius or prophet. The restrained balance valued in 18th-century culture was abandoned in favour of emotional intensity often taken to extremes of rapture, nostalgia, horror, melancholy, or sentimentality. Some—but not all—Romantic writers cultivated the appeal of the exotic, the bizarre, or the macabre, almost all showed a new interest in the irrational realms of dream and delirium or of folk superstition and legend. The creative imagination occupied the centre of Romantic views of art, which replaced the 'mechanical' rules of conventional form with an 'organic' principle of natural growth and free development.

The emergence of Romanticism has been attributed to several developments in late 18th-century culture, including a strong antiquarian interest in ballads and medieval romances. The immediate inspiration for the first selfdeclared Romanticsthe German group including the Schlegel brothers and Novaliswas the transcendental philosophy of Kant and Fichte, which stressed the creative power of the mind and allowed nature to be seen as a responsive mirror of the soul. This new German thinking spread via S. T. Coleridge to Britain and via Mme de Stael to France, eventually shaping American Transcendentalism.

English Romanticism had emerged independently with William Blake's then little-known anti-Enlightenment writings of the 1790s and with the landmark of William Wordsworth's 1800 Preface to *Lyrical Ballads*. In a second wave after the Napoleonic wars, Roman-ticism established itself in France and across Europe: by the 1830s the movement extended from Pushkin in Russia to Poe in the USA. Romanticism drew some of its energies from the associated revolutionary movements of democracy and nationalism, although the 'classical' culture of the French Revolution actually delayed the arrival of French Romanticism, and a strong element of conservative nostalgia is also evident in many Romantic writers.

The literary rebellion of Wordsworth in England and Victor Hugo in France declared an end to the artificiality of older conventions, breaking up the 18th-century system of distinct genres and of poetic diction. Lyric poetry underwent a major revival led by Wordsworth, Keats, Shelley, Pushkin, Leopardi, Heine, and others; narrative verse took on a new subjective dimension in the work of Wordsworth and Byron, but the theatre tended towards the sensationalism of melodrama. In fiction, Hoffmann and Poe pioneered the tale of terror in the wake of the Gothic novel, while the historical novels of Walter

Scott, Alessandro Manzoni, Victor Hugo, and James Fenimore Cooper combined bold action with nostalgic sentiment. A new wave of women novelists led by Mary Shelley, George Sand, and the Bronte sisters broke the imposed restraints of modesty in works of powerful imaginative force. The astonishing personality of Byron provided Alfred de Musset. Mikhail Lermontov, and other admirers throughout Europe with a model of the Romantic poet as tormented outcast. The growing international cult of Shakespeare also reflected the Romantic heroworship which, in the writings of Thomas Carlyle and R. W. Emerson. became a 'heroic' view of history as the product of forceful personalities like Napoleon.

Although challenged in the second half of the 19th century by the rise of realism and naturalism, Romanticism has in some ways maintained a constant presence in Western literature, providing the basis for several schools and movements from the Pre-Raphaebtes and Symbolists to expressionism and Surrealism. In a broader sense, the term 'romantic' may be applied to works and authors of other periods, by explicit or implicit comparison with a 'classical' standard: thus Shakespeare is more romantic than Moliere or Ben Jonson, both because he disregards the structural models 'of Greek drama and because it exploits freely the supernatural elements of folk legend: and in a different way, W. B. Yeats and D. H. Lawrence are more romantic than W. H. Auden and E. M. Forster, because they assert the absolute primacy of their personal visions, rejecting common norms of objectivity.

Rondeau: A medieval French verse form also used by some late 19th-century poets in English. It normally consists of 13 octosyllabic lines, grouped in stanzas of five, three, and five lines, The whole poem uses only two rhymes, and the first word or phrase of the first line recurs twice as a refrain after the second and third stanzas. Variant forms of the rondeau include those using 10-syllable lines and those having only 12 lines, but in all cases the refrain and the restriction to two rhymes are retained. An even more complicated form is the *rondeau redouble,* a 24-line poem also using only two rhymes in its six quatrains, with each line of the first stanza recurring in turn as the final fine of the following stanzas until the poem's opening phrase recurs after the last fine.

Rondel: A medieval French verse form related to the triolet and the rondeau. In its usual modern form, it is a 13-line poem using only two rhymes in its three stanzas. It employs a two-line refrain which opens the poem and recurs at lines 7 and 8, the first line also completing the poem. The rhyme scheme—with the repeated lines given in capitals. There is no fixed metre. This form was adopted by some poets in England in the late 19th century, including Austin Dobson and W. E. Henley.

Rotary press: A printing press carrying curved printing plates set into a rotating cylinder, which makes contact with the surface to be printed. Such presses may be *sheet-fed,* in which paper is supplied from a pile of sheets and fed into the press to be imprinted one by one; or *roll-fed* with paper feeding into the press from a continuous, roll, called a web. Rotary presses may be letterpresses, offset presses, or rotogravure presses.

Rough: A preliminary layout, such as that of a page or piece of advertising; often a handdrawn sketch.

Roundel: An English version of the rondeau, devised by A. C. Swinburne for his collection *A Century of Roundels.* It is a poem of eleven fines using only two rhymes in its three stanzas of 4, 3, and 4 lines. Lines 4 and 11 are formed by the repetition of the poem's opening word or phrase as a refrain, which may be rhymed with lines 2, 5. 7, and 9. The term was at one time a synonym for a rondeau or rondel.

Rounding: In bookbinding, the shaping of the back or spine of the book, so that it will be somewhat concave, making the fore-edge of the book somewhat convex; essential if the book is to lie flat in reading position.

Root mean square: Factor giving the effective value of an alternating current or voltage, taking account of its waveform.

Roundelay: A short dancing song with a refrain. The term covers the rondeau, the rondel, and various simpler forms, but commonly refers to such works as they are set to music.

rRune: A letter belonging to an old Germanic alphabet thought to have been used from the 2nd century AD, which is found in inscriptions on stones, coins, etc.

The runic alphabet came to be associated with magical powers, and so the term has sometimes been used to refer to any inscription, sign, or written message having magical properties or secret power.

Rostrum: (1) Platform raising actors and scenery, often to camera height. (2) A camera stand designed to illuminate and hold in specified position the artwork to be filmed.

Rostrum camera: A fixed film or TV camera mounted vertically for shooting complicated graphics and animation.

Rotary printer: A continuous contact printing machine in which both films are carried on a rotating sprocket at the time of exposure.

Rotations: Effects obtained by using the turntable on an animation stand.

Rotoseope: An instrument which projects a film frame by frame on to the table of an animation stand, so that it serves as a background to animation cels. (Strictly, a trade name)

Rough animation: The first tentative animation done as a test.

Rough cut: In editing, the first assembly of shots in their intended script order.

Routine: A special-purpose computer program, or part of a program, designed to perform specific, limited functions; when kept in storage for use in solving standard problems, often called library *routines* or *utility routines.*

Royalty: A share of revenue flowing from a work, generally a percentage of net or gross receipts, paid to its author by those selling the work, as when a publisher pays an author, composer, compiler, or editor a percentage of net or gross income from an article, book, periodical, or computerized database, or a company pays an inventor a percentage of proceeds for use of an invention. In publishing, for purposes of royalty computation, net *receipts* are billings to jobbers, retail booksellers, direct purchasers, and all others who are directly billed for manufactured books, minus sales taxes, allowances for returns of unsold books for credit, and allowances for uncollectibles. *Gross receipts* for royalty computation purposes are the list prices of books times the number of books ordered from the publisher by sellers or directly sold by the publisher, minus sales taxes, allowances for returns of unsold books for credit and uncollectibles.

As a practical matter, a wide variety of arrangements, varying from contract to contract, govern actual royalty computations, with many exceptions based upon such matters as discount schedules, modes of sale and place of sale tending to lower substantialy the amounts of royalties actually paid on gross receipts contracts. An *adva-*

nce paid by publisher to author is a prepayment of royalties made in anticipation of future income from that author's work.

RS232: An *EIA* interchange specification containing a selection of *V24* interchange circuits. *RS232* gives electrical characteristics and pin allocations in the 25-way connector.

RT60: The *reverberation time* for a 60 dB drop in amplitude.

RTL: Resistor Transistor Logic.

Rubricate: To apply red, as to print in red ink headings and decorations at the beginning of chapters and sections; a common practice in some older books.

Rumble: In audio disc reproduction, a very low frequency noise voltage, generated by the turntable drive mechanism and transmitted via the turntable to the pickup. A high-pass filter with a cut-off frequency around 20 Hz in the pickup output system can minimise the noise without impairing reproduction over the main audio frequency range.

Run: The instruction to commence execution of a programmed task, from the beginning unless otherwise specified.

Runaround: To set text around an illustration, rather than in normal width.

Run-in head: A head set on the same line as the text it introduces; generally a subhead.

Running heads: Headings printed across the tops of pages. carrying publication names, chapter titles, and sometimes key words, as in this dictionary.

Run-on: An instruction to compositors to set text without a paragraph or other break, even though a break is shown in copy; sometimes indicated by a mark between paragraphs. Also called *run-in.*

Racking: Another term for *framing.*

Run out: (1) A length of blank film stock at the end of each reel to protect the film from damage.

(2) The section of black film immediately following the last picture frame in the end section of an *Academy leader.*

Run time: Taking place when computer is run. (As opposed to when program is entered)

Run up: The length of film or tape that has to run through a projector or audio or videotape recorder before it is operating smoothly at normal speed.

Rushes: In motion picture practice, the first prints made from the newly processed picture or sound negative to check content and quality. Also called *dailies* or rush prints.

Russian formalism: A school of literary theory and analysis that emerged in Russia around 19 15, devoting itself to the study of literariness. i.e. the sum of 'devices' that distinguish literary language from ordinary language. In reaction against the vagueness of previous literary theories, it attempted a scientific descri-ption of literature as a special use of language with observable features. This meant deliberately disrega-rding the contents of literary works, and thus inviting 'strong disapproval from Marxist critics, for whom formalism was a term of reproach. With the consolidation of Stalin's dictatorship around 1929, Formalism was silenced as a heresy in the Soviet Union, and its centre of research migrated to Prague in the 1930s. Along with 'literari-ness', the most important concept of the school was that of defamiliarization: instead of seeing literature as a reflection' of the world, Victor Shklovsky and his Formalist followers saw it as a linguistic dislocation, or a 'making strange'.

S

S & F: a discreet abbreviation for a category of popular modern fiction known among cynics in the book trade as 'Shopping and Fucking'. This kind of romance, usually written by and for women, is distinguished by its shamelessly explicit descriptions of expensive clothes, jewellery, perfumes, cars, and other accessories of the very rich, naming actual brand names: several sexual encounters are also described in graphic detail. The genre established itself in the 1980s, following the huge commercial success of Judith Krantz's *Scruples.*

safe area: The area within a frame that is certain to be in vision when transmitted on television or video.

safelight: A source of visible light in a photographic darkroorn whose colour and intensity allow unprocessed sensitive materials to be handled without danger of unwanted exposure.

safety base: The almost nonflammable acetate or triacetate film base that has replaced the highly flammable nitrate base formerly used.

sag: In pulse reproduction, the extent to which a pulse amplitude falls over the time of the pulse duration. Usually expressed as a percentage of the pulse maximum value.

saga: the Norse name for various kinds of prose tales composed in medieval Scandinavia and Iceland and written down from the 12th century to the 14th. These usually tell of heroic leaders—early Norse kings or 13th-century bishops—or of the heroic settlers of Iceland in the 9th and 10th centuries; others, like the Vol*sunga saga,* relate earlier legends. The emphasis on feuds and family histories in some famous sagas like *Njals saga* has led to the term's application in English to any long family story spanning two or more generations: this may take the form of a lengthy novel like D. H. Lawrence's *The Rainbow* or of a novel-sequence such as John Galsworthy's *The Forsyte Saga.*

sale: 1. A contract passing title to goods or undertaking an obligation to supply goods or services in return for stated consideration, usually in the form of a price. 2. A lower than-normal offer of goods or services by a seller to one or more buyers; for example, the offering of a group of books at cut prices for a limited time by a bookseller.

sale on approval: A trial sale under a revocable form of contract in which the seller supplies goods to a potential buyer, who can return the goods to the seller for full refund or credit as specified in the form of contract; not really a binding sale or contract, but as a practical matter conditional upon the buyer's retention of the goods supplied. A standard form of sale by publishers to booksellers.

sales agent: An independent organization or proprietor that acts as agent for the goods or services of one or more firms; for example, commission agents representing publishers and selling to bookstores.

sales forecast: An estimate of sales that will be made within a specified period; a guess that is a vital part of all budgeting and other planning.

sales management: That part of management responsible for meeting the sales objectives of an organization, by developing sales organizations and techniques that successfully sell company goods and services.

salon: a French cultural institution consisting of a weekly social gathering at the private house of an aristocratic lady, at which social, artistic, and scientific questions are discussed. From the early 17th century to the early 19th, several important literary and philosophical salons provided a social base for French writers. The term can also refer to an exhibition of paintings by living artists, so that in a second literary sense the title *Salon* has been given to an essay on contemporary art and related matters: Diderot in the 18th century and Baudelaire in the 19th both wrote important Salons.

samizdat: A Russian word meaning 'self-publishing', applied since the 1960s to a clandestine mode of publication by which 'dissident' writings and other banned works have been secretly circulated, usually in typed carbon copies or photocopies. Novels by Alexander Solzhenitsyn and articles by Andrei Sakharov were among the important *samizdat* works of the 1960s and 1970s.

sample and hold: A circuit element which samples the instantaneous amplitude of an electrical waveform and retains (holds) the value. Commonly used in analogue-to-digital converters.

sample pages: Composed samples of forthcoming publications, set in type and laid out as specified by publisher or designer and set by compositor; they normally include enough material of sufficient variety to provide a good idea of how most of the pages in the forthcoming publication will look.

sampling: The process of describing a waveform in terms of its value at frequent and usually regular time intervals. To obtain complete information from the waveform, the sampling frequency must have a value at least twice the highest frequency in the waveform. An analogue signal waveform being sampled.

sandwiching: Mounting two or more pieces of film in a single slide mount to create effects.

sans serif: Without serifs; characterizing any typeface which does not have the tendrils or strokes called serifs projecting from the ends of letters, at angles different from those of the letters, and which usually has letters with an even thickness of body, rather than the varying, thicknesses that characterize serif typefaces.

Sapphics: lyric verses written in a Greek metre named after Sappho, the legendary woman poet of Lesbos. Sapphic verse uses stanzas of four lines, the first three having eleven syllables, the last having five. In the first three lines, the sequence of five metrical feet is: trochee; trochee or spondee; dactyl; trochee: trochee or spondee in the fourth line, a dactyl is followed by a trochee or a spondee. The metre was used frequently in Latin by Horace, but it is difficult to adapt to the stress-patterns of English. Sidney'. Swinburne, and Pound are among the poets who have attempted English Sapphics.

satellite: (1) A sub-station of a main location. (2) A station in space, often geostationary, providing a radio-frequency link between ground-based transmitters and receivers. (3) In broadcasting, a station that receives its programme signals by means of a radio link with a remote main station, and re-broadcasts them. (4) In space, a radio station located in a planned orbit in space round the earth, often *geostationary*. Satellites can act as *transponders*, thus forming a link between ground-based transmitters and receiving stations. Some can originate picture signals of various kinds, for transmission to earth.

Saticon TV: camera tube of the Vidicon format with a photosurface of doped selenium giving high resolution and reduced lag.

satin finish: A very smooth paper finish, with some of the texture of satin.

satire: a mode of writing that exposes the failings of individuals, institutions, or societies to ridicule and scorn. Satire is often an incidental element in literary works that may not be wholly satirical, especially in comedy. Its tone may vary from tolerant amusement, as in the verse satires of the Roman poet Horace, to bitter indignation, as in the verse of juvenal and the prose of Jonathan Swift. Various forms of literature may be satirical, from the plays of Ben jonson or of Moliere and the poetry of Chaucer or Byron to the prose writings of Rabelais and Voltaire. The models of Roman satire, especially the verse satires of Horace and juvenal, inspired some important imitations by Boileau, Pope, and Johnson in the greatest period of satire—the 17th and 18th centuries—when writers could appeal to a shared sense of normal conduct from which vice and folly were seen to stray. In this classical tradition, an important form is 'formal' or 'direct' satire, in which the writer directly addresses the reader with satiric comment. The alternative form of 'indirect' satire usually found in plays and novels allows us to draw our own conclusions from the actions of the characters, as for example in the novels of Evelyn Waugh or Chinua Achebe.

saturation: In marketing, the filling of a field; may describe an attempt to reach every possible buyer in a defined market using, every, available advertising, promotion, and selling tool; or may refer to the condition of a market that has bought heavily in a product area, and will buy relatively little more, at least for a time. (1) In magnetic devices, a condition where further increase in magnetising force produces no further increase in magnetic flux. (2) In thermionic and semiconductor devices, a condition where further change in control voltage produces no further increase in current. (3) In colour perception M television systems. Each discrete colour occupies a wavelength in the range of visible colours. A colour source generating a single wavelength is said to be saturated and, in practice, narrow-band sources would be similarly described. Mixtures of primary colour sources can produce another saturated colour, e.g. green and red can produce yellow. A mixture of a saturated colour, such as red, with white produces de-saturation, i.e. red becomes de-saturated to pink. De-sapration can be produced in another manner. Red, green and blue primaries, mixed in the correct proportions, produce white. Thus, if a saturated red, for example, is mixed with some green and blue, it will be de-saturated to pink. Yellow with some blue added becomes de-saturated.

saturation campaign: A massive promotional effort, aimed at using all available media to help sell a product in a specified market.

satyr play: a humorous performance presented in Athenian dramatic contests, following a trilogy of tragedies. The satyr play had a chorus of satyrs, and its action was a burlesque of some mythical story appropriate to the foregoing tragedies involving obscene language and gestures. Although fragments of satyr plays by Aeschylus and Sophocles have been found the only complete example to have survived is the Cyclops of Euripides.

save: A computer instruction to store information on magnetic disk or tape. The term is also used for saving a program to bulk storage such as a core store.

sawtooth: An electrical waveform which has a slow change in amplitude followed by a rapid return or vice versa.

sc: A proofreader's mark, instructing the printer to use small capitals; indicated either by the letters sc or by double underlining of the affected letter or word.

scaling: Determining by geometry or by use of a proportion wheel the final proportions of matter to be enlarged or reduced.

SCA: Subsidiary Communications Authorisation, Secondary channel used in stereo broadcasting in USA.

scan line: A horizontal line of *pixels* in a raster display.

scanner: (1) Equipment used to carry out *scanning. (2)* Specifically, abbreviation for *caption scanner. (3)* Mobile video production vehicle.

scanning: The process by which an area is systematically explored line-by-line, particularly in television, where an electron beam is used. In television, a process whereby, at the *camera tube,* an electron charge image of the field of view is explored line-by-line with an electron beam, which converts variations of luminance that are encountered, into electrical voltages. At the receiver, the display tube beam is swept in synchronism with the scanning beam in the camera, and it is amplitude-modulated with the demodulated video signal.

scanning line: In television, a single horizontal sweep of the camera tube beam. scanning speed In television, the speed with which scanning is effected. Often expressed as either (1) The time to complete a single line scan, (2) The time to effect a complete picture scan. In the UK 625-line system, a single line scan takes 64 μs, and a picture scan is completed in every 1/25 second.

scanning spot In television. (1) In a *camera tube, a* small area of the target that is covered by the diameter of the scanning electron beam. (2) In *display tube,* the area of the fluorescent screen that is covered by the modulated electron beam. In the case of colour tubes, the scanning spot may cover several *colour cells* or triads.

scansion: the analysis of poetic' metre in verse lines, by displaying stresses pauses, and rhyme patterns with conventional visual symbols. The simplest system, known as graphic scansion, marks stressed syllables unstressed syllables divisions between mettrical units or 'feet'(i), and major pauses or caesuras (ii) in a verse line, determining whether its metre is, for example, iambic or dactylic, and how many feet make up the line. In Greek and Latin quantitative verse, the symbols —and indicate long and short syllables respectively. Scansion also analyses the rhyme scheme in a poem or stanza, giving alphabetical symbols to the rhymes: The verb scan is applied not only to the activity of analysing metre, but also to the fines analysed: of a tine with an irregular or inconsistent metrical pattern it is said that it does not scan.

scattering: In *ionospheric* and *tropospheric* propagation, an effect produced due to lack of homogeneity at the point in the atmosphere where an incident wave is returned to earth, whereby some wave energy leaves at angles other than that indicated by *Snell's law.*

scatter loss: In *optical fibres, loss* of signal power due to scattering of light by particles and irregularities in the core and cladding materials.

scatter propagation: A system of radio communication using VHF and UHF, and scatter phenomena in the *troposphere,* for communication over paths beyond the radio horizon. How a narrow beam is radiated to just clear the horizon. A scatter zone is established in the troposphere at which a similar beam is directed from the receiving antenna. A useful proportion of the radiated energy is developed in the receiving antenna by *forward scatter.*

scatology: the study of excrement, e.g. in medicine or palaeontology. In the literary sense it means repeated reference to excrement and related matters, as in the coarse humour of Francois Rabelais or Jonathan Swift, whose works have passages of a scatological nature.

SCC: Single Chip Controller.

scenario: a brief outline of the plot, characters, and scene-changes of a play; or the script of a film. In the cinematic sense, a seenario is usually more detailed. whereas the theatrical scenarios of the *commedia* *dell' arte* were 'skeleton' summaries used as the basis *for improvisations*. A writer of scenarios, usually for the cinema is sometimes called a scenarist.

scene: The basic element of continuity sequence in a motion' picture or television production, planned for recording as continuous uninterrupted action. Also, the action that takes place at one time and place, or its setting. In a drama, a subdivision of an act or of a play not divided into acts. A scene normally represents actions happening in one place at one time, and is marked off from the next scene by a curtain, a blackout, or a brief emptying of the stage. In the study of narrative works, I scene' is also the name given to a 'dramatic' method of narration that presents events at roughly the same pace as that at which they are supposed to be occurring, i.e. usually in detail and with substantial use of dialogue. In this sense the scenic narrative method is contrasted with summary', in which the duration of the story's events is compressed into a brief account.

Scene Sync: Trade name for a system which permits movement of the foreground camera synchronised with the mask camera in *chromakey*, and *colour separation overlay* special effects.

Schauerroman: the German term for a Gothic novel or similar horror story, literally a 'shudder-novel'.

scheme: a term once used for a rhetorical figure usually one that departs from the normal order or sound of words but does not extend their meanings as a trope does. Some rhetoricians, however, have used the term to cover tropes as well.

scholarly press: A house primarily publishing works of intellectual and academic interest; often, though by no means always, a sponsored press.

Scholasticism: the methods and doctrines of the leading academic philosophers and theologians of the late Middle Ages in Europe. The school-men of the 12th, 13th, and 14th centuries attempted to reconcile,. Christian theology with the Greek philosophy of Aristotle. The leading figures of scholasticism included Peter Abelard, Albertus Magnus, Duns Scotus, and above all Thomas Aquinas, whose Summa Theologica is the most ambitious of scholastic works; his followers are called Thomists. During the Renaissance, the deductive logic of scholasticism was superseded by the inductive methods of modem science, while its theological concerns were challenged by the emergence of humanism.

Schmidt optical system: A large aperture optical projection system having a spherical concave mirror in combination with an aspheric correction lens.

Schmitt trigger: A pair of amplifying devices connected as a bistable multivibrator. A specific circuit con-figuration having a marked hysteresis so that it can give a sharply defined output to a slowly changing input.

science fiction: A work of imaginative fiction, relying heavily on extrapolation from current scientific knowledge and theory; contrasts with fantasy, which relies heavily on non-rational elements, often depending on existing human myths or new mythical materials developed by its author. This distinction is often blurred in publishing practice, with the terms quite often used interchangeably. A popular modem branch of prose fiction that explores the probable consequences of some improbable or impossible transformation of the basic conditions of human existence. This transformation need not be brought about by a technological invention, but may involve some mutation of known biological or physical reality, e.g. time travel, extraterrestrial invasion, ecological catastrophe Science fiction is a form of literary fantasy or romance that often draws upon earlier kinds of utopian and apocalyptic writing. The term itself was first given general currency by Hugo Gernsback, editor of the American magazine *Amazing Stories* from 1926 onwards, and it is usually abbreviated to SF, before this, such works were called, scientific romances' by H. G. Wells and others. Several early precedents have been claimed for the genre—notably Mary Shelley's *Frankenstein*—but true modern science fiction begins with Jules Verne's *Voyage au centre de la terre* and H. G. Wells's *The Time Machine*. Once uniformly dismissed as pulp trash, SF gained greater respect during the 1950s, as writers like Isaac Asimov, Ray Bradbury, and Arthur C. Clarke expanded its range. SF has also had an important influence on postmodernist fiction by writers not devoted to this genre alone: Thomas Pynchon, Kurt Vonnegut, Doris Lessing, and Italo Calvino are significant examples.

Science Fiction Writers of America: A professional organization of science fiction writers, representing its members in matters of Mutual interest and offering a series of annual awards called the Nebula Awards.

scientific and technical publishing: That branch of publishing concerned with the publication of nonfiction specialist publications for scientific and technical practitioners, teachers, and students, including reference work in those areas a very wide category, which contain's several kinds of content, including many business books, but excluding most lawbooks. Often shortened to *sci-tech.*

scintillation: (1) In HF propagation, short-period variations in received signal strength. (2) Unwanted rapid variations in an *oscillator* frequency, often produced by mechanical variations in the construction of the inductor or capacitor.

Scotchlite: A highly reflective beaded screen material for, reflex *projection.*

scoop: An exciting news story published exclusively or significantly ahead of competitors.

scoring: Partly cutting material, such as printing paper or cover materials, that must later be folded or separated, for later ease of handling. Also called *creasing.*

Scottish Chaucerians: the name given to a group of 15th and 16th—century Scottish poets who wrote under the influence of Geoffrey Chaucer, often using his seven-line rhyme royal stanza. The most important poets of this group were Robert Henryson, whose *Testament of Cresseid* continues and reinterprets the story of Chaucer's *Troilus and Criseyde,* and William Dunbar, whose *Lament for the Makaris* briefly pays tribute to Chaucer. Other figures are Gavin Douglas, Sir David Lyndsay, and King James I of Scotland. The term unfortunately diverts attention from the genuinely original character of these poets, and is thus not much favoured in Scotland.

scout: 1. One who searches for publishable literary properties on behalf of one or more publishing houses, in essence working as a freelance acquisitions editor; usually compensated by the publisher if a recommended property, such as book idea or manuscript, is contracted, and sometimes receiving a small salary or having an account from which to draw against commissions. Also called a *book* Scout. 2. One who locates and supplies books and book-related items to dealers and auctioneers, searching for specified items as well as buying speculatively whenever it seems appropriate. One who does such searching for other collectibles as well is often called a *picker.*

scrape flutter: A fault in magnetic recording resulting from stick/slip motion of the recording tape producing flutter.

scratch filter: In audio disc reproduction, the disc groove which is traversed by the stylus has, with modern discs, smooth walls but never perfectly smooth, and the groove can transmit a 'hiss' signal to the stylus. The effect is particularly pronounced with the older 78 rev/min discs. The energy in the hiss signal is predominantly of high frequency, and a low-pass filter can often be used to effect a compromise between reduction of hiss and loss of high-frequency signals.

scratchback: Technique in which part of the artwork, painted on a cel, is removed frame by frame under the camera while the latter runs backwards.

scratch pad: A temporary memory area used for holding partial results, etc.

screen: (1) A conducting surface, positioned with respect to an electric and/or magnetic field, so as to confine the field(s) within a boundary determined by the screen dimensions. (2) In cathoderay tubes, the surface of the tube, coated with phosphor materials, that is bombarded by the electron beam to produce the visual display.

screened cable: A central conductor, or a number of conductors insulated from an external screen formed by copper braiding or lapping or flexible metal.

screen dumping: Copying the contents of a visual display unit screen to a printer or disk.

screened loop antenna: A loop antenna in which the loop is enclosed in a conducting tube, itself a single-turn loop, in which there is a small gap to prevent circulating currents. Without the screen, a loop antenna behaves in two ways. A incident field will generate a circulating current in the loop, and the field will also generate a voltage in the mass of metal comprising the loop, as it would in a single conductor elevated above ground. By screening the loop, the 'elevated conductor' effect is eliminated without affecting the generation of loop current, providing a gap is introduced in the screening loop.

screamer: A very large and bold newspaper headline. Also called a *scarehead*.

screen: 1. A viewing surface; for example, the surface of a cathode ray tube in a computer system, or a movie screen. 2. A masking device used to eliminate specified areas of an image, such as a halftone screen used in converting a continuous-tone illustration into a halftone, or a screen in screenprocess printing.

screenplay: the script of a film, comprising dialogue with Instructions for sets and camera positions.

screen-process printing: A method of printing surfaces with ink forced through a stencil or screen in which images have been cut, with the ink forming the desired image; called silk screen printing when silk is used as the image-bearing material of the screen. Used most often for imprinting heavy stocks, such as cloth, plastic, and cardboard, which are not easily printed by faster, less expensive methods suitable for printing paper.

script: 1. A copy of the working text used in preparation of a play or film, which may or may not be formally published. 2. A kind of typeface, designed to closely resemble handwriting.

scriptible: a term used by the French critic Roland Barthes in his book S/Z, and usually translated as 'writerly'. In contrast with the easily readable or 'readerly' text the writerly text does not have a single 'closed' meaning: instead, it obliges each reader to produce his or her own meanings from its fragmentary or contradictory hints. Ideally—and the concept is very much a theoretical ideal rather than a description—the writerly text is challengingly open', giving the reader an active role as co-writer rather than as passive consumer. The nearest actual equivalents of this ideal would seem to be the more difficult works of modernism and postmodernism.

scrim: Gauze used to diffuse light. Also metal gauze used to provide protection for bare bulbs.

script: (1) The detailed scene-by-scene instructions for a film or television production, including description of the setting and action with dialogue and camera directions (= *scenario).* (2) A similar treatment for a tapeslide or multivision production. When the script also shows full details of the visuals, it is termed a *story board.*

scroll: (1) Portion of disc surface where the pitch of the grooves has been increased to separate bands. (2) Roll of transparent film for use on an overhead projector.

scrolling: Adding a new line of information and moving the others vertically.

SCR: Silicon Controlled Rectifier. A thyristor.

SECAM: A compatible colour television system in which the luminance signal is produced by amplitude modulation of the vision carrier, with a frequency-modulated sub-carrier providing the colour information. The system was developed in France and is the national standard system for colour television broadcasting. The name is derived from 'Sequential couleur a memoire', which relates to the modulation of alternate lines with the *colour-difference signals,* and their addition after a one-line delay in the receiver.

seal: A soft, durable, high quality, and very expensive leather made from sealskin and used in bookbinding.

search: 1. To locate and access data stored in a computer memory. 2. To look for a hard-to-find publication; a function often performed by a professional search service.

search software: Programming designed to provide access to data stored in a computer memory.

search time: The time taken to complete a search and find the required item or part of the programme.

SECAM: Sequential Couleur A Memoire. Sequential colour with memory. French television system.

second cover: The inside front cover; a preferred advertising position, usually carrying rates higher than those charged for text pages.

second detector: A term formerly used for the demodulator of a *superheterodyne* receiver. 'First detector' was a term for the frequency changer.

secondary emission: Electron emission produced by bombardment of a surface with high-velocity electrons or ions.

secondary emission factor: The ratio of the number of secondary electrons emitted for each primary electron. Different materials have differing factors. Aluminium, for example, has a factor of 4, whereas that for graphite is zero.

secondhand: Describing goods that are sold for a second or subsequent time; can apply to goods unused after original sale, but mainly refers to used goods for sale. Secondhand books may be described as *used* or *secondhand;* when they are valuable because they are scarce or old, they are often called *rare* or *antiquarian.*

secondary radiator: In antennas, that part of an antenna system that is energised by the fields from a primary radiator. Reflector and director elements are secondary radiators, as is an antenna of the form.

secondary service area: In LF and MF broadcasting, the area served by a transmitter in which the field strength ensures satisfactory reception by day, but degrades to acceptable by night.

second serial rights: The right to serialize a work after publication of the work in book form, as covered by contractual provisions in author-publisher contracts. In practice, these are second and subsequent serial rights, as the rights are usually sold on a nonexclusive basis.

secondary battery: A battery composed of secondary cells.

secondary cell: An electro-chemical cell which has to be recharged from a prime source before further electrical energy can be drawn from it.

secondary (transformer): A transformer winding other than the *primary.*

section: One of the subdivisions of a work; may refer to i body of matter within a chapter, and then sometimes introduced by the reference mark, § or to a group of chapters, and then used synonymously with *part.*

segment: In computer graphics, a number of display items which can be manipulated as a single unit.

segmented program: A computer program written in sections, and put into a computer system section by section, rather than all at once, as is usually the case.

segue: An indication that one section of music is to be played immediately after another one; this may be straight cut or cross-fade.

Selectavision: Trade name for a grooved capacitance videodisc system.

self-blimped: Describing a motion picture camera whose operating noise level is so low that no additional soundproof enclosure is necessary.

self clock: A data system requiring only one channel for data and the clock timing needed to receive that data.

Selsyn: Trade name for a servo system.

selection: A book chosen by a book club to be offered or sent to members. A *main selection* is a first-choice offer to members, often sold hard by the club; an *alternate selection* is a second-choice offer, several of which may be offered at once; a multiple offer of two or more books as a single selection is described by the number of books in the offer, as a *dual or* sometimes *triple* or *multiple selection; a* book provided free or for *a* very small charge is called a *book dividend.*

selective fading: In *ionospheric* propagation, a form of fading in which the individual frequency components over a band of frequencies of interest are attenuated unequally by the ionised region, thereby producing distortion of a modulated signal. Fading can be compensated for to a large extent by the use of AGC in the receiver, but distortion due to selective fading cannot.

selectivity: (1) Of a tuned system, the ability to resonate to a single frequency or band of frequencies, and discriminate against, adjacenL frequencies. (a) a single tuned circuit and, at (b) the overall frequency/voltage response for an input signal of constant amplitude and varying frequency. The selectivity is determined by the circuit Q factor (2) Of a receiver, the ability to discriminate between reception of desired signals, and undesired signals on adjacent frequencies. In a *superheterodyne* receiver, the selectivity is provided in two stages. The input selectivity is made adequate to reject signals on the image frequency, but the IF amplifying channel is where the adjacent channel selectivity is provided. The IF tuned circuits are arranged to provide a channel bandwidth for the required signals, and a high degree of rejection to signals from adjacent channels.

self capacitance: The capacitance presented between the terminals of any resistor, inductor, conductor or similar circuit element. The self-capacitance of an inductor is of particular significance if the inductor is to be tuned.

selfcover: A binding in which the front and back covers of the publication are part of the text, having been run through the press as part of a text sheet, falling into place as covers in the process of folding, trimming and binding the publication. Also called *selfwrapper*.

self-help book: A book focusing on the solution of personal problems through self-analysis and remedial activity, as recommended by the book's author, usually in emotional areas, using one or more popular psychological approaches.

self-mailer: A mailing piece that can be addressed and sent without an envelope.

self-oscillating mixer: In a *superheterodyne* receiver, a mixer produced by the local oscillator. The input signal is coupled to the oscillator circuit, which is operating under non-linear conditions and thus produces at a suitable output position, the required difference-frequency signal for processing in the IF amplifier.

self-publishing: The publishing of a work by its author; usually includes marketing and fulfillment responsibilities as well. Although self-publishers often claim they break even, few take into account the cost of their own time and labour.

self-reflexive: a term applied to literary works that openly reflect upon their own processes of artful composition. Such self-referentiality is frequently found in modem works of fiction that repeatedly refer to their own fictional status. The narrator in such works, and in their earlier equivalents such as Sterne's *Tristram* Shandy is sometimes called a 'self-conscious narrator'. Self-reflexivity may also be found often in poetry.

seller's market: A market in which sellers can command higher than normal prices and better than normal conditions because of relatively high demand or short supply.

semantics: the philosophical or linguistic study of meanings in language. The semantic aspect of any expression is its meaning as opposed to its form.

seme: an elementary unit of meaning, usually a defining feature or characteristic of something. A basic description of a person as, e.g, 'white, male, grey-haired, clean-shaven is a listing of semes. Some structuralist studies of fiction have analysed fictional characters in terms of the presence or absence of given semes. *Adjective:* semic.

semiotic: the, a term used by Julia Kristeva in La Revolution du *langage poetique* to designate the flow of pre-linguistic rhythms or pulsions' that is broken up by the child's entry into the Symbolic order of language. The unconscious energies of the semiotic are repressed and marginalized by patriarchal logic and rationality, but they may still disrupt the Symbolic order, transgressing its rigid categories. In Kristeva's psychoanalytic theory, the serniotic is associated with the mother's body, but she detects the anarchic energies of the serniotic in the writings of both female and male authors, especially those of the Symbolist and modernist avant-garde.

semiotics or semiology: the systematic study of signs, or more precisely, of the production of meanings from sign-systems, linguistic or non-linguistic. As a distinct tradition of inquiry into human communications sermiotics was founded by the American philosopher C. S. Peirce and separately by the Swiss linguist Ferdinand de Saussure, who proposed that linguistics would form one part of a more general science of signs: 'Semiology'. Peirce's term serniotics' is usually preferred in English, although Saussure's principles and concepts—especially the distinctions between signifier and signified and between *langue* and *parole*—have been more influential as the basis of structuralism and its approach to literature. Semlotics is concerned not with the relations between signs and things but with the interrelationships between signs themselves, within their structured systems or codes of signification. The semiotic approach to literary works stresses the production of literary meanings from shared conventions and codes: but the scope of serniotics goes beyond spoken or written language to other kinds of communicative systems such as cinema, advertising, clothing, gesture, and cuisine. A practitioner of serniotics is a semiotician. The term semiosis is sometimes used to refer to the process of signifying. For a fuller account, consult Terence Hawkes, Structuralism and Serniotics.

Senecan tragedy: a form of tragedy developed by the Roman philosopher-poet Lucius Annaeus Seneca in his nine plays based on Greek drama and further adapted by playwrights of the Italian, French, and English Renaissance. Seneca's plays were almost certainly closet dramas intended for recitation rather than stage performance. Composed in five acts with intervening choruses, they employ long rhetorical speeches, with important actions being recounted by messengers. Their bloodthirsty plots, including ghosts and horrible crimes, appealed to the popular English dramatists of the late 16th century, who presented such horrors on stage in their revenge tragedies. These were preceded by a purer form of English Senecan tragedy, notably in Thomas Norton and Thomas Sackville's Gorboduc, the first English tragedy. The conventional five-act structure of Renaissance drama owes its origin to the influence of Seneca.

sensation novel: a kind of novel that flourished in Britain in the 1860s. exploiting the element of suspense in stories of crime and mystery. The most successful examples are William Wilkie Collins's *The* Woman in White and Mary Elizabeth Braddon's *Lady Audley's* Secret.

sensibility: an important 18th-century term designating a kind of sensitivity or responsiveness that is both aesthetic and moral, showing a capacity to feel both for others' sorrows and for beauty. The term is also used in a different sense in modern criticism, the sensibility of a given writer being his or her characteristic way of responding—intellectually and emotionally—to experience. Its major significance, though, is as a concept or mood of 18th-century culture. *In* terms of moral philosophy, it signalled a reaction against Thomas Hobbes's view of human behaviour as essentially selfish: the 3rd Earl of Shaftesbury and other l8th-century thinkers argued that human beings have an innate 'benevolence' or sympathy for others. In literature, the quality of sensibility was explored and displayed in the 'novel of sensibility' in sentimental comedy, in graveyard poetry, and in the poems of William Cowper among others. The cult of sensibility is also apparent in late l8th-century primitivism and in the new interest in the sublime. At its self-indulgent extremes later criticized by Jane Austen in *Sense and Sensibility*—it is called sentimentalism. It was one of the cultural trends that gave rise to Romanticism. For a fuller account, consult Janet Todd.

sensitivity: (1) Of a receiver, the characteristics that determine the minimum input signal level necessary to provide a specified output signal/noise ratio, measured under specified conditions. (2) A general term for the response to an electronic control signal. For example, a diode, used as a capacitance for tuning purposes, might have its sensitivity expressed in terms of the control voltage, i.e. in pF/V. (3) In television camera tubes, the signal output can be expressed in terms of incident light, e.g. in A/ln.

sententia: a Latin term for an aphorism or maxim. Its English adjective, sententious, usually has a pejorative sense, referring to a style or statement that is condescending or self-important in giving advice; but it may be used neutrally to mean aphoristic'.

sentimental comedy: a kind of comedy that achieved some popularity with respectable middle-class audiences in the 18th century. In contrast with the aristocratic cynicism of English Restoration comedy, i, showed virtue rewarded by domestic bliss; its plots, usually involving unbelievably good middle-class couples, emphasized pathos rather than humour. Pioneered by Richard Steele in *The Funeral* and more fully in *The* Conscious *Lovers,* it flourished in mid-century with the French *comidie larmoyante* and in such plays as Hugh Kelly's *False Delicacy*. The pious moralizing of this tradition, which survived into 19th-century melodrama, was opposed in the 1770s by Sheridan and Goldsmith, who attempted a partial return to the comedy of manners.

sentimental novel: an emotionally extravagant novel of a kind that became popular in Europe in the late 18th century. Partly inspired by the emotional power of Samuel Richardson's *Pamela, or Virtue Rewarded,* the sentimental novels of the 1760s and 1770s exhibit the close connections between virtue and sensibility, in repeatedly tearful scenes; a character's feeling for the beauties of nature and for the griefs of others is taken as a sign of a pure heart. An excessively sentimental example is Henry Mackenzie's *The Man* of *Feeling,* but Oliver Goldsmith's *The Vicar* of *Wakefield* and Laurence Sterne's *A Sentimental journey* are more ironic in Europe, the most important sentimental novels were J.J. Rousseau's *La Nouvelle Hiloise* and J.W. von Goethe's *The Sorrows of Young Werther*. The fashion lingered on in the early Gothic novels of Ann Radcliffe in the 1790s.

separate luminance camera: In colour television, a camera in which the luminance signal is derived separately from the colour signal tubes, by means of its own tube.

septet: a stanza of seven lines, such as the English rhyme royal stanza.

sequential access: Ability to locate data within a computer only by reading through the stored data in sequence, in contrast to random *access*.

sequential colour television: A system in which the primary colour signals are transmitted sequentially. See *field sequential system*.

sequential scanning: In television, a system in which the scanning lines follow a successive line-by-line sequence from top to bottom of the picture.

serisitometry: The scientific study and measurement of the effect of light on photographic materials, especially the relation between exposure and the resultant density after processing.

serial: 1. Any periodically issued work that has no defined limit to the number of its issues, such as magazines, newsletters, looseleaf services, and annuals, and sometimes including works appearing at intervals of more than a year. 2. A multi-part work, in periodical or broadcast form.

serialization: The running of a work in parts in a periodical, as when a forthcoming book is run as a series of articles prior to or concurrently with book publication in a newspaper or magazine.

series: A group of books or booklets on a single subject or theme, with common physical characteristics and formats and often carrying the name of one or more general editors.

serif: Characterizing any typeface which has tendrils or strokes called *serifs* projecting from the ends of letters, at angles different from those of the letters. Serif typefaces usually have varying letter body thicknesses, in contrast to *sans serif* typefaces, which usually have even thicknesses and have no serifs.

service area: Of a broadcast transmitter, the area around the transmitter within which the field-strength is at or above a minimum planned value.

service area diagram: In broadcasting, a diagram showing a boundary defining an area within which a transmitter provides a prescribed field strength.

service charge: A special charge for services performed, beyond the price paid for goods or services; for example, a bookseller's charge for a rush order of a book.

separation: Acoustic isolation between instruments essential to a certain degree in multitrack recording to give control over relative balance between instruments.

sepmag: A magnetic sound record, on tape or perforated film separate from the picture film with which it is associated.

sequential access: A mode of data retrieval where each byte of data is recovered in the order in which it was written to the disk.

serial communication: A data communication scheme needing only one wire (and return) where the data is sent one bit at a time.

servo: A control system involving feedback, which operates ' to correct any error between the input and an output sensor.

sestet: a group of six verse fines forming the second part of a sonnet following the opening octave. More rarely, the term may refer to a stanza of six lines, such as the Burns stanza or the stanza used in a sestina. Sestina a poem of six 6-line stanzas and a 3-line envoi linked by an intricate pattern of repeated line-endings. The most elaborate of the medieval French fixed forms, It uses only six repeating them in a different order in each stanza so that the ending of the last fine in each stanza recurs as the ending of the first line in the next. The *envoi* uses all six words, three of them as line-endings. The established pattern of repetition for the six stanzas is as follows: 1-ABCDEF, 2-FAEBDC, 3-CFDABE, 4-ECBFAD. 5-DEACFB, 6-BDFECA. The form was introduced into English by Sir Philip Sidney in his *Arcadia*. A modern example is W. H. Auden's 'Paysage Moralise. Even more remarkable as a technical feat is A. C. Swinburne's 'The Complaint of, a rhyming double sestina with twelve 12-line stanzas and a 6-line *envoi*.

set: 1. To compose matter, although Originally describing composition using metal type, the term now refers to any form of composition. 2. A group of related books, sold as a single unified whole, *although* also often available individually; may be any combination of books SO described by their publisher, such as the works of a single author or multiple parts of the same work, like the volumes of an encyclopedia.

set level: A continuous tone at exactly signalling level, used to adjust recording level. It is used in multivision control systems.

set-off: During a press run, the unintentional transfer of wet ink from a recently printed sheet to the back of the sheet below it; occurs when the stock has not properly absorbed the ink or the inking is too heavy. Also called *offset.*

set solid: Describing type that is set on a body of the same size, without leading, or spacing; for example, 10 points type set on a 10 point body is set solid.

set-top converter: In cabled distribution systems, an apparatus, connected between the system outlet and a receiver, for converting the system frequencies to those suitable for the receiver.

set up: (1) The complete system. (2) In motion picture production, the arrangement of setting, actors, lights, microphones and cameras ready to record a scene; also, a specific camera position. (3) To get into a state of readiness to operate. (4) In a TV system, to differentiate between zero level or true black, and the actual black level of the reproduced picture.

sewing: In bookbinding, the use of thread to Join publication sheets or leaves together; although still done by hand in some binding operations, mainly a machine process. Most modem books use the *Smythe sewing* method, which uses a continuous thread to sew each signature together through the fold of the sheets in the signature, and to join all the signatures in the book together side by side. For greater strength, as needed by such hard-used publications as children's books and some texts, the *side sewing* method is used, with all signatures and leaves joined together by threads sewn through the side of the book through the gutter; the binding is then very strongly sewn, but the book cannot lie flat. *Saddle stitching,* in which stitches are placed vertically through the spine of folded signatures, once a common sewing process, is now largely a mechanical binding method, using staples instead of thread. Sewing is sometimes called *stitching,* but in modem usage that term usually refers to mechanical binding.

sex differential: Differences in pay for substantially similar work Performed by men and women, with women receiving less pay than men because of sex discrimination; an illegal Practice.

sex discrimination: Discrimination against those of one sex in favour of another an illegal practice, although often difficult to prove; for example, failure to hire qualified women for sales jobs because they are women, even though some other reason is alleged by the employer.

SFD: Society of Film Distributors (UK).

SFX: Sound effects.

shading: In television, distortion of a picture signal whereby an unwanted variation in luminance takes place over the picture area. Some camera tubes generate shading, and shading correction signals can be inserted into the signal output.

shadow area: In VHF and UHF broadcasting, term sometimes used for a region within a service area, which has an obstruction between receiving sites and the transmitter, resulting in a degree of shielding and a reduced signal strength at the receivers.

shadowboard: A black board suspended below the camera on an animation stand, containing a hole through which the lens protrudes to prevent reflection of the camera in the platen glass.

shadow box: A box drawn to enclose copy, that creates a three-dimensional illusion, often through weighted or wavy lines

shadowmask: A display tube for colour TV having a mosaic of *RGB* phosphors to which the electron beam is directed through a perforated metal screen.

shadow-mask tube: In colour television, a three-gun display tube in which the colour cells are masked by a metal sheet. Holes in the sheet ensure that the three electron beams are directed to their appropriate colour phosphors.

shakeout: A business or financial trend forcing some companies into troubled business positions, and others out of business, as when companies which have been weakened by not moving with new technology and market conditions find their competitive positions undermined and are therefore unusually vulnerable to adverse economic conditions, or when a group of small new companies in a rapidly developing new field find undercapitalization and overexpansion a disabling combination when interest rates are high and investment money hard to find.

shannon: Unit of information in a *binary* system.

sharpness: The clarity and definition of line achieved by printed Material, especially illustrative maternal.

Shavian: characteristic of the work of the frish playwright George Bernard Shaw.

shaving: Trimming a book's contents so closely as to cut into the top or bottom type on the page.

shedding: Magnetic recording material losing particles from its magnetic coating.

sheet: Any single piece of material, usually paper, on which printing is placed. Also see *in sheets.*

sheet-fed: Describing a printing press in which the stock to be printed is fed into the press in sheets, rather than from a continuous roll which is cut into sheets after printing.

shelf life: 1. The length of time materials can be stored without deterioration; for example, the length of time before papers and other printing materials become dry, or before chemically treated materials deteriorate, and thereby become unusable. 2. The length of time a publication is kept by a retail bookseller, before being returned to its publisher for credit, when returns privileges apply.

SHF: Super High Frequency, 3 GHz30 GHz.

shielding: In Computer graphics, defining an opaque *window* in which to display a message.

shift register: A series of *bistables* capable of storing and transmitting a pattern of ones and zeros, one bit at a time at each *clock pulse.*

shield law: A statute providing reporters, authors, and others engaged in legitimate news-gathering activities with protection of the confidentiality of their sources of information as against judicial and executive attack; such statutes exist or are proposed in a number of states.

shingling: To create a composed page out of many small pieces of composed material by overlapping; for example, when a library card file is transferred to microform, the print area on each card is captured and the white area covered by the printed copy on other overlapped cards.

shipping charges: Costs incurred for the shipment of goods to purchasers, as when a publisher incurs charges for shipments to booksellers. Such charges may be absorbed by the publisher or passed on to the purchaser; a matter of considerable long-term contention between publishers and booksellers.

shoot: To operate a camera.

short end: The portion of a roll of film or magnetic tape remain ing after the main part has been used.

short story: a fictional prose tale of no specified length, but too short to be published as a volume on its own, as novellas sometimes and novels usually are. A short story will normally concentrate on a single, event with only one or two characters more economically than a novel's sustained exploration of social background. There are similar fictional forms of greater antiquity—fables, lais, folktales, and' parables—but the short story as we know it flourished in the magazines of the 19th and early 20th centuries, especially in the USA, which has a particularly strong tradition.

shot: A scene photographed or record as one continuous action.

shot effect or shot noise: Noise due to a random fluctuation of current about a mean value.

shotgun microphone: A highly directional microphone.

short discount: Any discount that is smaller than a normal trade book discount offered by publishers to booksellers and jobbers; scientific, technical, business, law, and other professional books often carry considerably smaller discounts than do trade books.

short page: A page set with fewer lines of type than the full normal depth of the page; for example, the last page in a chapter.

short run: A job consisting of relatively few impressions for the shop running it, as when a small job shop runs 100 copies of a leaflet, or a much larger shop runs several thousand impressions, rather than the hundreds of thousands of impressions it is accustomed to running.

short story: A brief story, not long enough to stand alone as a book, and shorter than a full novel; whether to call a medium-length story a short story, a novella, or a short novel is often purely a matter 'of choice by authors, editors, and publishers, there being no firm distinctions between the categories.

show copy: A selected copy of a completed programme, video, tapeslide, multivision or film, intended for presentation to an audience. For a motion picture production it is often termed a *show print*.

shows: in addition to its initial trochaic inversion, a metrical variation at the end, which would be described in traditional prosody as the substitution of a pyrrhic and a spondee for the final two iambs. Some more modem theories of versification, however, have rejected the concept of the foot and along with it that of substitution, accounting for such metrical variations in terms of demotion, promotion, and the 'pairing' of stressed and unstressed syllables. In this view, the ending of Keats's line illustrates a permissible variation in English iambic verse, whereby the occurrence of two stressed syllables together can be compensated by the pairing of two unstressed syllables. In Greek and Latin quantitative verse, some kinds of substitution are governed by the principle of 'equivalence' whereby one long syllable is equal to two short syllables, so that under certain conditions a spondee, for example, can stand in for a dactyl.

shred: To physically destroy printed materials by putting them through a shredding machine, usually as part of reconversion back to pulp for reuse. More generally, the term has come to mean the physical destruction of printed materials by any means.

shunt: (1) To connect two components in parallel, e.g. a resistor placed across an ammeter to increase its range. (2) To place a load across terminals.

shutter: A device to cut off light in an optical instrument, particularly (1) In a camera where it is opened and closed to effect the exposure. (2) In motion picture equipment, a rotating blade which interrupts the light in a camera or projector while the film pulldown occurs. (3) In slide projection, a device to cut off the light while the slide is being changed or if there is no slide in position. See also *snap.*

shuttle search: The ability to play back a film, video or audio-tape in either direction and reproduce the picture over a wide range of speeds.

SIAD: Society of Industrial Artists and Designers.

sibilance: the marked recurrence of the 'hissing' sounds known as sibilants. The effect, also kjiown as sigmatism ;ifter the Greek letter *sigma, is* often exploited in poetry, as in Long-fellow's lines

Ships that pass in the night, and speak each other in passing;
Only a signal shown and a distant voice in the darkness

sic: A word, generally enclosed in brackets, inserted in quoted material to indicates at a seerling error in form or content either was intended by the original author or occurred in the original source, and was not introduced in the current work; from the Latin, meaning "thus" or "so."

sideband: A range of frequencies generated by modulating a carrier wave. A range of frequencies generated by modulation of a carrier wave with signals such as speech, music or video.

side-frequency: A single frequency component of a sideband, or one of the side frequencies resulting from *amplitude modulation* of a carrier wave with a sinusoidal signal. With sinewave amplitude modulation of a carrier, side frequencies are generated, one higher and the other lower than the carrier frequency, spaced from the carrier by a frequency equal to the modulating frequency. Frequency modulation of a carrier with a single sinewae signal results in the generation of an infinite range of side frequencies, extending to zero on one side of the carrier, and to infinity on the other, spaced from the carrier and each other by the frequency of the modulation. Fortunately the more remote side frequencies are of such a low level that they can be ignored but, for good quality reception, it is necessary to use a number ot side frequencies in the channel. The side frequencies necessary for good quality reproduction of a 15 kHz signal using a deviation of 75 kHz, and their relative amplitude.

sidehead: A heading that appears above its following body of copy, but flush left or somewhat indented rather than centered.

side lobe: In antennas, a lobe in the radiation pattern, other than the main forward lobe and any back lobe.

side lock: In colour television receivers, a fault condition whereby the receiver *colour sub-carrier* generator locks on to a side frequency instead of the *burst* frequency. The sub-carrier is modulated by the line scanning frequency and thus produces side frequencies spaced at integral multiples of the line frequency on either side of the sub-carrier frequency.

sidestitching: A kind of mechanical binding, in which wire or staple stitches are set into a publication near its spine to hold its contents; when a work so bound is opened, it cannot lie flat.

siemens: Unit of *e* equivalent to mho.

sign: a basic element of communication, either linguistic or non-linguistic; or anything that can be construed as having a meaning. According to the influential theory of the Swiss linguist Ferdinand de Saussure, every sign has two inseparable aspects: the signifier, which is the materially perceptible component such as a sound or written mark, and the signified, which is the conceptual meaning. In a linguistic sign, according to Saussure, the relationship between signifier and signified is 'unmotivated' or arbitrary, that is, it is based purely on social convention rather than on natural necessity: there is nothing about a horse which demands that it be called 'horse', since the French call the same thing tin cheval. Saussure's theory deliberately leaves out the referent or real external object referred to by a sign. The alternative theory of the American philosopher C. S. Peirce has more room for referents and for motivated' signs. Peirce calls the unmotivated sign a symbol, while identifying two further kinds of sign: the icon, which resembles its referent, and the index, which is caused by its referent. *Verb: signify.*

signal: The electrical characteristics of voltage or current changes that transmitted over a suitable path, convey information or exercise a control function.

signal adapter: In HF cabled distribution systems, a device for processing distributed signals so that they are suitable for receivers designed for VHF or UHF reception.

signal generator: General term for a particular range of equipment, generating signals suitable for measurements and test of systems, equipment or components. A signal generator is, basically a generator of an AC voltage, controllable with respect to frequency and amplitude. An RF signal generator covers a specified range of frequencies and usually includes provision modulating the generated RF voltage.

signal slicer: A form of limiter with two boundary values, the amplitudes between the slicing values being transmitted.

signal tilt: In *cabled distribution systems,* a difference in level between signals in a band of frequencies, at any point in system. When a band of signals is launched into a cable network the higher frequencies in the band experience greater attenuation, than the lower frequencies as the signals traverse the network This tilt can be compensated by an equalising network, or when relaunched by an amplifier.

signal-to-noise ratio: The relationship of the wanted signal to the unwanted interference, usually expressed in dB. In television the interference is referred to as 'noise' though it cannot be heard, but is roughly equivalent to graininess on a photographic picture.

signature: A single sheet of printed material, usually paper, which is printed on both sides and which when folded and trimmed becomes a set of consecutive leaves and pages, as when a single sheet printed on both sides and folded once becomes a two-leaf, four-page signature, or a single sheet folded four times becomes a sixteen-leaf, thirty-two page signature.

signified: the conceptual component of a sign, as distinct from its material form, the signifier. The signified, also known in French as the *signi*fie, is the idea conventionally indicated by the signifier, rather than the actual external object or referent.

signifier: the concretely perceptible component of a sign, as distinct from its conceptual meaning. In language, this may be a meaningful sound, or a written mark such as a letter or sequence of letters making up a word. The term often appears in its French form, signifiant.

SIL: Single-In-Line. A type of integrated component construction.

silver-fork novel: a kind of novel that was popular in Britain from the 1820s to the 1840s, and was marked by concentration upon the fashionable etiquette and manners of high society. The term was used mockingly by critics of the time, and has been applied to works by Theodore Hook, Catherine Gore, Frances Trollope, Lady Caroline Lamb, Benjamin Disraeli, and Susan Ferrier.

simile: an explicit comparison between two different things, actions, or feelings, using the words 'as' or 'like', as in Wordsworth's line:

I wandered lonely as a cloud

A very common figure of speech in both prose and verse, simile is more tentative and decorative than metaphor. A lengthy and more elaborate kind of simile, used as a digression in a narrative work, is the epic simile.

simple PAL: In colour television, a decoding process for the PAL system that relies on the eye of the observer for optically-integrating the switched, line-by-line hue errors.

simplex channel: A communications channel capable of carrying only one body of information, in contrast to a *multiplex* channel, which is capable of carrying two or more bodies of information simultaneously.

Simul-sync: A method of avoiding the time delay caused by the distance between the recording and replay heads on a tape recorder by replaying from the record head.

simultaneous colour television: A system in which the primary colour signal components are transmitted simultaneously, as distinct from a *sequential* system. NTSC, PAL and *SECAM* are examples of simultaneous systems.

SINAD: Signal to Noise And Distortion.

sine-squared pulse: A pulse having a shape equal to the square of one half-cycle of a sinewave. The pulse is defined by y = K sin^2 where 2T is the duration of the pulse, K is the amplitude and t lies between 0 and 2T. The half-amplitude duration of the pulse is then T. The frequency spectrum of the pulse, from which it is seen that, for a video bandwidth 5 MHz or so, as in the UK System 1, a T test pulse has most of its energy outside the frequency range of interest. For this reason, a 2T pulse, with virtually all its energy in the band of interest, is used for most tests.

sine wave: Waveform showing variation in a simple harmonic manner.

single copy order: An order from a bookseller or a direct purchaser to a publisher for a single copy of a book; some trade publishers regard fulfillment of such orders inordinately costly, although many professional and reference publishers, selling more expensive books and organized to handle such orders, regard them as an essential and indispensable part of their business.

single frame: (1) One individual image in a strip of images. (2) To expose or project one picture at a time at a comparatively slow rate.

single hop: In *ionospheric* propagation, a communications link between transmitter and receiver using a single path, earth-ionosphere-earth. Long-distance paths involve multiple hops by reflection from the ground back to the ionosphere

single outlet store: A retail seller with only one place of business, as is true of most independent bookstores.

single shot: Exposing film, one frame at a time, as in animation work.

single-sideband transmission: A system of transmission in which only the upper or lower sideband, produced as a result of *amplitude modulation, is* transmitted. With this system the carrier is either wholly or partially suppressed. For envelope demodulation it is necessary to re-insert the carrier which, is either locally generated or, if partially suppressed, is extracted amplified and re-inserted at high level. There are three main advantages arising from SSB operation. Only half of the DS bandwidth is occupied and, as a result, selective fading effects are less serious. Power consumption takes place only during modulation.

single standard: A TV monitor, video tape recorder or other equipment, capable of accepting video signals of only one standard, *NTSC, PAL* or *SECAM.*

single system: Method of motion picture production in which both picture and sound are simultaneously recorded on the same strip of film.

single-wire transmission line: A *waveguide* consisting of a single conductor, coated with a dielectric material.

sink: Term for a thermal radiating system intended to extract heat by conduction from a heat-generating surface and disperse it b radiation from a large area.

sinkage: The amount of space left blank at the top of a page, beyond the margins normal for the work, as at the start of a chapter or for graphic material that will not occupy a full page.

sixteenmo (16mo): An American book size, approximately 6"—7", high.

sixtyfourmo (64mo): An American book size, approximately 3"—3½" high.

sizing: A glazing or coating material, such as starch, glue, or clay, which is used to make materials less porous, as when applied to printing paper or book cloth. Also the process of applying such material. Also called size.

sjuzet: the term used in Russian Formalism to denote the plot of a narrative work, as opposed to the events of its story. The *sjuzet is* the finished arrangement of narrated events as they are presented to the reader, rather than the sequence of such events as reconstructed in their 'true' sequence and duration.

skald: an Old Norse word for a poet, usually applied to a Norwegian or Icelandic court poet or bard of the period from the 9th century to the 13th. Skaldic verse is marked by its elaborate patterns of metre, rhyme, and alliteration, and by its use of kennings.

Skeltonics: verses written in the manner favoured by John Skelton, whose lively satirical poems use irregular short fines of two or three stresses, and often extend the same rhyme over several consecutive lines. A similar effect of vivid colloquial wordplay is often found in modem dub poetry.

sketch: a short composition, dramatic, narrative, or descriptive. In the theatre, a sketch is a brief, self-contained dramatic scene usually comic.

As a kind of prose narrative, a sketch is more modest than a short story, showing less development in plot or characterization. The term is also applied to brief descriptions of people or places.

skew: Picture distortion in which the verticals are not at right angles to the horizontals. In video recording it can result from mechanical error in the tape motion or tension. The term also refers to the non simultaneous arrival of data on several data lines.

skid: A large wooden or metal platform, so constructed as to be movable by machine, used to store and stack materials, such as books in a warehouse or stock in a printing shop.

skin effect: An effect experienced in a conductor carrying an alternating current. The current tends to concentrate on the outside surface of the conductor to an increasing degree as the frequency is raised, and this reduction of the area through which the current is passing has the effect of raising the resistance.

skip area: In *ionospheric* propagation, a zone round a transmitting radiator in *which skip distance is* experienced.

skip distance: In *ionospheric* propagation, the minimum ground distance from a transmitting radiator at which radio waves of a specific frequency can be received, in a specified direction, at a particular state of ionisation. Within this distance there is a so-called 'silent zone', ranging from the region where the ground-wave ceases to be useful, out to the point where the wave is first returned from the ionosphere. Signals can usually be received within the silent zone due to *scattering*, but they will be of low field-strength compared with the returned wave.

skip frame: In cinematography, printing only frames selected at regular intervals from the original record to produce the effect of speeding up action.

slander: Malicious spoken defamation of the character of another of actionable at law, which must be provable through evidence given by other than the one defamed; contrasts with libel, which must be published.

slate: Chart or board with information regarding the production, its title, scene and take numbers, etc., reproduced at the beginning or end of each *take* photographed on film or recorded on tape.

slant polarisation: In antennas and propagation, a form of *polarisation* in which the electric field can be resolved into vertical and horizontal components. This type of polarisation is used by some VHF, FM sound tranmitters, and has similar advantages to *circular* or *elliptic polarisation* for this type of broadcasting; namely, it is possible to use either vertical or horizontal receiving antennas.

slave: A unit designed to function only as ordered by a 'master' unit, e.g. a videotape recorder that is controlled by another VTR.

slavelock (to): In television broadcasting, to synchronise video signals derived from remote and local sources, at the mixing point. The local pulse generator controls the remote generator.

slave narrative: a written account by an escaped or freed slave of his or her experiences of slavery. A special American form of autobiography, the slave narrative appeared as an important kind of abolitionist literature in the period preceding the Civil War. The outstanding example is the *Narrative of the Life of Frederick Douglass.*

sleeper: Something unexpectedly popular, such as a book that suddenly catches buying attention or a moving picture that becomes an unexpected hit.

slew rate: Rate of change of voltage.

slide: The complete assembly of a still picture transparency in a mount, which may also contain a mask.

slide mount: A metal or plastic receptacle, often glazed, for holding a picture image on film.

slider: A form of potentiometer.

sliding frequency: Also known as *gliding frequency.*

slit: In photographic sound, a narrow aperture through which the film is exposed in recording and scanned in reproduction.

slit loss: In photographic sound, the reduction in amplitude at higher frequencies which results from the finite height of the slit in recorder or reproducer. Note that slit height is measured in the direction of film travel.

slick magazine: A magazine printed on a very glossy stock; normally rather expensively printed, and featuring considerable illustration. Such magazines as a group are also called *slicks.*

slide: A photographic print carrying a single image, capable of being shown by projection.

slidefilm: A filmstrip, composed of many slides, often accompanied by a soundtrack; commonly used in educational and training materials.

sliding scale: A schedule in which one value varies according to changes in another, often at specified break points; for example, the increase of an author's royalties according to the volume of books sold, or an increase in a discount according to number of books purchased. Sometimes called a *graduated scale.*

slip: In television, term sometimes used for partial loss of line or field *synchronism.*

slipease: A book box or bag, open at one end; if a bag, often one made of transparent plastic.

slip sheet: The placement of leaves of paper or other material between newly printed leaves, to prevent set-off or *offsetting,* which is the deposit of unabsorbed ink from one printed sheet to the back of another sheet, or to separate bodies of printed material.

slope: Steepness of filter curves normally expressed in dB/octave.

slope: (1) Relating to the frequency/amplitude response of systems or devices. For example, the attenuation regions of low, high or bandpass filters will have a slope, often expressed as so many decibels per octave. (2) In cabled distribution systems.

slope defector: A form of demodulator for a frequency-modulated signal.

slot array: An array of slot radiators. Slots cut into the skin of mobile vehicles, or in a cylindrical tower structure, can often form more convenient antenna arrays than can be obtained by the erection of dipoles.

slot-fed dipole: A half-wave dipole, fed symmetrically at the centre by connecting the two quarter-wave halves to the outer conductor of a transmission line. The line outer conductor has a slot, a quarter wavelength long between the points of attachment for the antenna. One form of a slot fed dipole. The inner conductor of the transmission line is connected to the outer conductor as shown, at a suitable point to effect impedance matching.

slot loading: Mechanism where tape or film can be loaded laterally instead of lacing or threading.

slot radiator: A slot in a conducting sheet, acting as a radiator. Slot, cut from a sheet having linear dimensions very large compared with the wavelength. It will be noted that the metal removed from the sheet could become a half-wave dipole. A plan view of (a) and the radiation pattern of the electric field that would be obtained from a slot in a sheet of finite dimensions. A vertical slot radiates a horizontal electric field and a vertical magnetic field. The feed-point impedance for the slot is about 470 ohms.

There are two main practical points concerning slot radiators. Firstly, the high feed-point impedance can be reduced by using a 'folded slot'; the folded dipole is similarly used for impedance changing. Secondly, there is seldom a need for radiation from both sides of the slot, and one side can be boxed-in to produce a unidirectional radiation pattern from the open side of the slot.

slo-mo: Abbreviation for *slow motion.*

slotted line: A length of co-axial *line,* in the wall of which is a longitudinal slot, through which a probe can be inserted to determine the field configuration within the line. Used for measurements of impedance, SWR, etc. The probe is mounted on a carriage so that it can traverse the slot and be used to measure the field intensity at measured linear intervals along the line.

slow-scan television: A system of image transmission and reception, using similar methods to broadcast television, but at a much slower rate. Scanning is usually sequential, and a complete field may take several seconds to complete, the display being produced by a tube having a long-persistance screen By adjusting picture rate and definition it is possible to reduce the channel bandwidth to a value within 3 kHz. The system is thus usable over normal telephone and radio speech links.

slow motion: Photography by a motion picture camera with the film running faster than normal, so that when the result is projected at normal speed, the action appears to be slowed down.

slug: 1. A line of type, cast from a single piece of metal. 2. A piece or strip of metal used to provide spacing in metal type composition; sometimes used more widely to describe any spacing wider than that resulting from leading of one to three points. Also called a *slugline.*

slushpile: A body of unsolicited manuscripts in the hands of a publisher or agent; though in form a term of derogation, in fact a prime source of salable material for many agents and publishers. Many trade publishers now rely upon agents to read unsolicited manuscripts, but many professional and reference publishers continue to derive significant numbers of new books from such unsolicited, or over-the-transom, manuscripts. Also called slush.

smearing: In television, term for a distortion of picture signal voltage transitions, whereby a vertical edge between white and black generates a trailing slow voltage change instead of a sharp transition.

Smith chart: A graphical method for the determination of impedance, reactance and phase, based on the relationship (a) is the angle relationship between resistance, reactance and impedance. At (b) A normalised value for impedance as the diameter of a circle, positions such as A, B and C can indicate the effects of a change in frequency, and the relative values of reactance and resistance.

smoothing: Term for minimising the ripple in a DC supply which is derived from an AC supply and a rectifying system.

SMPTE: Society of Motion Picture & Television Engineers (USA).

S/N: Signal-to-Noise (ratio).

snap: A very rapid picture change effect achieved with the use of shutters in slide projectors.

Snell's law: Relating to the change of ray path direction at a boundary between two media with differing refractive. The ratio of the sines of the incident and refracted angles equals the ratio of the refractive index of the second medium to that of the first. Of considerable value in dealing with radio wave propagation in the *ionosphere.*

SNOBOL: A computer language that is especially useful in dealing with symbolic equations, and especially strings, which are sets of symbols that are to remain exactly as they appear in a program and are usually enclosed in quotation marks for identification; an acronym for string-oriented symbolic language.

snoot: Conical hood to reduce the width of the beam from a light source.

snow: In television picture display, term for the visual effect of *noise* on the displayed picture.

soak test: A test on equipment or components, involving prolonged operation under normal operational conditions.

socialist realism: a slogan adopted by the Soviet cultural authorities in 1934 to summarize the requirements of Stalinist dogma in literature:

the established techniques of 19th-century realism were to be used to represent the struggle for socialism in a positive, optimistic fight, while the allegedly 'decadent' techniques of modernism were to be avoided as bourgeois deviations. The approved model was Maxim Gorky's novel.

Society of Children's Book Writers: A professional organization of writers of children's books, representing its members in matters of mutual interest and offering annual book awards.

Society of Illustrators: A professional organization of illustrators representing its members in matters of mutual interest and offering annual awards in the graphic arts.

sociology of literature: a branch of literary study that examines the relationships between literary works and their social contexts, including patterns of literacy, kinds of audience, modes of publication and dramatic presentation, and the social class positions of authors and readers. Originating in 19th-century France with works by Mme de Stael and Hippolyte Taine, the sociology of literature was revived in the English-speaking world with the appearance of such studies is Raymond Williams's *The Long Revolution,* and is most often associated with Marxist approaches to cultural analysis.

Socratic: pertaining to the Greek philosopher Socrates. His manner of feigning ignorance in order to expose the self-contradictions of his interlocutors through cross-examination is known as Socratic irony. Ms method of seeking the truth by such processes of question-and-answer is illustrated in the Socratic *Dialogues* of his follower, Plato.

SOF: Sound-On-Film. Term used to indicate synchronised picture and sound on film.

soft edge: A diffuse or graduated boundary to a picture image area, as in *matte* or *wipe* effects.

soft-edged masks: Graduated neutral density masks used in slide mounts to blend adjacent projected images imperceptibly so that very large composite images can be made without visible joins.

soft focus: Producing an image with less than the maximum sharpness of which the system is capable.

software: (1) The program of instructions which the hardware of a computer obeys. (2) The audio and visual programme material used in AV productions. The programmes, routines and documentation for computers and data processing equipment.

soft copy: 1. News material that is somewhat short on hard facts and long on uncorroborated speculation 2. Copy that is not yet cameraready in form, though it may be complete in content. 3. Copy supplied in impermanent, rather than permanent form; for example, an on-screen printout that is not captured on paper.

soft typesetting: In computerized composition, the production of composed material on an editing screen for examination, but without commitment to actual production of typesetting; images so produced can either be erased or composed.

software package: A body of programming data, and related materials designed for computer use. In publishing, often a computerized database, with programming related to storage in and retrieval of data from the computer memory in which the database is stored, and related print materials, such as indexes, catalogues, directories, and looseleaf reporters.

solar cell: A photoelectric device that converts incident radiation from the sun into electrical energy.

solarisation: Originally, a photographic effect in which the picture image is partially reversed in tone with light or dark edges at highlight and shadow boundaries; a similar effect produced by video methods.

solecism: a grammatical error or, more loosely, any mistake that exposes the perpetrator's ignorance. *Adjective:* solecistic.

sole proprietorship: A major form of ownership, in which a single person is the only owner of a business, and carries both unlimited rights and liabilities in regard to that business.

solid state: Not using liquids or gases, hence semiconductor technology generally.

soliloquy: a dramatic speech uttered by one character speaking aloud while alone on the stage. The soliloquist thus reveals his or her inner thoughts and feelings to the audience, either in supposed self-communion or in a consciously direct address. Soliloquies often appear in plays from the age of Shakespeare, notably in his *Hamlet* and *Macbeth. A* poem supposedly uttered by a solitary speaker, like Robert Browning's 'Soliloquy of the Spanish Cloister, may also be called a soliloquy. Soliloquy is a form of monologue, but a monologue is not a soliloquy if the speaker is not alone. *Verb: solilo*quize.

solid matter: 1. Material that is set solid, in which type is set on a body its own size, without leading. Also called *solid copy.* 2. Text to be composed without illustrations or major breaks. Also called *straight matter.*

sonnet: a lyric poem comprising 14 rhyming fines of equal length: iambic pentameters in English, alexandrines in French, hendecasyllables in Italian. The rhyme schemes of the sonnet follow two basic patterns.

(1) The Italian sonnet comprises an 8-line 'octave of two quatrains, followed by a 6-line 'sestet' usually rhymed. The transition from octave to sestet usually coincides with a 'turn' in the argument or mood of the poem. In a variant form used by the English poet John Milton, however, the 'turn' is delayed to a later position around the tenth line. Some later poets—notably William Wordsworth—have employed this feature of the 'Miltonic sonnet' while relaxing the rhyme scheme of the octave to abbaacca. The Italian pattern has remained the most widely used in English and other languages.

(2) The English sonnet comprises three quatrains and a final couplet. An important variant of this is the Spenserian sonnet which links the three quatrains by rhyme. *In* either form, the 'turn' comes with the final couplet, which may sometimes achieve the neatness of an epigram.

Originating in Italy, the sonnet was established by Petrarch in the 14th century as a major form of love poetry, and came to be adopted in Spain, France and England in the 16th century, and in Germany in the 17th. The standard subject-matter of early sonnets was the torments of sexual love, but in the 17th century John Donne extended the sonnet's scope to religion, while Milton extended it to politics. Although largely neglected in the 18th century, the sonnet was revived in the 19th by Wordsworth, Keats, and Baudelaire, and is still widely used. Some poets have written connected series of sonnets, known as sonnet sequences or sonnet cycles: of these, the outstanding English examples are Sir Philip Sidney's *Astrophel and Stella,* Spenser's *Amoretti,* and Shakespeare's Sonnets, later examples include Elizabeth Barrett Browning's *Sonnets from the* Portuguese and W. H. Auden's 'In Time of War'. *A* group of sonnets formally linked by repeated lines is known as a crown of sonnets. Irregular variations on the sonnet form have included the 12-line sonnet sometimes used by Elizabethan poets, G. M. Hopkin's curtal sonnets of 10½ lines, and the 16-line sonnets of George Meredith's sequence *Modern Love.*

sorts: Additional pieces of metal type, beyond those normally available to compose a job, as from a second font of the same type or from standing type.

soubrette: the stock character of the heroine's maidservant in French comedy of the 17th and 18th centuries. The soubrette usually protests against the delusions of her master, ingeniously scheming on behalf of her young mistress. The character of Dorine in Moliere's *Le* Tartuffe is a model for the type, which originated in the *commedia dell* arte.

sound: The range of audio frequencies that can be propagated in gases, solids and liquids. A subjective experience produced when the ear responds to air pressure variations. A minimum sound pressure of 0.02 mPa at I kHz corresponds to the threshold of hearing, the smallest sound pressure that the ear/brain system can detect. Very high sound pressures, of the order of 20 x 103 mPa or more, are painful and dangerous in that they can damage the hearing mechanism of the ear.

sound drum: Roller used to control uniformity of movement of film where a scanning beam slit scans, or a magnetic head reads, the sound track.

sound gate: The gate used instead of a sound drum to keep the film sound track aligned with the scanning beam.

sound head: (1) In motion picture equipment, a mechanism for transporting the film and reproducing the photographic or magnetic sound record. (2) In audio or video equipment, the mechanism for recording/reproducing the audio information.

sounding: In *ionospheric* propagation, determination of the characteristics of the ionosphere by the use of a radio wave directed into the ionosphere, and observation of the returning signals.

sound mixer: In audio broadcasting, an apparatus for processing a number of sound sources, so that their individual signal values may be adjusted, and they can be combined in any required manner.

sound-in-syne: In television, a system for sending the sound channel of a television transmission in the video channel, by using the *line sync pulse* interval. The audio analogue signal is sampled at intervals, and the coded amplitude samples are transmitted during the line sync interval. At the receiving point, the digital signals are extracted and converted back to analogue form. The system is used within a broadcasting system or network and, at the transmitter, the pulses are removed from the video waveform and the reconstituted audio signal is used to modulate the sound transmitter.

sound track: The defined area along the length of a recording medium such as film or magnetic tape which carries the audio information. Also, the sound record itself.

source code: A program written in a high-level language; needs *compiling* or *assembling* before use.

source book: A book composed mostly of primary, or source materials, rather than analytical and interpretive writings; for example, a book mainly composed of historical documents.

source document: A document supplying primary information, rather than information secured from secondary sources. In electronic data processing, any document providing data used in a computer system.

source language: The language in which a computer program was first written, such as FORTRAN or COBOL, which must be translated by an assembler or compiler into the object language, or machine language, used by the computer.

source program: The program written by a computer programmer, usually in a symbolic language such as FORTRAN or COBOL; source programs are translated by an assembler or compiler into object programs, written in machine languages that computers use.

space diversity: In radio reception, a method of diversity reception in which signals from a single source are derived from two or more antenna systems, spaced apart horizontally or vertically by several wavelengths. The tub signals are processed in receivers and either combined or the strongest signal is selected. The system is very effective for minimising the effects of fading along an HF or *scatter-propagation* path.

space seller: One who sells advertising space in printed media, such as newspapers and magazines; closely allied to but not identical with a *time seller,* who sells advertising time in broadcast media, such as television and radio.

spacing loss: In magnetic recording, the loss of high frequencies due to imperfect contact between the reproducing head and the magnetic medium.

Spasmodic School: a title applied mockingly by the Scottish poet and critic W. E. Aytoun in 1854 to a group of poets who had lately achieved some popularity In Britain: P. J. Bailey, Sydney Dobell, Alexander Smith, and others. Their work is marked by extravagant attempts to represent emotional turmoil sometimes in a manner derived from Byron. Dobell's dramatic poem Balder includes the notorious line:

Ah! Ah! Ah! Ah! Ah! Ah! Ah! Ah! Ah! Ah!

The term has sometimes been extended to the comparable' emotional intensities of Tennyson's *Maud,* and of some poems by Elizabeth Barrett Browning.

speaker support module: Slide sequence for use with a live presenter.

special effects: General term for scenes in which an illusion of the action required is created by the use of special equipment and processes rather than in reality. Also, video mixer enabling sections from two or more pictures to be montaged and displayed on the same screen.

special interest: Describing a publication aimed at in audience of professionals or consumers sharing one or more specific subject interests; for example, an investment publication aimed at both investment professionals and private investors, or a series of war books intended for military history buffs.

special order: An order placed by a bookseller with a publisher that requires some kind of special handling on the part of the bookseller, such as a rush order placed by telephone for a book out of stock or an order for a book on short discount, which the bookseller would not usually stock, booksellers often charge customers an additional fee, above the price of the book ordered, for such special orders.

special sales: Sales made by a publisher outside the publisher's normal distribution channels, often requiring special pricing and handling; for example, premium sales are designated "special" by many publishers. This designation is a matter of individual company practice, as kinds of sales called "special" by some publishers are quite routine for others.

specifications (specs): 1. A physical description of a proposed, forthcoming, or published work, itemizing all main design elements, such as kind of binding, trim size, type sizes, and anticipated page count. 2. More generally, detailed, written, or drawn descriptions of work to be done or products in being, used for several purposes, including bidding, standard-setting, and repair information.

specific performance: The legally enforceable performance of contractual obligations precisely as agreed upon in a contract, with no material deviation.

spectral characteristics: In colour television, general term for the colour response of a colour channel, with respect to wavelength. The term is equally applicable to coloured light sources and lamps used in television broadcasting, but lamps are usually described in terms of the *colour temperature.*

spectrum: (1) A range of wavelengths or frequencies of acoustic, visible or electromagnetic radiation. (2) Specifically a display of visible light radiations arranged in order of wavelength. A range of frequencies or wavelengths exhibiting common characteristics. For example, the visible light spectrum, the radio frequency spectrum and the *audio frequency* spectrum. Non-sinusoidal signals have an associated spectrum. A pulse, for example, has a frequency spectrum containing the *fundamental* and *harmonic* frequency components.

spectrum analyser: Am instrument for measurement of a signal characteristic in a band of frequencies. This type of instrument usually has a *swept-frequency oscillator* as a signal source applied to the system under test. The sweep is locked to the horizontal sweep of a *cathode-ray tube* display. A narrow-band filter at the output of the system being tested provides the vertical deflection of the cathoderay tube beam. Device to display the frequency distribution and levels of a signal.

speech act theory: a modern philosophical approach to language, which has challenged the long-standing assumption of philosophers that human utterances consist exclusively of true or false statements about the world. Initiated by the English philosopher J. L. Austin in lectures published posthumously as How to Do Things with Words, speech act theory begins with the distinction between 'constative' utterances and performatives. Further analysis reveals that a single utterance may comprise three distinct kinds of speech act: in addition to its simple 'locationary' status as a grammatical utterance, it will have an illocutionary force, and probably a perlocutionary force. Since Austin's death in 1960, speech act theory has been developed further by J. R. Searle in *Speech Acts* and other works, and applied to problems of literary analysis by Mary Louise Pratt in Toward a *Speech Act Theory of Literary Discourse.*

speech level: The signal level produced by a microphone, relative to a specified level of voltage or power, measured at a point in a transmission path by a meter having specified characteristics.

speech pressure: In audio, at a point in space, the acoustic sound pressure due to speech, measured under specified conditions.

speech track: A voice track as opposed to music or effects.

Spenserian stanza: an English poetic stanza of nine iambic fines, the first eight being pentameters while the ninth is a longer line known either as an iambic hexameter or as an alexandrine. The rhyme scheme is *ababbcbcc.* The stanza is named after Edmund Spenser, who invented it probably on the basis of the ottava *rima* stanza for his long allegorical romance *The Faerie Queene.* It was revived successfully by the younger English Romantic poets of the early 19th century: Byron used it for Childe *Harolirs Pilgrimage,* Keats for 'The Eve of St Agnes' and Shelley for *The Revolt of Islam* and *Adonais.*

SPG: Sync-Pulse Generator.

spherical aberration: Of an electron beam, a focusing system defect in which electrons at different radial distances from the beam axis focus at different distances from the lens.

spherical wave: A wave originating from a point source. At a distance remote from the source, the curvature of the wave-front has virtually vanished and the wave becomes a plane wave.

spinoff: 1. The development of additional or auxiliary products from an earlier or primary product; for example, the development of a line of single-subject books from a multi-subject encyclopedia, or of several special interest magazines from one general interest magazine. 2. The transfer of some portion of corporate stock and some corporate activities to a newly formed corporation, for such purposes as preparation for sale or liquidation of the operations involved, or for expansion of those operations.

spiral binding: A kind of mechanical binding, consisting of a continuous wire in the form of a spiral drawn through many holes drilled into the side of a book, usually a softcover.

split page: The front page of the second section of a newspaper; sometimes used to describe the front page of each section of a multi-sectioned newspaper.

split run: A periodical run, carrying different content in different parts of the run; for example, a regional edition carrying much the same material as a national edition, but also containing regional news and advertising not carried by the national edition; or five different ad pages in the same slot in the publication, each for a different area edition.

spoilage: Losses caused by the spoiling of goods due to such causes as the mildewing of paper in a warehouse, over-inking, and uneven trimming sponsored book: See subsidy publishing.

spike: To reject copy, from the original newspaper practice of literally impaling such copy on a spike; article copy so rejected by an editor is described as *spiked.*

SPL: Sound Pressure Level.

splice: A physical join in the medium, film or tape.

split beam: In *cathode-ray tubes,* a tube containing one gun producing a beam which is split to provide two traces, each subject to the same horizontal deflection system, but having separate vertical deflection systems.

split screen: A shot in which two or more separate images appear in different areas of the same picture.

split screen switch: In television broadcasting, a device having two video inputs and a switching signal input. The output contains signals from both input sources, so switched that the two pictures are presented as one on a screen, split either vertically or horizontally, depending on the switching rate.

splitter: In cabled distribution systems, a device in which input signal energy is divided into two or more outlet paths. Some forms of splitter can be used for combining two or more signal sources into a single signal path.

spoilers: Pins used to prevent head-to-tape contact during rewind or fast-forward.

spool: A flanged hub on which film, magnetic tape or ribbon is wound.

spool, to: To wind a film or tape at a speed higher than the normal speed of reproduction.

sporadic-E: An abnormal degree of ionisation occurring in the *E-region,* at random times, of varying ionisation density and random duration. Sporadic-E can sometimes support long-distance propagation of VHF and UHF waves beyond the distances normally associated with *tropospheric* propagation.

spot: A single commercial broadcast time purchase, in contrast commercial messages accompanying sponsored broadcasts. In *cathode-ray tubes,* the small area of the screen surface bombarded by the electron beam.

spot wobble: In television display, a system for imparting a small vertical oscillatory motion to the *scanning spot.* If the beam spot diameter is made small, horizontal definition can be improved, but gaps appear between the lines. Spot wobble can close the gaps. The system is almost essential for large-screen displays where a large picture area shows the line structure very clearly.

spotting: (1) Locating individual sounds or words in it, sound recording. (2) Retouching with an opaque medium to eliminate small transparent defects, such as pinholes, in the heavy density areas of a photographic image.
(3) Marking slides to indicate their correct orientation for projection.

spondee: a metrical unit consisting of two stressed syllables. Spondees occur regularly in several Greek and Latin metres, and as substitutes for other feet, as in the dactylic hexameter but in English the spondee is an occasional device of metrical variation. The normal alternation of stressed and unstressed syllables in English speech makes R virtually impossible to compose a complete fine of true spondees. Some English compound words like *childbirth* are spondaic, although even these do not have exactly equal stresses. The occurrence of adjacent stressed syllables in English verse may be accounted for more convincingly in terms of demotion, rather than in the doubtfully applicable terms of classical quantitative feet.

Spoonerism: a phrase in which the initial consonants of two words have been swapped over, creating an amusing new expression. It takes its name from the Revd W. A. Spooner, Warden of New College, Oxford. His reputed utterances, like the accusation that a student had 'hissed my mystery lectures', appear to have been inadvertent slips, but Spoonerisms may also be used for deliberately humorous effect: W. H. Auden referred dismissively to Keats and Shelley as 'Sheets and Kelly', while a feminist theatre group toured Britain in the 1970s under the name Cunning Stunts.

spot wobble: Vertical oscillation of the scanning beam in a television display to render the raster spacing less obvious.

sprocket: A toothed drum engaging with the perforation holes of film or paper tape for transport.

sprocket holes: Deprecated term tor *perforations* in motion picture film.

spread: Any two facing pages in a Publication; can be used to create a single large advertisement or illustration.

spring season: In trade bookselling, approximately the period from mid-January to mid-June, although many books sell as well through the summer as in the spring, or even better; the second most import in season of the year for booksellers and trade publishers, the first being the fall season.

sprinkled edges: Book edges spattered with specks or dots of colour, for decorative purposes.

sprung rhythm: the term used by the English poet Gerard Manley Hopkins to describe his peculiar metrical system, based on the accentual verse of nursery rhymes and on medieval alliterative metres. It counts the number of strong stresses in a line, regardless of the number of unstressed syllables, and permits the juxtaposition of stressed syllables more frequently than normal English duple or triple metre. Hopkins saw his metre as having four kinds of foot, each beginning with a stressed syllable: the stressed monosyllable, the trochee, the dactyl and the first paeon; additional unstressed syllables or 'outrides' were also permitted. Hopkins's aim was to make use of the energies of everyday speech, and his sprung rhythm may be regarded as a kind of free verse based partly on accentual metres.

spur feeder: In *cabled distribution systems,* a feeder supplying signals to subscribers' feeders or looped system outlets.

spur feeder amplifier: In *cabled distribution systems,* an amplifier used to raise signal levels to compensate for signal loss in a *spur feeder.* The functions of *splitting* and *signal tilt* compensation are sometimes combined in this amplifier.

spurious emission: An undesired radiation from a transmitter.

spurious response: In receivers, any undesired signal at the receiver output.

square-law detector: A *demodulator* system for AM signals in which the output is proportional to the square of the input voltage.

square wave: A periodic voltage variation which, for equal periods of time, is at one of two values. Electrical waveform switching virtually instantaneously between two voltage levels, with the 'on-off ratio' not necessarily of equal duration.

squeezezoom: Device to manipulate the geometry of a television image for artistic effect; specifically a trade name, but loosely used for other equipment to perform similar functions.

squelch: A circuit in a FM radio receiver which *mutes* the output when the incoming radio signal falls below a preset amplitude.

squib: another word for a lampoon: a short satirical attack upon a person, work, or institution.

S-signal: In stereophonic sound transmission, the difference between right and left audio channels, used to amplitude modulate a sub-carrier which is then suppressed for transmission, leaving only the sidebands.

stability: General term for the ability of a system to remain operational at its designed state. Design of equipment or components for stable operation requires not only the correct electrical performance, but resistance to the effects of mechanical and thermal shock, effects due to supply power variations and accidental overload. For example, a power supply is preferably of a constant voltage under all conditions of load current variation. An oscillator should remain at its designed frequency and amplitude. An amplifier should not operate under conditions where a negative feedback can become positive.

stack: A store in a microcomputer for holding program count or data in a first in, last out manner, used to ensure orderly return from *nested subroutines.*

stage left: On the actor's left looking at the audience.

stage right: On the actor's right looking at the audience.

stage weight: Weight used to keep french scenery braces steady.

stagger-tuned amplifier: A system of wideband amplifier design in which several stages of amplification are used, each stage being tuned to different frequencies. Useful for muiti-stage, wideband amplifiers, requiring careful adjustment of Q values and resonance frequencies.

staircase video signal: In television, a test signal in which each line scan includes a series of uniform steps increasing in signal amplitude. This signal provides a very useful test for differential gain and a number of other features. It is often included in a repetitive line scan with pulse and bar signals.

standard cell: A primary cell characterised by its constancy of *EMF* over a long period of time, used as a voltage reference.

standard frequencies: Radiated transmissions on 16 kHz, 20 kHz, 200 and 250 kHz, 2.5 MHz, 5 MHz, and every 5 MHz up to 25 MHz. These transmissions have a frequency precision of a Very high order, and the transmissions are modulated with various types of information, again, with very accurate tone frequencies and time intervals.

storage tube An electron tube in which signal information can be stored by conversion to an electric charge on a suitable electrode. A television camera is an "ample of a storage tube in which the charges stored on the target are 'read off' by the scanning beam.

store: Device or system into which data can be entered for retrieval later. General term for a device or equipment into which data can be placed, for later access and/or retrieval. The term *memory* is also used for a store, but is deprecated.

storage tube: A cathode ray tube which does not require *refreshing* to maintain its display.

story: in the everyday sense any narrative or tale recounting a series of events. In modern narratology, however, the term refers more specifically to the sequence of imagined events that we reconstruct from the actual arrangement of a narrative plot. In this modern distinction between story and plot, derived from Russian Formalism and its opposed terms *fabula* and *sjuzet,* the story is the full sequence of events as we assume them to have occurred in their likely order, duration, and frequency, while the plot is a particular selection and re-odering of these. Thus the story is the abstractly conceived raw material' of events which we reconstruct from the finished arraangement of the plot: it includes events preceding and otherwise omitted from the perceived action, and its sequence will differ from that of the plot if the action begins *in medias res* or otherwise involves an anachrony. As an abstraction, the story can more successfully than the style of the narration could be.

story board: Chart consisting of a series of still pictures, usually drawings, summarising the contents of a proposed film, video or slide production.

stop out: To apply protective material to clean up and make minor alterations in plates; also the material so applied.

storage: 1. The holding of information or materials for future use; for example, the holding of bits of information in a computer memory videodisc, microform, or card file. 2. An area or device in which computerized data may be held, such as a specified area in a central processing unit, a disc, or a drum.

stored program computer: A computer in which programmed instructions are stored in its own main core, rather than stored externally, such as on tape.

straight receiver: Term sometimes used for a simple receiver involving direct amplification and demodulation of signals without *frequency-changing.* Also known as a TRF receiver.

stream of consciousness: the continuous flow of sense-perceptions, thoughts, feelings, and memories in the human mind: or a literary method of representing such a blending of mental processes in fictional characters, usually in an unpunctuated or disjointed form of interior monologue. The term is often used as a synonym for interior monologue, but they can also he distinguished, in two ways. In the first sense, the stream of consciousness is the subject-matter while interior monologue is the technique for presenting it; thus Marcel Proust's novel A la *recherche du temps perdu* is about the stream of consciousness, especially the connection between sense-impressions and memory, but it does not actually use interior monologue. In the second sense, stream of consciousness is a special style of interior monologue: while an interior monologue always presents a character's thoughts 'directly', without the apparent intervention of a summarizing and selecting narrator, it does not necessarily mingle them with impressions and perceptions, nor does it necessarily violate the norms of grammar, syntax, and logic; but the stream of consciousness technique also does one or both of these things. An important device of modernist fiction and its later imitators, the technique was pioneered by Dorothy Richardson in Pilgrimage and by James Joyce in *Ulysses,* and further developed by Virginia Woolf in Mrs Dalloway and William Faulkner *in The Sound and the* Fury.

streamer: An advertising display poster, wider than it is tall, used in point-of-purchase advertising.

stress: the relative emphasis given in pronunciation to a syllable, in loudness, pitch, or duration. The term is usually interchangeable with accent, although some theorists of prosody reserve It only for the emphasis occurring according to a metrical pattern. In English verse, the metre of a line is determined by the number of stresses in a sequence composed of stressed and unstressed syllables. In quantitative verse, on the other hand, the metrical pattern is made up of syllables measured by their duration rather than by stress.

stretching: In television, signal processing whereby an input signal experiences an increase in gain as the signal level increases or decreases. Of particular importance where processing a video signal, because it could produce a change in video/sync-pulse amplitude ratio. Stretching is sometimes used as a deliberate pre-distortion of an input signal to a power amplifier which, to obtain full output, may cause *crushing*.

string: In computer practice, a type of *variable* consisting of a sequence of characters, correctly referred to as a literal, enclosed in quotation marks, e.g. DAY = "TUESDAY".

stripe: A narrow band of magnetic material applied to photographic motion picture film for sound recording and reproduction.

stripline: Transmission line circuit elements produced on circuit: boards by printed circuit techniques.

strobing: A disturbing effect in film or television arising from the field or frame sampling rate distorting motion, particularly of rotating objects.

stroboscope: (1) Pulsed light source used to measure speed of rotation or frequency of repetition or to freeze the motion of objects. (2) A disc with equally spaced marks around its circumstance used to check the rotational speed of objects, such as checking tape or turntable speed in the presence of AC lighting.

strikeon composition: Typewriter or other direct-impact composition.

stringer: A writer employed part-time by a publication, being paid either on a part-time basis, or by the article accepted for publication.

stripping: 1. Putting together or altering an existing piece of copy or reproduction copy. 2. Preparing a negative for platemaking in the offset printing process. 3. Removing the covers of unsold paperbacks for return to the publisher, in lieu of returning the whole book for credit.

strong-stress metre: another term for the metre of accentual verse, in which only the stressed syllables are counted while the unstressed syllables may vary in number. The, term thus encompasses the Old Germanic alliterative metre, various kinds of popular English metre, and G. M. Hopkins's sprung rhythm.

strophe: a stanza, or any less regular subdivision of a poem such as a verse paragraph. In a special sense, the term is applied to the opening section of a Greek choral ode. In the Pindaric ode, sometimes imitated in English, the strophe is followed by an antistrophe having the same number of lines and the same complex metrical arrangement; this is then followed by an epode of differing length and structure, and the triadic pattern may then be repeated a number of times. In choral odes, the chorus would dance in one direction while chanting the strophe, then back again during the antistrophe, standing still for the epode.

structuralism: a modern intellectual movement that analyses cultural phenomena according to principles derived from linguistics, emphasizing the systematic interrelationships among the elements of any human activity, and thus the abstract codes and conventions governing the social production of meanings. Building on the linguistic concept of the phoneme—a unit of meaningful sound defined purely by its differences from other phonemes rather than by any inherent features—structuralism argues that the elements composing any cultural phenomenon are similarly 'relational': that is, they have meaning only by virtue of their contrasts with other elements of the system, especially in *binary oppositions of paired opposites. Their meanings can be established not by referring each element to any supposed equivalent in natural fearity, but only by analyzing its function within a self-contained cultural code. Accordingly structuralist analysis seeks the underlying system or *langue* that governs individual utterances or instances. In formulating the laws by which elements of such a system are combined. It distinguishes between sets of interchangeable units and sequences of such units in combination, thereby outlining a basic syntax of human culture.

Structuralism and its 'science of signs' are derived chiefly from the linguistic theories of Ferdinand de Saussure, and partly from Russian Formalism and the related narratology of Vladimir Propp's *Morphology of the Folktale*. It flourished in France in the 1960s, following the widely discussed applications of structural analysis to mythology by the anthropologist Claude Levi Strauss. In the study of literary works, structuralism is distinguished by its rejection of those traditional notions according to which literature expresses an author's meaning or 'reflects' reality. Instead, the 'text' is seen as an objective structure activating various codes and conventions which are independent of author reader and external reality. Structuralist criticism is less interested in interpreting what literary works mean than in explaining how they can mean what they mean, that is, in showing what implicit rules and conventions are operating in a given work. The structurafist tradition has been particularly strong in narratology, from Propp's analysis of narrative 1unctions to Greirnas' theory of actants. The

French critic Roland Barthes was an outstanding practitioner of structuralist literary analysisnotably in his book S/Z and is famed for his witty analyses of wrestling, striptease, and other phenomena in *Mythologies*; some of his later writings, however, show a shift to poststructuralism, in which the overconfident 'scientific' pretensions of structuralism are abandoned. For more extended accounts of this enterprise, consult Terence Hawkes, *Structuralism and Serniotics*, Jonathan Culler, *Structuralist Poetics*, and Robert Scholes, *Structuralism in Literature: An Introduction*

structured programming: Computer programming that emphasizes program segments placed in hierarchical order, as in the language Structured COBOL, rather than focusing on individual instructions in a fixed sequence.

stub: In antennas, a length of transmission line connected in parallel with the main feed to an antenna, to introduce a required reactance at the point of connection. A line with an impedance Z_0 connected to an antenna at a point where the impedance is R + iX. If Z_0 equals R, a stub exhibiting an impedance of, -jX can be connected as shown to improve the power match between the feeder and the load.

stuffer: A mailing piece that is included in a mailing primarily devoted to other purposes; often, selling material included with non-sales mailings, as when a selling piece—the ubiquitous *statement stuffer*—included in a mailing of bills, or statements, to customers.

Sturm und Drang: the name'Storm and Stress'given to a shortlived but important movement in German literature of the 1770s. An early precursor of Romanticism, it was passionately individualistic and rebellious. maintaining a hostile attitude to French neoclassicism and the associated rationalism of the Enlightenment. The term is taken from the title of a play by F. M. Klinger. but the leaders of the movement were J. G. Herder and J. W. von Goethe. Herder, inspired by the primitivism of J.J. Rousseau, encouraged the cult of Ossianism and praised the 'natural' qualities of Shakespeare and of folk song. Goethe's play *Gotz von Berlichingen*, a Shakespearean chronicle play about a leader of the 16th-century peasants' revolt, is the major dramatic work of the *Sturm und* Drang period, while his sentimental novel of hopeless love and suicide, *The Sorrows* of *Young Werther* is its most significant novel. A belated product of the movement is Friedrich Schiller's play *Die Rduber*, which influenced the later development of melodrama.

style: 1. A set of composition rules, as set forth by a generally accepted published manual of style or by a specific publisher, compositor, or printer, which is then called a *house style.* When developed into a formal set of rules in written form, to help guide editors, authors, and compositors, the written list of rules" is" called a, style *sheet.* 2. The distinctive tone, rhythms, and mode of expression that characterize the work of a particular writer, making it stand out from all other such work; agonized over by many writers, sought after by many editors, and always a matter of individual assessment. Any specific way of using language, which is characteristic of an audior, school. period, or genre. Particular styles may be deftned by their diction, syntax. Imagery, rhythm. and use of figures, or by any other linguistic feature. Different categories of style have been naraed after particulair authors, periods, and professions. while in the Renaissance a scheme of three stylistic 'levels' was adopted, distinguishing the high or grand'stylefrom the middle or 'mean' style and the low or 'base' style.

The principle of decorum held that certain subjects required particular levels of style, so that an epic should be written in the grand style whereas satires should be composed in the base style. Since the literary revolution of Romanticism. however, this hierarchy has been replaced by the notion of style as an expression of individual personality.

stylistics: a branch of modem linguistics devoted to the detailed analysis of literary style. or of the linguistic choices made by speakers and writers in nonliterary contexts.

sub-audio frequencies: Frequencies below the range of audio frequencies normally used for speech and music. This imprecise definition refers to very low frequencies below about 15 Hz, and down to zero frequency. Such frequencies are often used control functions.

sub-carrier: A frequency within the passband of a range of signal frequencies, which is modulated with another signal or signal frequencies. (1) In colour television, a carrier frequency that is modulated to provide colour information. In the UK standard System I PAL, the colour Subcarrier has a frequency of 4,43361875 MHz, and this frequency is within the luminance channel. (2) In FM stereophonic sound, a sub-carrier on a frequency of 38 kHz is amplitude-modulated by 'left minus-right' signals, and the resulting sidebands only are transmitted. By reducing the deviation of the *L+R* signals, the L-R information can be transmitted and received in the same channel bandwidth as was used for the former *L+R* signal at full deviation.

subhead: A heading on a body of copy, such as a chapter subsection, usually set in type different from that used in the body of the copy, and often larger and bolder than that copy, but subordinate in size and placement to such main heads as titles and chapter and section headings. A work may include several types of subheads, ranked in a hierarchy according to the work's design.

subgenre: any category of literary works that forms a specific class within a larger genre: thus the pastoral elegy may be regarded as a subgenre of elegy, which is in turn a subgenre of lyric poetry.

subjective grading scales: In television and sound, grading scales for assessment of received broadcast quality, *impairment*, or for comparison purposes.

sublime: A quality of awesome grandeur in art or nature. which some 18th century writers distinguished from the merely beautiful. An anonymous Greek critical treatise of the 1st century AD, *Peri hypsous* provided the basis for the 18thcentury interest in sublimity, after Boileau's French translation in 16 72. 'Longinus' refers to the sublime as a loftiness of thought and feeling in literature, and associates it with terrifyingly impressive natural phenomena such as mountains, volcanoes, storms, and the sea. These associations were revived in Edmund Burke's influential *Philosophical Enquiry into the Origin of our Ideas of the Sublime and Beautiful*, which argues that the sublime is characterized by obscurity. vastness, and power, while the beautiful is light, smooth. and delicate. The 18th-century enthusiasm for the sublime in landscape and the visual arts was one of the developments that undermined the restraints of neoclassicism and thus prepared the way for Romanticism.

subliminal advertising: An advertising technique that seeks to influence the actions of its audience by striking at the unconscious rather than the conscious, by such techniques as flashing an advertising message on a television screen so quickly that it can be registered by viewers without their becoming aware that it has been shown.

submission: A manuscript sent to a publisher by an author or agent, whether the work 'is under contract or on speculation, partial or complete, and whatever its size; a book outline, a completed book, and a brief magazine or newspaper article are all submissions. Occasionally used to describe manuscripts sent to agents. The offer of a work to more than one publisher at a time is called a *multiple submission*.

subplot: a secondary sequence of actions in a dramatic or narrative work, usually involving characters of lesser importance. The subplot may be related to the main plot as a parallel or contrast, or it may be more or less separate from it. Subplots are especially common in Elizabethan and Jacobean drama, a famous example being that of Gloucester and his sons in Shakespeare's *King Lear*; but they are also found in long novels such as those of Dickens.

subprogram: A portion of a larger computer program, capable of being handled and translated into machine language independently.

subroutine: A group of instructions within a computer system, operating to perform standard functions for many programs

subscriber: One who buys something to be supplied in series, such as a periodical publication, the right to access a body of information periodically, or tickets to a concert series. That which is purchased is a *subscription.*

subscriber: In cabled distribution systems, the ultimate user of signals available at a system outlet.

subscribers' feeder: In cabled distribution systems, a feeder used to connect a system outlet to a *spur feeder.*

subscribers' tap-off: In cabled distribution systems, a unit connecting a subscriber's feeder to a *spur feeder.*

subscription books: Books sold as a connected series, with periodic delivery of volumes; may be sold and paid for in full on sale or sold by the unit and paid for as individual books are delivered.

subscription library: A membership library, in which dues-paying members support or partly support the library with their dues and in return enjoy the use of the library.

subscription list: The body of current subscribers to a set of publications that is supplied serially. Those engaged in mail order selling usually consider recently expired and cancelled subscribers to be part of these lists for selling purposes, although such former subscribers are held and accounted for separately.

subsidiary: A corporation that is wholly owned or directly controlled by another corporation.

subsidiary communications authorisation chennel: (US) In frequency modulation stereophonic broadcasting, a *sub-carrier* used in addition to the usual *multiplex* signal for stereophony to provide background music for public use. Sometimes termed 'storecasting'. The UK version of the *GE-Zenith* system does not use this extra sub-carrier.

subsidy publishing: 1. A mode of financing publication in which publications are wholly or partly financed by private or public grants; for example, a work in oral history, funded by government grant and destined for publication by a university press which could not otherwise fund such an expensive project; or a work sponsored, or funded, by a private corporation or institution, which may publish the work or arrange for publication. Also called a *sponsored publication.* 2. Sometimes used as a euphemism for vanity publishing.

subtitle: An additional book title, following the main title; often further explaining the content and intent of the book, and attempting to catch the interest of potential readers.

substitution: a term used in traditional prosody to denote the use of one kind of foot in place of the foot normally required by the metrical pattem of a verse fine. In English verse, the kind of substitution most Commonly referree to by prosodists is the replacement of the first iamb in an iambic line by a trochee; this 'initial trochaic inversion', as it is called, appears in Tennyson's line:

Far on the ringing plains of windy Troy.

The substitution of an anapaest for an iamb, or of a dactyl for a trochee, is called trisyllabic substitution, since it increases the number of syllables from two to three. The feet known as the spondee and the pyrrhic are sometimes invoked as substitute feet, where stressed or unstressed syllables occur in pairs.

subtext: any meaning or set of meanings which is implied rather than explicitly stated in a literary work, especially in a play. Modern plays such as those of Harold Pinter, in which the meaning of the action is sometimes suggested more by silences and pauses than by dialogue alone. are often discussed in terms of their hidden subtexts.

succes d'estime: a high reputation enjoyed by a work on the basis of critics' favourable judgements: thus a critical success rather than a merely commercial one. Another kind of reputation for which the French have a phrase is the **succes de.**

sudden ionospheric disturbance: In HE propagation, short-duration disturbance similar to *Dellinger effect.*

sum signal: In FM stereophonic broadcasting, the signal produced by adding the A and B signals.

sun-spot cycle: An approximately 11-year cycle between successive maximum or minimum numbers of sunspots. The ionisation densities in the ionosphere appear the to be related to the sun-spot cycle, providing higher ionisation densities and better propagation conditions during the peak period of a cycle.

supergain array: In antennas property of an array whereby the gain obained in particular directions is larger than would be obtained with a uniform distribution of element spacing, element currents and phase.

superheterodyne reception: Originally *supersonic* heterodyne reception. A method of reception with which the input signal frequency is changed to another, generally lower, frequency by a heterodyne process in which the signal frequency is beat with a locally-generated oscillation.

The essentials of a superheterodyne receiver. The input signal level is usually raised with an amplifier that also provides enough selectivity to reject the image frequency. The mixer and local oscillator provide the beat frequency, termed the intermediate frequency, which has a frequency equal to the difference between the two input signal frequencies to the mixer. The intermediate frequency amplifier system determines most of the signal amplification, the channel bandwidth and the adjacent channel rejection.

superior: Type set smaller and somewhat above the line of which it is part, accompanying type on that line, as is a reference mark, such as an asterisk, *. Also called superscript.

super-regenerative reception: A system of reception using positive *feedback* in a signal-frequency tuned amplifier circuit, to a degree where oscillation would normally take place. The build up of RF amplitude in the tuned system is periodically suppressed at a *supersonic* rate, thus providing a large gain to the signal voltage. The suppression frequency is sometimes termed the quench frequency.

supplement: 1. An additional section of a newspaper or other periodical, beyond the basic news sections; for example, a weekend news review section or a Sunday magazine section. 2. An updating portion of a publication; for example, a pocket part added to a lawbook, or a body of loose pages interleaved periodically into a looseleaf reporter.

supplier: A firm or person selling goods to businesses, for use or resale; usually describing, a firm that sells such goods to its customers on a long-term basis.

suppressed carrier system: In transmission, an *amplitude modulation* system in which the transmitter radiates sidebands only, with the carrier wholly or partially suppressed. For demodulation at the receiver, a carrier is re-inserted with the sideband signals.

suppression: The withdrawal of a forthcoming or published work from publication; may result from an act of government censorship, from legal action aimed at the work, such as an injunction or preliminary injunction stopping the work's publication or sale, or from a voluntary act of the publisher.

surface acoustic wave: A wave generated and propagated on the surface of *piezoelectric* solids. The wave velocity is independent of frequency, and is of a value comparable with the velocity of sound through the material. The wave is generated, propagated and received. The dimensions and disposition of the interleaved transducer elements determine the bandwidth and other characteristics of the device. An application of the device is as a *bandpass fillter,* and the small size and mechanical stability makes this type of filter very suitable for the *intermediate-frequency* amplifier of receivers. These filters are also used for time-delay, oscillator and other functions.

surface wave: In propagation, a wave that travels over a surface to a degree determined by the electrical properties of the surface and the frequency. At very low radio frequencies, the ground wave and surface wave are nearly the same and difficult to distinguish.

surfiction: a term coined in 1973 by the American experimental writer Raymond Federman to designate a new kind of liction which is now more often referred to as postmodernist. Rather than attempt to mirror some preexisting reality, surfiction abandons realism in favour of metafiction. selfconsciously advertising its own lictional status. Federman proposed that 'the new fiction will not attempt to be meaningful, truthful, or realistic'. He reprinted his 1973 manifesto 'Surfiction—A Position' in a volume of essays, *Surfiction: Fiction* Now... *and Tomorrow,* which also included contributions from Ronald Sukenick and John Barth. The term's reference is broadlysimilar to that of Robert Scholes's 'fabulatloh, although it has not been so widely adopted.

surprinting: The printing of additional material over already-printed material, as when selling or headline material is printed over text in an advertisement or on a magazine cover.

Surrealism: an antirational movement of imaginative liberation in European art and literature in the 1920s and 1930s. launched by Andi6

Breton in his *Manifeste du Surrealisme* after his break from the Dada group in 1922. The term *surrialiste* had been used by the French poet Guillaume Apollinaire in 1917 to indicate an attempt to reach beyond the limits of the 'real'. Surrealism seeks to break down the boundaries between rationality and irrationality. exploring the resources and revolutionary energies of dreams, hallucinations, and sexual desire. Influenced both by the Symbolists and by Sigmund Freud's theories of the unconscious, the surrealists experimented with automatic writing and with the free association of random images brought together in surprising juxtaposition. Although surrealist painting is better known, a significant tradition of surrealist poetry established itself in France, in the work of Breton, Paul Pluard, Louis Aragon, and Benjamin P6ret. Surreafism also attempted to become an international revolutionary movement, associated for a while with the Communist International. Although dissolved as a coherent movement by the end of the 1930s, its tradition has survived in many forms of postwar experimental writing, from the theatre of the absurd to the songs of Bob Dylan. The adjectives surreal and surrealistic are often used in a loose sense to refer to any bizarre imaginative effect.

survivalist: Describing works predicting apocalyptic events, such as nuclear war and world economic collapse, and outlining recommended modes of survival past their occurrence

swash letters: Capital letters in italic typefaces, carrying flourishes on top, bottom, or both.

swatch: A small physical sample, as of cloth for book covers or colours for colour printing.

sweep: In *cathoderay* display devices, term for the repetitive movement of the cathode beam over the phosphor screen. In a television display tube, two simultaneous sweeps take place, one tracing lines horizontally, and another moving vertically at a slower rate, tracing an assembly of lines into fields.

swinging burst: In PAL colour television. The colour burst for a PAL system is at a phase angle of 135° for one line, and at 225° on the next line, as the V-signal alternates in phase by 180° with each line. This gives rise to the expression.

syllabic verse: verse in which the fines are measured according to the number of syllables they contain, regardless of the number of stresses. This syllabic principle operates inthe poetry of the Romance languages and of Chinese and Japanese; but in English, purely syllabic verse occurs only in rare experiments such as those of Marianne Moore, W. H. Auden, and Thom Gunn. The counting of syllables in the line is one element of English prosody, but not the dominant principle, English verse being either purely accentual, in which case the number of syflables per line does not matter. or accentualsyflabic, in which case the number of stresses is counted as well as the total number of syllables. English accentualsyllabic verse can tend towards either the syllabic or the accentual principle. thus Alexander Pope and other poets of the early 18th century were quite strict in counting the ten syllables of their pentameters, which can therefore be called decasyllabic lines; but other English poets like Shakespeare and Keats allowed themselves more variation in the syllable-count, so that it is more accurate to call their pentameters fivestress lines. The conventions of European syllabic verse give us the names of certain standard fines: the hendecasyflable is important in Italian verse, as the 12-syllable alexandrine is in French, while octosyllabic verse is very common in many languages including English.

syllepsis: a construction in which one word is applied to two other words or phrases, either ungrammatically or in two differing senses. In the first case, the verb or preposition agrees grammatically with only one of the two elements which it governs, e.g. 'He works his work, I mine'. In the second case, the word also appears only once but is applied twice in differing senses, as in Pope's *The Rape of the Lock:*

Here, thou, great Anna, whom three realms obey

Dost sometimes counsel takeand sometimes tea.

A more farfetched instance occurs in Dickens's *Pickwick Papers* when it is said of a character that she 'went home in a flood of tears and a sedan chair'. There is usually a kind of pun involved in this kind of syllepsis. The term is frequently used interchangeably with zeugma, attempts to distinguish the two terms having foundered in confusion: some rhetoricians place the ungrammatical form under the heading of syllepsis while others allot it to zeugma. It seems preferable to keep zeugma as the more inclusive term for syntactic 'yoking' and to reserve syllepsis for its ungrammatical or punning varieties.

syllogism: a form of logical argument that derives a conclusion from two propositions sharing a common term, usually in this form: all x are y; z is x; therefore z is y. For example: all poets are alcoholics; Jane is a poet; therefore Jane is an alcoholic. In this deductive logic, the conclusion is of course reliable only if both premises are true.

Syllogistic reasoning was cultivated in medieval scholasticism, and is sometimes found in Chaucer and Shakespeare.

symbol: in the simplest sense, anything that stands for or represents something else beyond itusually an idea conventionally associated with it. Objects like flags and crosses can function symbolically, and words are also symbols. In the serniotics of C. S, Peirce. the term denotes a kind of sign that has no patural or resembling connection with its referent, only a conventional one: this is the case with words. In literary usage, however, a symbol is a specially evocative kind of image; that is, a word or phrase referring to a concrete object, scene, or action which also has some further significance associated with it: roses, mountains, birds, and voyages have all been used as common literary symbols. A symbol differs from a metaphor in that its application is left open as an unstated suggestion: thus in the sentence She was a *tower of strength,* the metaphor ties a concrete image to an identifiable abstract quality. Similarly, in the systematically extended metaphoric parallels of allegory, the images represent specific meanings: at the beginning of Langland's allegorical poem *Piers Plowman,* the tower seen by the dreamer is clearly identified with the quality of Truth, and it has no independent status apart from this function. But the symbolic tower in Robert Browning's poem '"Childe Roland to the Dark Tower Came", or that in W. B. Yeats's collection of poems *The Tower,* remains mysteriously indeterminate in its possible meanings. It is therefore usually too simple to say that a literary symbot 'stands for' some idea as if it were just a convenient substitute for a fixed meaning; it is usually a substantial image in its own right, around which further significances may gather according to diflicring interpretations. The term symbolism refers to the use of symbols. or to a set of related symbols; however, it is also the name given to an important movement in late 19thcentury and early 20th-century poetry: for this sense, *see* Symbolists. One of the important features of Romanticism and succeeding phases of Western literature was a much more pronounced reliance upon enigmatic symbolism in both poetn and prow fiction, sometimes involving obscure private codes of meaning, as in the poetry of Blake or Yeats. A wellknown early example ofthis is the albatross in Coleridge's 'The Rime of the Ancient Mariner. Many novelistsnotably Herman Melville and D. H. Lawrencehave used symbolic methods: in Melville's *MobyDick* the White Whale becomes a focus for many different suggested meanings. Melville's extravagant symbolism was encouraged partly by the importance which American Transcendentalism gave to symbolic interpretation of the world.

Symbolic: the, a term used by the French psychoanalyst Jacques Lacan and by the literary theorist Julia Kristeva to designate the objective order of language, law, morality. religion, and all social existence, which is held to constitute the identity of any human subject who enters iL Drawing on Freud's theory of the Oedipus complex and on the structuralist anthropology of Claude UviStrauss, Lacan developed an opposition between the 'Imaginary' state enjoyed by the infant who has no distinct sense of a self opposed to the world, and the Symbolic Order in which the cbild then becomes a separate subject within human culture. The Symbolic is the alm of distinctions and differences—between self aind others subject and objectand of absence or 'lack', since in it we are exiled from k1rie completeness of the Imaginary, and can return to it only in fantasized identifications. The infant's entry into the Symbolic is associated with the 'splitting' of the subject by language, which allots distinct subject-positions' for us to occupy in turn. In Kristeva's literary theory, the Symbolic is opposed to the disruptive energies of the semiotic, which have theirsource in the Imaginary state.

Symbolists: an important group of French Poets who, between the 1870s and the 1890s, founded the modem tradition in Western poetry. The leading Symbolists—Paul Verlaine, Arthur Rimbaud, and Stephane Mallarme—wrote in reaction against realism and naturalism, and against the objectivity and technical conservatism of the Parnassians. Among the minor Symbolist poets were Jules Laforgue and Tristain Corbiere. The Symbolists aimed for a poetry of suggestion rather than of direct statement, evoking subjective moods through the use of private symbols, while avoiding the description of external reality or the expression of opinion. They wanted to bring poetry closer to music, believing that sound had mysterious affinities with other senses. Among their influential innovations were free verse and the prose poem. Their chief inspiration was the work of the pcwt Chades Baudelaire, especially his theory of the 'correspondences' between physical and spiritual realms and between the different senses: Baudelaire had also promoted Edgar Allan Poe's doctrine of 'pure' poetry, which the Symbolists attempted to put into practiot. As a selfconscious movement, French symbolism declared itself under that name only in 1886, forming part of the socalled decadence of that period. It appeared in drama too, notably in the works of the Belgian playwright Maurice Maeterlinck in the 1890s; and some of its concerns were reflected in novels by J.K. Huysınans and Wouard Dujardin. The influence of symbolism on European and American literature of the early 20th- century was extensive: Paul Valery in French. Rainer Maria Rilke in German, and W. B. Yeats in English carried the tradition into the 20th century, and hardly any major figure of modernism was unaffected by it.

symbolic language: Language used in programming which is easily understood by humans, in contrast to machine languages which are far less easily understood by humans, but usable by computing machines.

symmetrical deflection: In *cathode-ray tubes* with electric beam deflection, the application of balanced positive and negative potentials to the deflector plates to effect beam deflection, to maintain the mean potential at the deflector zone at zero.

synaeresis or syneresis: a form of contraction or elision in which two adjacent vowel sounds are run together into a single diphthong or vowel: thus 'the effect' becomes *th'effect,* and 'seest' becomes seest. The device is used in poetry for the sake of conformity to the metre, especially in syllabic and accentualsyllabic verse. A distinction is sometimes made between synaeresis, which creates diphthongs, and sinizesis. which creates simple vowels.

synaesthesia: a blending or confusion of different kinds of senseimpression, in which one type of sensation is referred to in terms moreappropriate to another. Common synaesthetic expressions include thedescriptions of colobrs as 'loud' or 'warm', and ofsounds as smooth'. This effect was cultivated consciously by the French Symbolist but is often found in earlier poetry, notably in Keats.

sync: Abbreviation used with several terms associated with *synchronism.*

synchronic: concerned only with the state of something at a given time, rather than with its historical development. In modern linguistics. The synchronic study of language as it is has generally been preferred tathe diachronic study of changes in language that dominated the concerns of 19th-century philology.

syncope: a kind of verbal contraction by which a letter or syllable is ornilted from within a word. Obvious cases are *heav'n* for 'heaven' and *o'er* for 'over': but the term also covers the omission of sounds without indication in the spelling. The device is especially common in syllabic and accentualsyllabic verse, where it keeps the word within the metrical scheme.

syndication: The sale of written or broadcast work to many publishers or broadcasters at the same time; for example, the sale of a newspaper column to many newspapers or of a radio program to many stations for simultaneous publication or broadcast.

synecdoche: a common figure of speech by which something is referred to indirectly, either by naming only some part or constituent of it or—less often—by naming some more comprehensive entity of which it is a part. Usually regarded as a special kind of metonymy. synecdoche occurs frequently in political journalism and sports commentary, but also has literary uses like Dickens's habitual play with bodily parts: the character of Mrs Merdle in *Little Dorrit is* referred to as'the Bosom'.

synergy: The achievement of far more through the combination of two or more factors than could have been accomplished by those factors alone; for example, the achievement of very substantial business successes resulting from the combination of two companies, successes that could not have been achieved by either company acting alone.

synopsis: a bljef summary or pr6cis of a work's plot or argument.

synonym: a word that has the same—or virtually the same—meaning as anotherword, and so can substitute for it in certain contexts. This identity ofneaning is called synonymy.

syntagm or syritagma: a linguistic term designating any combination of units which are arranged in a significant sequence. A sentence is a syntagm of words. Language is said to have two distinct dimensions: the **syntagmatic** or 'horizontal' axis of combination in which sequences of words are formed by combining them in a recognized order, and the paradigmatic or 'vertical' axis of selection, from which particular words are chosen to fill given fimctions within the sequence. The syntagmatic dimension is therefore the 'linear' aspect of language.

syntax: the way in which words and clauses are ordered and connected so as to form sentences: or the set of grammatical rules governing such wordorder. Syntax is a major determinant of literary style: while simple English sentences usually have the structure 'subjectverbobject', poets often distort this syntax through inversion, while prose writers can exploit elaborate syntactic structures such as the periodic sentence.

synthesis: any compound produced by uniting two or more elements: or the process of combining things into one. Synthesis, which brings elements into combination, is the opposite of analysis, which breaks something down into its constituent parts. In philosophical dialectic. the synthesis is the product of the opposition between a thesis and its antithesis.

T

tabs: (1) In computing, tabulation, setting printout or text on a printer or visual display unit in vertical columns. (2) Markers, often metal clips, attached to the edge of motion picture film to identify or cue a position. (3) Openable curtains on a stage. (US term is drapes).

tabular setting: Composition of matter containing many tables graphs, and columns of numbers, which is considerably more difficult' than normal composition, and which therefore is often classified as special work by compositors, justifying special charges.

TAC: Television Advisory Committee (UK).

tachometer: A transducer which converts speed of rotation into a scale reading or an electrical signal related to speed.

tail: The final section of a roll of film or tape.

tailpiece: A decorative illustration inserted at the end of a chapter or other book section.

tailrhyme stanza, a stanza that combines longer lines with two or more short lines or 'tails'. Chaucer's parody, the *Tale of Sir* Thopas. uses a sixline version. Tailrhyme is also known as caudate rhyme, and in French as *rime couee.*

take: A scene or part of a scene photographed without a break in the action.

takeout book: A book that so fills the available market that no work on the same subject is thought by Potential publishers to be capable of commercial success for some years thereafter; for example, a major biography of a minor figure, purchased by scholars and libraries and likely to foreclose purchase of a second book on the same figure.

takeover: The acquisition of one business by another, whatever the form used in making the transaction and whether or not the transaction was effected amicably.

takeover candidate: A company that is being studied by one or more potential acquirers, in terms of the desirability and feasibility of a takeover attempt.

take-up: That part of a machine handling film or tape at which material is wound up after passing through.

talkback: Communication between director and technical and production staff in studios.

talk-back circuit: ln broadcasting, a speech communication circuit between control room and studio for purposes of directing the use of facilities.

talking book: A record of someone reading a book aloud; often used by unsighted or poorly sighted people.

talk show: A broadcast interview program, on radio or television; a prime vehicle for book publicity, through the device of the author interview.

tanka, a traditional form of Japanese lyric poem consisting of 31 syllables arranged in fines of 5, 7, 5, 7. and 7 syllables. It has had fewer Western imitators than the haiku.

tank circuit: Term used for the tuned circuit at the output stage of a transmitter. Often used for the tuned output system of other circuits, such as crystal *oscillators.*

tan tale or tall story, a humorously exaggerated story of impossible feats. Several tall stories attributed to the German Baron Miinchhausen appeared in the 1780s, but the form flourished in the oral tradition of the American frontier in the 19th century. several tall tales being published byMark Twain, George Washington Harris and others.

tape: Storage or recording medium in the form of a long narrow strip, either a magnetic-coated plastic base or a paper strip with punched holes.

taper: In, *waveguides,* term for a change in cross-section introduced gradually over a length of guide.

tape reader: In computer systems, a machine designed to read tapes with magnetized surfaces and perforated paper tapes carrying data to be stored in computer memories.

tapered distribution: In antennas, used in some multi-element arrays, such as a broadside array, in which the current in each of a line of radiating elements differs in value for each element, with respect to amplitude and, possibly, phase. The current in elements at the centre of the line generally has a maximum value, with lower values of current in elements along the line, tapering to minimum values at the end elements. Careful determination of current values and phase can minimise side-lobes.

tape-slide: A sequence of slides synchronised with, or controlled by, an accompanying audio tape.

tape splice: A join in film or tape in which the ends are joined by adhesive tape.

tape transport: Mechanism for driving and guiding audio or video magnetic tape in a recorder/reproducer.

target: In television *camera tubes,* the electrode that is charged by the light input and scanned by an electron beam to provide an output signal.

target area: (1) In broadcasting, the target service area intended to be served with a broadcast programme. (2) In television *camera tubes,* the area of the target scanned by the electron beam, with due regard for the *aspect ratio.*

target company: A takeover candidate company that has been selected by a potential acquirer as a desirable and feasible takeover target, whether or not that company has evidenced any desire to be taken over.

targeting: Directing marketing efforts, at sharply defined audiences or markets; for example, emphasizing advertisements in special interest rather than general interest magazines, or focusing on selling home computer books through computer stores, rather than general bookstores. Targeting does not imply neglecting other markets, but is rather a matter of focusing efforts on those markets thought likely to be most responsive.

target population: In research, the population that is being studied, or the population to which the results of an experiment will be applied.

TASC: Television Advisory Technical Sub-Committee (UK).

task force: A group assembled to get a specific job done, in contrast to a continuously operating group performing ongoing functions.

TBC: *time-base corrector.*

TDM: Time Division Multiplex.

TDS: Time Delay Spectrometry.

teacher's manual: A publication supplementing educational materials, directed at helping a teacher to use those materials effectively; for example, a guide accompanying a textbook or set of audiovisual materials, containing a suggested course outline, examination questions, and answer keys.

teaching machine: A machine developed for individualized instruction, and using programmed instruction, computer-assisted instruction materials, or both.

tearing: In television, a break-up of part or whole of a picture by partial failure of line synchronism.

tear sheet: A sheet torn from a publication and sent to advertisers and others as evidence of execution of placement instructions, in advance of receipt of the publication itself.

technical writei: A writer concerned with the translation of scientific and technical ideas and information into comprehensible written material.

telecine: In television, apparatus used as a video signal source derived from cinema film.

Telecom: The *British national* telecommunications service.

telecommunications: Communications over suitable transmission paths, using electrically-derived signals from sound, visual images, data or control information.

telecine: Equipment for replaying motion picture film into a television system. See also *flying spot scanner.*

telegraphy: A system of communication using coded digital signals, either direct as signal voltage variations, or as a form of modulation of a carrier wave.

telemetry: The transmission and reception, over a suitable path, of measureable quantities by means of suitably-coded signals.

telephony: A telecommunications system for transmission and reception of audio-frequency signals, such as speech and music

telephoto lens: Camera objective lens of long focal length and comparatively short back focus.

teleprinter: An apparatus comprising a keyboard similar to that on a typewriter, and a printing receiver, for sending and receiving *alpha-numeric* characters over *a* communication link.

teleprompter: Television prompter providing the script for an artist to read while looking directly at the camera.

telerecording: Transferring a television or video presentation to motion picture film.

Teletel: French viewdata service.

Teletex: An intercommunicating system between text-only terminals, such as telex, not involving video display.

teletext: In television, a system for transmitting pulse-coded signals during the *field blanking* interval, which can be stored in the receiver and recalled on demand to display information in *alpha-numeric* form. The system originated in the UK, the BBC and IBA versions using the same standards, but being termed 'Ceefax' and 'Oracle' respectively. Suitable receivers can provide access to many hundred 'peges' of information.

teletype: A teletypewriter, a term for *teleprinter.*

television: System of transmitting electrical signals for the reproduction of a visible image at a distance, often with associated sound.

television camera: An equipment including optical and electronic apparatus necessary for translating an optical image into electrical voltages or currents, suitable for television transmission.

television receiver: A receiving equipment comprising apparatus for receiving television signals, generating beam *sweep* and *modulation* signals for the display tube, and reproducing the accompanying sound.

television rights: The right to adapt a published work for television broadcasting purposes; one of the subsidiary rights sold or leased by an author to others, and covered by author-publisher contracts.

television standard: A specification for the parameters of a television system. A Standard will specify the number of lines, number of pictures per second, polarity of modulation, type of modulation used for the sound channel, etc.

television standards converter: Equipment for converting television signals from one standard to another. At one time, conversion was carried out by establishing an image on a display tube with signals of one standard and, using a camera, scanning the displayed image using another standard. The method lost some definition, and beat effects between differing line rates could produce *moire* effects. The more recent method is to digitise the signals and store a field. The stored signals can then be read out at any rate.

television transmission system: A system conforming to a specification, that generates a video signal, necessary synchronising information, and method of transmission with an associated sound channel.

television tube: A *cathode-ray tube* designed for the display of a received picture transmission. A black-and-white system requires a single-gun tube and a phosphor screen that emits a white light with a *colour temperature* around 6500 K. A colour display tube has three guns, each aiming its beam at one only of the three primary colour phosphors which display on the screen.

telex: System of international teleprinter communication over public telegraphy links.

Telidon: Canadian viewdata service.

Telset: Finnish viewdata service.

temperature inversion: In *tropospheric* propagation, an increase in temperature with height above ground. Normally, temperature falls with height but, particularly after a day of clear sky, the earth can radiate the heat it has acquired and produce a temperature inversion. The effect is to produce a ray path for VHF and UHF waves that curves towards the ground and thus produces extended transmission range beyond the *radio horizon.*

template: A drawing and lettering guide or pattern used in artwork and drafting.

tender: 1. An offer to pay a debt or perform a contractual obligation. 2. An offer to purchase, often encountered in company takeover situations, in which one company makes an offer to buy the stock of another at stated price.

tenor, the subject to which a metaphorical expression is applied. In a **metaphor** like *the ship* of *state,* the state is the tenor, while the metaphoricalterm *ship is* called tfie'vehicle' This distinction between tenor and vehicle was formulated by the critic I. A. Richards in *The Philosophy of Rhetoric,* where he argues that the total meaning of a metaphor is the product of a complex interaction between them.

tentelometer: Trade name for a tape tension measuring instrument.

tera: A prefix denoting a factor of 10^{12}.

tercet, a unit of three verse lines, usually rhyming either with each other or with neighbouring fines. The three-line stanzas of *terza rima* and of the villanelle are known as tercets. The sestet of an Italian sonnet is composed of two tercets.

terminal: A communications device whi^h can be attached to a computer system from some distance away and used to access that computer, for both input and output.

termination: An impedance connected at the end of a transmission line or waveguide.

terza rima a verse form'consisting of a sequence of interfinked tercets rhyming. Thus the second fine of each tercet provides the rhyme for the first and third lines of the next; the sequence closes with one fine rhyming with the middle line of the last tercet. The form was invented by Dante Afighieri for his *Divina Commedia,* using the Italian hendecasyllabic line. It has been adopted by several poets in English perstameters, notably by P. B. Shelley in his 'Ode to the West Wind'.

tesla: Unit of magnetic induction.

test card: In television, a stationary pattern used for assessment of the overall quality of a displayed picture.

testimonial: An endorsement, such as a celebrity's recommendation of a forthcoming book.

test tape: A prerecorded magnetic tape for the alignment and testing of tape recorders/reproducers.

tete-beche: A system for interleaving two *asymmetric-sideband* signals, whereby the carrier of one channel is situated near the upper limit of the common channel bandwidth, and the second carrier is situated near the lower frequency limit.

tetralogy, a group of four connected plays or novels. Ancient Greek dramatic festivals presented tetralogies comprising three related tragedies and a satyr play. Shakespeare's major history plays fall into two tetralogies, the first comprising the three parts of *Henry VI* and

Richard III, the second comprising *Richard 11, Henry IV* Parts 1 and 2, and *Henry V.* Lawrence Durrell's *Alexandria Quartet* is a tetralogy of novels.

tetrameter, a verse line of four feet. In English verse, this means a line of four 'stresses, usually iambic or trochaica a very common form.

text, the actual wording of a written work, as distinct from a reader's interpretation of its story, theme, subtext etc; or a sPcciflc work chosen as the object of analysis.

textbook: A book used as part of a course of study; may be a book written specifically for that purpose, and used solely in that connection, or a book selected for course use but designed for other purposes. Also called a text.

textbook publisher: A publisher issuing works primarily designed for use as part of course material; many such publishers also issue nonbook educational materials, as well as other kinds of published works.

textfiche (tf): Microfiche positives that may be enlarged to function as if they were pages in a book; developed and sold both as book alternatives and supplements as when a conventionally bound book is designed to be accompanied by a fiche which contains art prints or supporting documentary materials.

textual criticism,a branch of literary scholarshipthat attempts to establish the most accurate version of a written work by comparing all existing manuscript and/or printed versions so as to reconstruct from them the author's intention, eliminating copyists' and printers' errors and any corrupt interpolations.

texture, a term used in some modern criticism to designate those concrete' properties of a literary work that cannot be subjected to paraphrase, as distinct from its paraphrasable structure' or abstract argument. The term is applied especially to the particular pattern of sounds used in a poem: its assonance, consonance, alliteration euphony, and related effects. Often, though, the term aim covers diction, imagery, metre, and rhyme.

THD: (1) Total Harmonic Distortion. (2) Third Harmonic Distortion.

theatre In the round, a form of theatrical Presentation in which the audience Is placed around a central acting area or stage, as in a circus or boxing match.

theatre of cruelty, a term introduced by the French actor Antonin Artaud in a series of manifestos in the 1930s, collected as Le *Thatre et son double*. It refers to his projected revolution in drama. whereby the rational 'theatre of psychology' was to be replaced by a more physical and primitive rite imended to shock the audience into an awareness of life's cruelty and violence. The idea. derived Partly from Surrealism, was that the audience should undergo a catharsis through being possessed by a 'plague' or epidemic of irrational responses. Artaud's own attempts to put this theory into dramatic practice failed, and he was locked up for some time as a lunatic.

theme, a salient abstract idea that emerges from a literary work's treatment of its subjectmatter, or a topic recurring in a number of literary works. While the subject of a work is described concretely in terms of its action, its theme or themes will be described in more abstract terms. The theme of a work may be announced explicitly, but more often it emerges indirectly through the recurrence *of* motifs.

thermal shock: The effect produced on the electrical performance of a system as a result of a rapid change of temperature. The effect is of particular significance with tuned circuits. If temperature is raised, the linear dimensions of inductor and capacitors will change and, unless compensation effects have been employed, a resonance frequency change will take place. Of particular importance with *oscillator* circuits and precision *filter* systems.

thermography: The creation of raised lettering by, means of applying heat to wet ink fixed on printed sheets; the result closely resembles embossing, but is far less expensive to produce.

thesaurus: 1. A list or book of synonyms and antonyms. 2. A list 0 book of special terms; for example, a descriptive list of index term useful in accessing a computerized database. prepared

thesis, an argument or proposition, which may be opposed by an antithesis; or a scholarly essay defending some proposition. usually a dissertation submitted for an academic degree. The thesis *of* a literary work is its abstract doctrinal content, that is, a proposition forsweehpichobt argues.

think tank: A public or private organization primarily engaged medium and long-term analysis and recommendation in policy are affecting government, business, and other major sectors of society.

third cover: The inside back cover, a preferred advertising position, usually carrying rates higher than those charged for text pages.

third-person narrative, a narrative or mode of storytelling in which the narrator is not a character within the events related, but stands I outside'those events. In a thirdperson narfative. all characters within the story are therefore referred to as 'he' she', or 'they': but this does not of course, prevent the narrator from using the first person 'I' or we' in commentary on the events and their meaning. Third-person narrators are often omniscient or'all-knowing' about the events of the story, but they may sometimes appear to be restricted in their knowledge of these events. Third-person narrative is by far the most common form of storytelling.

thirty (30): Symbol used ill newspaper writing for "the end."

thirtytwomo (32mo): An American book size, approximately 4"—5" high. Also see book size.

three phase: A three (or four) wire means of distributing AC electricity power supplies with the waveform in each of the three wires 120° out of phase. The fourth wire is the neutral in a star system.

three-plane registration: In slide projectors, the exact positioning of each slide mount in three dimensions, vertical, horizontal and along the optical axis.

three quarter binding: A binding with back and corners in leather, the leather of the corners extending over half to three-quarters of the covers, but not all the way to meet the back of the book.

threnody, a dirge or lament for the dead. A writer or speaker of threnodies is a threnodist.

threshold frequency: Of a *photoelectric* device, a frequency of incident radiation, below which there is no useful electrical output.

threshold howl: Acoustic feedback produced by sound from loudspeakers re-entering microphone.

thriller: A genre novel, usually stressing such matters as extralegal activities, international espionage, violence, and sex.

throat: Of a driven-horn *loudspeaker,* the small-area end of the horn where the driving unit is attached.

through-loss: In *cabled distribution systems,* the loss experienced in a feeder at a point where another feeder connection is made, e.g. at a distribution point.

throughput: The amount of work which can be performed by a production system In a specified time. The term, synonymous with capacity, is used in the computer industry.

throw: The distance from the projector aperture to the centre of the screen.

thumb index: An index marker, in the form of a small tab affixed flush to the fore-edge of a page being marked, with a die cut into the preceding pages so that the book may be opened at the flush tab; used in substantial reference books, such as encylopedias and dictionaries.

thumbwheel: A, rim-operated rotary control; in computer graphics it controls the movement of a line, either horizontally or vertically, across the display surface.

Thyristor: A controlled semiconductor switch often used as a power control device, e.g. in lighting dimmers.

Tic-tac: Viewdata type system used in France.

tickler file: A file of items kept in timed sequence, as a reminder of what must be done when; for example, an outside salesperson's monthly file, indicating which customers are to be called on and when in the coming month, which is added to and subtracted from as work proceeds.

tide page: That page of a book carrying its full tide, the name of its author or authors, and the name of its publisher, plus any other publishing information required by the author-publisher contract or desired by the publisher; often the second printed page of a work, following the half-title page in the front matter, but sometimes the first printed page.

tie-in: The issuance of a work in two or more media, so as to enhance sales by the timing of issuance and joint promotion; for example, the issuance of a work as a hardcover or softcover book simultaneously or in the same time period as a movie. Such issuance may be arranged at the start of a project, but more often results from subsidiary rights sales.

tie-in sale: 1. A sale of subsidiary rights linked, formally or informally, with the sale of other subsidiary rights, as when sale of movie rights is accompanied by the sale of paperback rights to the same conglomerate. 2. A sale requiring that the purchaser buy other goods and services from the seller; an illegal practice in the United States.

tie line: A communications channel directly !inking' two or more locations, rather than being part of a network.

tier: In antenna arrays, an array in which antenna elements are erected in a vertical plane. Sometimes referred to a *stack.*

trope, a figure of speech, especially one that uses words in senses beyond their 1iteral meanings. The theory of rhetoric has involved several disputed attempts to clarify the distinction between tropes and schemes. The most generally agreed distinction in modern theory is that tropes change the meanings of words, by a 'turn' of sense, whereas schemes merely rearrange their normal order. The major figures that are agreed upon as being tropes are metaphor, simile, metonymy, synecdoche, irony, personification, and hyperbole: litotes and periphrasis are also sometimes called tropes. The figurative sense of a word is sometimes called its tropological sense, tropology being the study of tropesand especially of the spiritual meanings concealed behind the literal meanings of religious scriptures. In a second sense, the term was applied in the Middle Ages to certain additional passages introduced into church services. The most important of these, the *quem* quaeritis trope in the Easter Introit, is thought to have been the origin of liturgical drama.

tropopause: Of the *ionosphere,* the upper boundary of the troposphere, at a height of about 10 km.

troposphere: The lower part of the atmosphere, extending from ground level to the tropopause. The troposphere is characterised by the large movements of air and water-vapour masses, also the temperature and pressure variations associated with weather. Propagation of VHF and UHF waves in the troposphere relies on radiation from an elevated site above ground, to a range limit decided by the distance to the *radio horizon* and the height of the receiving antenna system.

troubadour, a poet of southern France writing in Provenqal in the late Middle Ages. The troubadours, mostly aristocratic poets rather than wanderig minstrels or *jongle*urs, flourished in the period 1100-1350, composifig elaborate lyrics of courtly love which had an extensive influefice on Western poetry and culture. Among the best known are Guillaume d' Aquitaine, Arnaut Daniel, and Bertran de Bom. Their favoured poetic forms included the aubade, the *chanson,* and the *pastourelle.* From the late 12th century onwards they found imitators in northern France and in Germany.

trouvere, a poet of northern France in the late Middle Ages. The *trouveres* flourished in the late 12th an yearly 13th centuries, and were in many respects the followers of the Provencal troubadours, although their repertoire extended beyond love lyrics into narrative verse, especially the *chanson de geste* and the verse romance. The term covers some of the professional entertainers known as *jongleurs,* but applies mainly to poets of higher rank. The most important was Chretien de Troyes, who established the Arthurian romance of 'courtly love with his *Lancelot;* other notable *trouveres* include Conon de Bethune, Thibaud de Champagne, and Blondel de Nestewho. according to legend, discovered the imprisoned Richard the Lionheart by singing under his window.

truncation, the shortening of a metrical verse line by omitting a syllable or syllables from the full complement expected in the regular metrical pattern. This may occur at the beginning of the line or, more usually. at the end. In English verse, truncation is most often found in trochaic verse, where the final unstressed syllable is commonly not employed.

trunk-bridge amplifier: In *cabled distribution systems,* an amplifier for raising signal levels in a *trunk feeder* cable, and providing a distribution point.

trunk feeder: In *cabled distribution systems,* feeder cable between the head end and a distribution point, or between distribution points.

trunk feeder amplifier: In *cabled distribution systems,* an, amplifier connected into a *trunk feeder* to compensate for signal loss on the cable. The amplifier often provides correction for *signal till,* when signals are relaunched.

truth table: In binary logic, a table relating the logic state produced at the output of a logic element, by each combination of logic states at its input.

TTL: (1) Through 'Me Lens, a camera viewfinder system. (2) Transistor-Transistor Logic. A common low cost integrated circuit logic family operating from 5 V.

TTY: Teleprinter (Teletype, Telewriter).

tumbling: In computer graphics, moving three-dimensional object on a display by continually changing its axis of rotation.

tuned antenna: A *standing-wave antenna* which normally would have a resonance frequency higher than required, but is tuned by the inclusion of series inductance and possible *top-loading.* Tuned antennas are used at MF, LF and VLF due to the practical difficulty involved in. the use of an elevated conductor a quarter-wave high.

tungsten-halogen lamp: An efficient lamp consisting of a tungsten filament in a quartz or hard-glass envelope containing a halogen (bromine or iodine) to avoid internal blackening of the envelope due to the deposition of tungsten from the filament.

tungsten lighting: Lighting with incandescent lamps having tungsten filaments, including tungsten-halogen types.

tuning: The process of changing the resonance frequency of a circuit or, simultaneously, circuits by variation of capacitance, inductance or both. Receiver tuning consists generally of' mechanical variation of variable capacitors, but many receivers use *capacitance diodes* and *electric tuning.*

turnstile antenna: A pair of horizontal centre-fed dipoles, forming a right angle, fed in such a manner that they are in phase quadrature. This arrangement of horizontal dipoles has an omnidirectional radiation pattern in the horizontal plane, and is sometimes stacked to increase gain and reduce beam-width in the vertical plane.

turn, the English term for an abrupt change in the mood or argument of a poem, especially in a sonnet also an older word for a trope.

turnaround time: The time it takes to do a job, from beginning to end.

turnkey: Supplying a complete system, self-contained and ready to use; e.g. a computer with both the hardware and the software required for an application.

turnkey system: *A* computer system installed ready for use, tailored and debugged by its outside supplier, and ideally ready for the user to simply "turn the key" to commerce operations.

turntable: (1) A constant-speed rotating platform to carry a disc, typically a gramophone record, during reproduction. (2) A mechanism fitted to an animation table or camera to produce *rotations.*

turret: A rotatable mount on a camera or projector allowing any one of two or more lenses to be brought into position on the optical axis as required.

TV: Television.

tweeter: In audio reproduction, a loudspeaker intended to operate on high *audio frequencies* only. This type of speaker is seldom used alone, and is usually part of a loudspeaker assembly consisting of two or more speakers. The tweeter is not designed, for the large air movements associated with reproduction of low frequencies, and it is necessary to keep the lower audio frequencies out of the tweeter. A cross-over network is used to divide the band into two or more parts, separated at about 1 or 2 kHz, with the higher frequencies being fed to the tweeter.

twelvemo (12mo, or duodecimo): An American book size, approximately 7"—8" high.

twentyfourmo (24mo): An American book size, approximately 5"—6" high.

twinkle: In slide projection, a rapid image intensity fluctuation effect.

twinning stand: A stand which supports one automatic slide projector on top of another, which actually bears its weight.

twin-T: network A network consisting of two T-networks connected in parallel.

two-duration control: The control of two slide-projectors to give fast and slow dissolve changes by means of cue tones of 1000 Hz but of two different durations, typically 50 ms and 450 ms.

TWT: Travelling Wave Tube amplifier.

TX: Transmission.

type, a fictional character who stands as a representative of some identifiable class or group of people. Although some uses of the term equate it with the stereotyped stock character of literary and folk tradition. other uses distinguish between this 'twodimensional' stock character and the more individualized type: in the work of the Hungarian Marxist critic Georg Lukacs, 'typicality' is a quality combining uniquely individualized with historically representative features. LukAcs found this typicality in the characters of early 19th-century realist novels like those of Balzac; similarly, the realist fiction of George Eliot and Henry James is inhabited by such types. who are certainly not mere stock characters. In two other senses, the term is used in reference to literary forms as a synonym for genre, and in reference to religious allegory as'another word for emblem or symbol.

typeface: 1. The surface of a piece of metal type, in the shape *of* the character to be printed; also called the *face.* 2. More generally, the characteristics of a particular example of printed type. 3. The full range of type *of* a particular design, such as Bódoni, or of a general family, such as roman or italic.

typescript: Writing produced by a typewriter, generally used only to emphasize that material is typed, not handwritten, as the term manuscript has in the last century broadened to include typed material.

typesetter: One who sets type; also a typesetting machine.

types of emission: Radio frequency emissions take place over a wide range of frequencies (See Appendix A), and various forms of *modulation* are in use. The types of emission are classified in Appendix **B.T-number:** A system of calibration of the light transmission of a lens based on its actual transmission at various diahragm settings. (cf. *f-number).*

type specimen: A sample of printing produced by use of a specific typeface, usually contained in sample books supplied by printers to customers.

typographer: One with design skills in typography; may be a compositor, designer, or printer.

typographical error (typo): Any error in typing or composition, at any stage of print production, from the typing of an original manuscript to a misprint found in a finished publication, and to whomever attributable.

typography, the arrangement of printed words on the page. Typographical factors—most obviously the lack of a righthand margin in most verse, and the spaces between stanzas—have some influence on readers' understanding of literary works. The exploitation of typography for special effects is found in pattern poetry and modern concrete poetiry, and in some experimental prose works like those of the Scottish roovelist Alasdair Gray.

typology, a system of interpretation Eipplied by early Christian 'theologians to the Hebrew scriptures, by which certain events, images, and personages of pre-Christian legend could be understood as prophetic 'types' or 'figures' foreshadowing the life of Christ. Typology—literally the study of types—is thus a method of rereading t1he Old Testament anachronisticatly in terms of the New Testament. so that Adam, Isaac, Jonah, and other characters are prefigurings of Christ, the Tree of Knowledge in Eden is a type of the Cross, and so on,. By the 13th century an elaborate system of allegory had been constructed, dividing the sense of anything in the Old Testament into four levels of meaning: the literal, the allegorical, the moral or tropological, and the anagogical. In the standard illustration of this scheme, Jerusalem is literally a city. allegorically the Church, tropologically the soul of the believer, and anagogically the heavenly City of God. Typological allegory is an important element in many literary works of medieval Christianity, including Dante's *Divina Commedia* and in some later sermons and religious verse.**tab:** An index marker, in the form of a small projecting piece affixed to a page or a piece of a page cut by a die so that it projects beyond the outer edge of the page it is marking. Also called an *index guide.*

U

Unit cost: The cost to a producer, distributor, or retailer of a single designated unit in a group of substantially identical units. In publishing the cost is often computed as the sum of all direct costs involved in a book divided by the number of books produced, but this producing method of assessing costs is rapidly being replaced by estimates that take into account such factors as overhead costs, opportunity costs, and profit expectations.

University press: A publisher affiliated within institution of higher education, whether formally part of the institution or independently organized and publishing under the name of the institution.

Unopened: Book edges that have neither been trimmed by machine during bindery operation, nor cut open by hand after the book was finished.

Unpublished work: A written work that has not yet been published; Linder the United States Copyright Act and the Universal Copyright Convention, such work completed after January 1, 1978 enjoys copyright protection even without registration.

Unsolicited manuscript: A manuscript sent by an author to a publisher or agent unrequested; that is, a work arriving over *the transom.*

Many trade publishers will not read such manuscripts, which they call slash, but most agents will read and evaluate the commercial prospects of such manuscripts, although sometimes for a fee from the author. Professional and educational publishers, however, derive a substantial portion of their lists from such unsolicited manuscripts.

V

Variorium edition: Originally an edlition of an author's works containing explanatory notes by various commentators and editors. In recent usage, however, the term has come to mean an edition that includes all the variant readings from manuscript and other versions.

Video publishing: That branch of publishing focusing on the creation of materials capable of being stored on videodisc or in a computer memory, and retrieved to be printed out on a television screen..

Volume: In sound broadcasting, the amplitude of programme or other audio signals in the sound channel. The amplitude is related to a measurement by means of a peak-programme meter and/or a *VU-meter*.

Volume compression: In audio, a circuit system for compressing the dynamic range of audio signals, according to a specified law.

Volume discount: A discount rising as quantities ordered rise; for example, a discount offered by a publisher to booksellers based on the quantities of books purchased.

Volume expansion: In audio, a circuit system for expanding the dynamic range of audio signals.

Volume unit (VU): In audio, usually in its abbreviated form 'VU unit'. A unit used for expressing the level of a speech or music signal voltage. The level is compared with a reference volume level, and the difference expressed in decibels.

W

Web printing: Printing on presses designed to accept roll-fed paper, rather than paper fed in sheets.

Weighting: An adjustment of measured values to allow for certain other features of operation. For example, the disturbing effects of *noise* signals varies with frequency, and a measured performance over a frequency range may be weighted to allow for the varying disturbance of the noise. The term generally applied to a network that has frequency-response characteristics that perform the weighting adjustment.:

Well published: Describing a publication that has been well designed and executed by its publisher; sometimes also used to describe a book that has been effectively publicized and sold.

Word of mouth: Recommendation of publications by readers to other potential readers; a process devoutly desired by all authors, publishers, and booksellers.

Word processing (wp): The process of producing typed or otherwise composed material within an organization, often including some editing and composition functions; with the advent of new recording, storing, retrieving, and composing technology, some of the work formerly done by typists, editors, and compositors has merged, justifying a new name for the combined functions.

Workbook: A book designed to provide problems for solution, such as a set of problems accompanying a textbook; often intended to be written in, with problems worked out in the book itself.

Y

Young adult book (YA): A book aimed at a readership roughly in the middle school and early high school age range; the line between young adult and adult often is hard to draw, and many YA books appeal to a substantial adult audience.

Z

Zinc etching: The process of creating an etching on a plate made of zinc; also the resulting image on the plate, and a print made using that etching.

Zit: A break or blemish in printed material.